Frommer's

Best Beach Vacations

Vacations

H*awaii*

By Rick Carroll

A Beachscape Publishing, Inc. production for
MACMILLAN TRAVEL USA

Frommer's Best Beach Vacations: *Hawaii*

Publishers/Editors Gary Stoller and Bruce Bolger
Managing Editor Martin Everett
Design Director Audrey Razgaitis
Beach Consultant Dr. Stephen Leatherman
Copy Editor Marita Begley
Research Editors Teresa Stoller and Betty Villaume
Map Designer John Grimwade
Cartographer Joyce Pendola
Graphic Design Sun Design/Lauri Marks

Frommer's Best Beach Vacations: Hawaii is produced for Frommer's by Beachscape Publishing, Inc. Please address any comments or corrections to Beachscape at 145 Palisade St., Dobbs Ferry, N.Y. 10522; tel. 914-674-9283.

Also Available:
Best Beach Vacations: Florida
Best Beach Vacations: California

Coming in 1996:
Best Beach Vacations: New England
Best Beach Vacations: New York to Washington, D.C.
Best Beach Vacations: Carolinas & Georgia

Macmillan Travel
A Simon & Schuster Macmillan Company
1633 Broadway, New York, NY 10019-6785

Library of Congress Catalog Card No. 95-79431
ISBN 0-02-860497-0

Manufactured in the United States of America

10 9 8 7 6 5 4 3 2 1

About the author

Rick Carroll has spent most of his life at the beach. He grew up at Laguna Beach, Calif., lived at Santa Cruz and Stinson Beach, Calif., and now lives and works at Lanikai Beach on Oahu's Windward Coast. A former reporter for the *San Francisco Chronicle*, Carroll frequented San Francisco's North Beach. He covered Hawaii and the Pacific for United Press International and won a National Headliners Award from the Atlantic City Press Club for his reporting from the Philippines during the Marcos era. A recipient of the Lowell Thomas Award for distinguished travel writing, he has written five guidebooks, including *Great Outdoor Adventures of Hawaii*. He is the founder of the Hawaii Travel News Network, which provides news of the islands on the Internet at: http://www.cyber-hawaii.com/travel/.

A word from the author

Many kind people in Hawaii helped me to write this book, and I thank all of them. I am grateful to friends and colleagues who prevented errors or offered new information. They include Hawaii's lifeguards, especially Ralph Goto, Larry Silva, Norman Hunter, and Pua Mokuau, and sailors, surfers, and maritime experts, including Rick Maxey, Ralph Blancato, Randy Hilario, Jerry Kermode, Fred Henunings, and Sonny Kaukini Bradley.

I am indebted to Yoshihiko Sinoto for his archaeological insights and to Stephen Leatherman of the University of Maryland for his beach observations. For historical reference, I looked to John R.K. Clark's resource books on the beaches of Oahu, Maui, the Big Island, Kauai, and Niihau. No Hawaii book is possible without the *Hawaii Dictionary*, by Mary Kawena Pukui and Samuel H. Elbert, and *Hawaii Place Names*, by Mary Kawena Pukui, Samuel H. Elbert, and Esther T. Mookini.

I offer thanks to Hawaii's public relations professionals for their support: Ruth Ann Becker, Nancy Daniels, Mary Dikon, Sheila Donnelly, Nikki Dugan, Sonia Franzel, Julia Gajcak, Donna Jung, Ruth Limtiaco, Joyce Matsumoto, Linn Nishikawa, Noelani Whittington, and Connie Wright.

I must acknowledge the graceful expertise of New York editor Martin Everett, who's never been to Hawaii but literally knows his way around the islands now. Finally, special thanks to my wife/editor/critic Marcie, who makes life at one of Hawaii's best beaches a joy.

RICK CARROLL

Table of

Beach Rating System. VI
Overview. VIII

Oahu

1. Kailua. 1
2. Ala Moana. 10
3. Haleiwa. 20
4. Malaekahana. 30
5. Makaha. 39
6. Waikiki. 48

Maui

7. Hamoa 61
8. Kapalua. 71
9. Wailea. 80
10. Kamaole III. 91
11. Maluaka. 102
12. Kaanapali. 111

Kauai

13. Hanalei Bay. 127
14. Kalapaki. 139
15. Poipu. 150
16. Anini. 164
17. Tunnels. 172

Big Island

18. Hapuna. 182

Contents

19. **Kahalu'u**. **195**
20. **Waipio**. **209**
21. **Leleiwa**. **215**
22. **Volcano Coast**. **226**

Lanai

23. **Hulopoe**. **235**

Molokai

24. **Papohaku**. **244**

Niihau

25. **Keamano**. **254**

Beach Locator Maps

Oahu. . . . . **XV**
Maui. . . . . **XVI**
Kauai. . . . . **XVIII**
Big Island. . . . . **XX**
Lanai. . . . . **XXI**
Molokai. . . . . **XXII**
Niihau. . . . . **XXIII**

The Best Beach Vacations Rating System

Going to the beach is a great American pastime. Whether for a vacation or just a day, Americans flock to the nation's shores in search of the inexplicable pleasure that comes with a stay by the water. That's about all we have in common regarding our love of beaches, for each person has his or her own special tastes. Some come for serenity, others for action, and there are a hundred variations in between. *Best Beach Vacations* is designed to help you find the beach experience that's right for you, be it for a day, a weekend, or an entire vacation.

Best Beach Vacations uses a unique rating system that systematically evaluates each beach area according to the categories that matter most to beach lovers: **Beauty, Swimming, Sand, Hotels/Inns/B&Bs, House Rentals, Restaurants, Nightlife, Attractions, Shopping, Sports,** and **Nature**. A quick review of the ratings will help you quickly narrow your selection. The overview and service information in each chapter provide everything you'll need to start planning your beach experience.

To select the beaches featured in this book, we began with information gathered by professor Stephen Leatherman, sometimes called Dr. Beach, a coastal geologist and director of the University of Maryland's Laboratory for Coastal Research. For years, Leatherman has collected information on water quality, scenic beauty, sand conditions, surf, temperature, and tourist amenities at beaches around the United States—data he uses to determine an overall rating for each beach. Using that data, along with their own knowledge and input from regional and local sources, the authors visited each beach and combed nearby areas to personally evaluate all of the

Beauty	A
Swimming	B
Sand	C
Hotels/Inns/B&Bs	B
House rentals	A
Restaurants	B
Nightlife	B
Attractions	B
Shopping	C
Sports	A
Nature	A

other important elements that go into a stay at a beach.

The ratings at the beginning of a chapter summarize the entire area. Within each chapter, individual beaches are listed. Each has its own description with more specific ratings. It's easy to use the rating system, because it's based on the A through F scale that's used for grade-school report cards; if you see NA (not applicable) in a ratings category, it means that that particular feature does not apply to this beach.

Here are the criteria used to formulate a grade for particular aspects of each beach or beach area.

Beauty: overall setting, sand, and views offshore.

Swimming: water quality, temperature, and wave conditions.

Sand: texture, color, and cleanliness.

Amenities: rest rooms, food concessions, other facilities, and the presence of lifeguards.

The grades for all other categories are based on the quality and quantity of offerings in or around the beach area. The rating for **Attractions**, for example, assesses the quality and quantity of all types of things to do in the area surrounding the beach.

Best Beach Vacations makes every attempt to warn readers of specific safety concerns in each area. However, readers should visit all beaches mindful of the potential dangers posed by water, wave, and sun, and take appropriate precautions.

We hope you have a wonderful beach vacation.

—*Gary Stoller and Bruce Bolger*

Best Beach Vacations:

A beach is a beach is a beach, right? Not if the destination is Hawaii.

With 132 islands (7 of them inhabited) in the tropical Pacific and a general coastline of 750 miles, America's fiftieth state has beaches of almost every size, shape, and color. The variety is astonishing.

The Big Island of Hawaii, for example, has 266 miles of coastline, the longest in the Hawaiian archipelago, with sand that is black, gold, white, green, and black-and-white. On the island's southeast coast, new beaches are being created daily when red-hot lava hits the sea.

Oahu's most famous beach is Waikiki, but who, outside of a few sun-burned *kama ainas*, has ever heard of Malaekahana? You will. The island of Kauai has more than 80 excellent beaches, but can you name three? Everyone likes to go to the beach on Maui, but which one's best for snorkeling— Kaanapali, Kamaole, or Kapalua?

For anyone planning a beach vacation in Hawaii, the abundance of choice poses a delightful dilemma. First, you must choose your island destination, then zero-in on the beach of choice. There's a big difference between the beach at Kapalua and Kaanapali. Or Hanalei and Kalapaki, for that matter.

Choosing a beach in Hawaii was much easier in the days when folks arrived by steamship. They disembarked at the pier that led to the Moana Hotel on Waikiki Beach. In 1927, the Royal Hawaiian Hotel opened a few hundred yards away and gave beach goers a choice.

In 1959, only 250,000 people visited Hawaii. Most stayed in Waikiki at new hotels like The Waikikian, the Outrigger, and the Reef. In the 1960s, the choice of beaches became complicated. Tourists began

Overview

arriving by jet, and new hotels opened on neighboring islands on new beaches few had ever heard of or could pronounce. Kaanapali Beach, the first planned resort, opened on Maui in 1963. The following year, Laurance Rockefeller built the Mauna Kea Beach Hotel at the Big Island's Kaunaoa Beach. Many other resort hotels followed. During the past ten years, more than a dozen multimillion-dollar resorts have opened in Hawaii, which many believe has the finest tropical beach resorts in the world.

More than six million people now hit the beach in Hawaii each year. To accommodate the many visitors, more resorts are being planned. A new Four Seasons beach hotel is going up on Uluweuweu

BEACH RANKINGS

Here are Hawaii's 25 best beach areas, ranked in the order of the author's personal preference:

1. Kapalua, Maui
2. Kailua, Oahu
3. Hanalei Bay, Kauai
4. Hamoa, Maui
5. Kamaole III, Maui
6. Hapuna, Big Island
7. Wailea, Maui
8. Poipu, Kauai
9. Kaanapali, Maui
10. Waikiki, Oahu
11. Ala Moana, Oahu
12. Kalapaki, Kauai
13. Kahalu'u, Big Island
14. Haleiwa, Oahu
15. Maluaka, Maui
16. Hulopoe, Lanai
17. Tunnels, Kauai
18. Waipio, Big Island
19. Papohaku, Molokai
20. Anini, Kauai
21. Malaekahana, Oahu
22. Leleiwi, Big Island
23. Makaha, Oahu
24. Volcano Coast, Big Island
25. Keamano, Niihau

Beach, the black-sand cove next to Ka'upulehu Beach on the Big Island of Hawaii. Never heard of either beach? Don't worry, that's what *Best Beach Vacations* is for.

Another small problem you already may have noticed: Hawaiian words have more vowels than consonants, causing a kind of weird dyslexia for English-speaking people. Most beachgoers don't know Kahalu'u (on the Big Island) from Maupulehu (on Kauai)—both great beaches, by the way. Take the time to learn how to pronounce your favorite beach. The beaches were poetically named by early Hawaiians for such natural elements as big waves that crash, a rock that looks like a sea turtle, or red-hot sunsets in the sea.

This book contains information about more than a hundred beaches on all seven inhabited islands: Oahu; Maui, Kauai, the Big Island of Hawaii, Lanai, Molokai, and even the "forbidden" island of Niihau. These beaches are tropical, made of coral sand, lava rock, and erosional runoff. They are red, black, and gold, and there are a few true white-sand beaches.

The older the island, the better looking the beach. Kauai and Oahu, the two oldest isles, are the most eroded, which creates spectacular mountains, valleys, and beaches, especially on the north shores. The Big Island, youngest of the chain, is primarily a large lump of lava. Kauai, one of the oldest inhabited islands, is between 3.8 and 5.6 million years old, compared with the Big Island, which is less than a million years old and still growing.

ISLANDS AT A GLANCE

OAHU: With 50.3 miles of sandy shore and 594 known surfing sites, it has the best and most popular beaches in Hawaii. More than 30,000 people go to Waikiki Beach every day. Oahu has the world's best surfing beaches, the only beach with a major shop-

BEST BEACHES FOR:

HOUSE RENTALS: Chapter 13, Hanalei Bay.

RESTAURANTS: Chapter 6, Waikiki.

LODGING: Chapter 9, Wailea.

NIGHTLIFE: Chapter 6, Waikiki.

ATTRACTIONS: Chapter 22, Volcano Coast.

SHOPPING: Chapter 2, Ala Moana.

FISHING: Chapter 19, Kahulu'u.

BOATING: Chapter 12, Kaanapali.

SURFING: Chapter 3, Haleiwa.

DIVING: Chapter 8, Kapalua.

BICYCLING: Chapter 15, Poipu.

GOLF: Chapter 18, Hapuna.

HISTORY: Chapter 18, Hapuna.

NATURE: Chapter 7, Hamoa.

ping mall in its backyard, and the most dangerous surf in the islands.

KAUAI: Some of the world's most beautiful beaches are found on Kauai's 41.2 miles of sandy shoreline. Kauai has Hawaii's longest beach, it's most inaccessible beach, a beach with sand that barks like a dog, and 330 known surf sites, second only to Oahu.

MAUI: Ringed by 32.6 miles of sandy shoreline, it has more than 80 beaches. Most consist of black or gold sand, and there is even a rare red-sand beach. Except for four-mile-long Kaanapali Beach, Maui's beaches are mostly small pocket beaches tucked between black lava points.

BIG ISLAND: With 266 miles of raw, rugged lava coast, it has only 19.4 miles of sandy shoreline and very few great beaches. Although most beaches are made of black lava, the Big Island does have a green-sand beach as well as the newest beaches on earth, now being created on the southeast coast because of the continuing eruption of Kilauea volcano.

LANAI: With 18.2 miles of sandy shoreline, it has long, empty beaches ideal for beachcombing and one small gold-sand beach that's perfect for swimming, snorkeling, tanning, and watching spinner dolphins at play.

MOLOKAI: It has 23.2 miles of sandy shoreline, but most of the island's beaches are rendered inaccessible by either sea cliffs, fish ponds, or private property. But it does have one great North Shore beach, several pocket beaches, and 180 surfing sites.

NIIHAU: Most of the "forbidden" island of Niihau is still *kapu* (off limits), except for two special gold-sand beaches where you can encounter native Hawaiians, find precious Niihau shells, and snorkel in lagoons with friendly tropical fish.

WHEN TO GO

Average temperatures change little throughout the year, with rainfall generally limited to short showers in the summer and an occasional winter storm that can bring several days of rain and gray skies. However, with numerous microclimates based on each area's orientation in relationship to the trade winds, temperature, rainfall, and wind can vary greatly. Average water temperature at Honolulu's Waikiki Beach in the afternoon is 77 in March and 82 in August. The peak tourism seasons are winter and summer.

HOW TO GET THERE

Most major U.S. airlines offer service to Honolulu, usually via the West Coast gateways of Los Angeles, San Francisco, and Seattle. There is also some nonstop service to Maui and the Big Island. Other islands are reached by regional carriers specified in each chapter.

SERVICE INFORMATION

Following are a few notes about the service information provided in this book.

HOTELS/INNS/B&Bs

Hawaii has everything from lavish hotels and mass-market resorts to intimate B&Bs, motels, and remote campgrounds. Lodgings fall into four price categories, based on double-occupancy peak-season nightly rates (before taxes):

Very expensive	More than $180
Expensive	$111 to $180
Moderate	$76 to $110
Inexpensive	$75 or less

HOUSE RENTALS

Generally speaking, house rentals are not available as extensively as they are on the mainland, and many of the offerings are for condominiums, not single-family homes.

RESTAURANTS

Some things to try if you're determined to eat like the natives: a plate lunch, two scoops of rice, and teriyaki chicken.

Restaurants fall into four price categories based on the approximate cost of an appetizer, main course, and dessert for one person at dinner (not including drinks, tax, and tip):

Very expensive	More than $50
Expensive	$31 to $50
Moderate	$16 to $30
Inexpensive	$15 or less

SAFETY

Any dangers associated with Hawaiian beaches are minimized by awareness and care. Too often, travelers let down their guard, yet a few simple precautions can reduce the chances of a problem. Sunburn is the biggest threat to beach goers, so use plenty of sun block or tanning lotion and cover up with clothing during extended periods on the beach.Watch out for spiky kiawe tree thorns, which fall on the beach and can pierce bare feet.

Swimmers may encounter the Portuguese man-of-war, a stinging jellyfish, and sharp coral causes nasty cuts. Sharks are seldom if ever encountered by swimmers in Hawaiian waters, although surfers, whose dangling legs on boards resemble turtles and other edible marine life, should be on guard.

Wherever you hit the beach in Hawaii, remember that you are on an island in the middle of the Pacific Ocean. Waves and surf here are different than in the Atlantic, the Pacific, and the Gulf of Mexico. Hawaii's beaches are found on every point of the compass, and ocean conditions vary on each island and beach, every day. Generally safe for swimming in the summer, Hawaii's ocean water can be *extremely* dangerous in winter and during high surf, usually in December and January. Always check with the lifeguard before entering the water. Lifeguards are posted on major beaches on Oahu, Maui, Kauai, and the Big Island of Hawaii.

Crime is a reality in metropolitan areas and near areas frequented by tourists. Keep hotel and car doors locked at all times, and don't leave valuables in your car or on the beach.

Oahu
Chapters 1–6

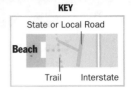

KEY

State or Local Road

Beach

Trail   Interstate

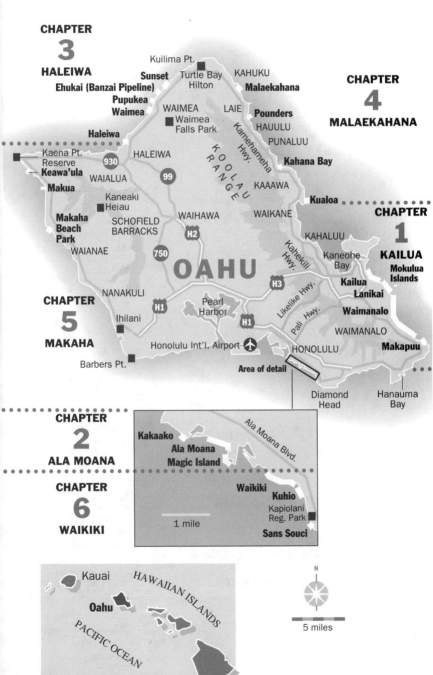

CHAPTER 3
HALEIWA

Kuilima Pt.

Sunset Turtle Bay Hilton   KAHUKU

Ehukai (Banzai Pipeline)   **Malaekahana**

Pupukea   LAIE

Waimea   WAIMEA   **Pounders**

Waimea Falls Park   HAUULU

Haleiwa   PUNALUU

Kaena Pt. Reserve   HALEIWA   **Kahana Bay**

Keawa'ula   (930)   WAIALUA   KAAAWA

Makua   (99)

Kaneaki Heiau   WAIHAWA   WAIKANE   **Kualoa**

Makaha Beach Park   SCHOFIELD BARRACKS

WAIANAE   (H2)   KAHALUU

CHAPTER 4
MALAEKAHANA

Kahekili Hwy.   Kaneohe Bay

CHAPTER 1
KAILUA

(750)   **OAHU**   (H3)   **Mokulua Islands**

NANAKULI   (H1)   Pearl Harbor   **Kailua**

Lanikai

Ihilani   (H1)   Likelike Hwy.   Pali Hwy.   **Waimanalo**

Honolulu Int'l. Airport ✈   WAIMANALO

Barbers Pt.   **HONOLULU**   **Makapuu**

Area of detail

Diamond Head   Hanauma Bay

CHAPTER 2
ALA MOANA

Kakaako

Ala Moana Blvd.

Ala Moana Magic Island

CHAPTER 6
WAIKIKI

Waikiki   **Kuhio**

Kapiolani Reg. Park

1 mile

Sans Souci

CHAPTER 5
MAKAHA

Kauai   HAWAIIAN ISLANDS

Oahu

PACIFIC OCEAN

N

5 miles

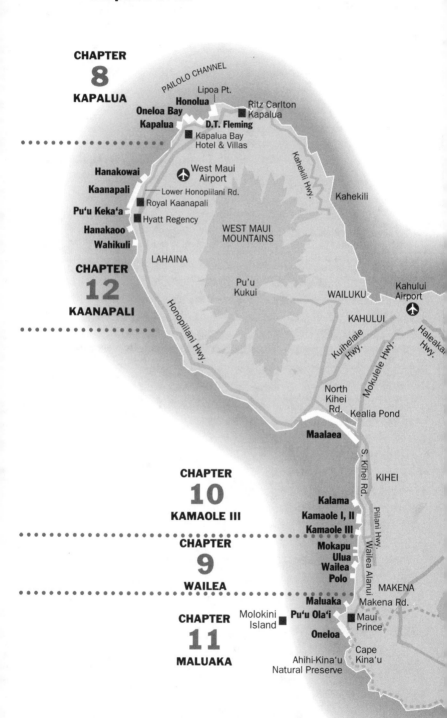

Maui

Chapters 7–12

CHAPTER 8 KAPALUA

PAILOLO CHANNEL

Lipoa Pt.

Honolua

Oneloa Bay

Ritz Carlton Kapalua

Kapalua

D.T. Fleming

Kapalua Bay Hotel & Villas

West Maui Airport

Hanakowai

Kaanapali

Lower Honopiilani Rd.

Royal Kaanapali

Pu'u Keka'a

Hyatt Regency

Hanakaoo

WEST MAUI MOUNTAINS

Wahikuli

LAHAINA

CHAPTER 12 KAANAPALI

Kahekili Hwy.

Kahekili

Pu'u Kukui

WAILUKU

Kahului Airport

KAHULUI

Honopiilani Hwy.

Kuihelaie Hwy.

Mokulele Hwy.

Haleakala Hwy.

North Kihei Rd.

Kealia Pond

Maalaea

S. Kihei Rd.

KIHEI

CHAPTER 10 KAMAOLE III

Kalama

Kamaole I, II

Kamaole III

CHAPTER 9 WAILEA

Mokapu

Ulua

Wailea

Polo

Piilani Hwy.

Wailea Alanui

MAKENA

Maluaka

Makena Rd.

CHAPTER 11 MALUAKA

Molokini Island

Pu'u Ola'i

Maui Prince

Oneloa

Cape Kina'u

Ahihi-Kina'u Natural Preserve

N

3 miles

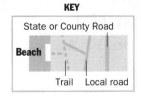

HAWAIIAN ISLANDS

Oahu

Maui

PACIFIC OCEAN

Baldwin Ave.

Hana Hwy.

MAKAWAO

PUKALANI

M A U I

CHAPTER

7

HAMOA

Waianapanapa

Hana Airport ✈

Hotel Hana-Maui ■

Haleakala
Crater

Hana

Kaihalulu

HANA

Koki

Skyline Trail

Hamoa

Mokae
Cove

Piilani Hwy.

Kauai

Chapters 13–17

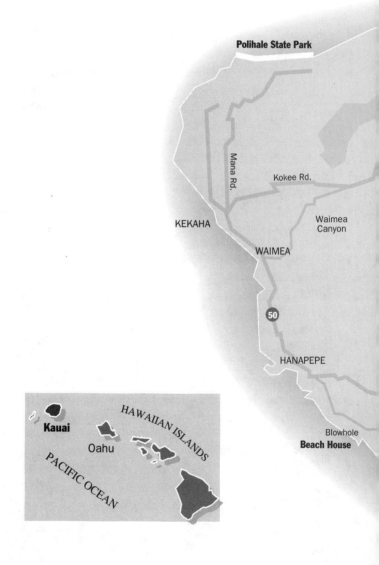

Polihale State Park

Mana Rd.

Kokee Rd.

KEKAHA

Waimea
Canyon

WAIMEA

50

HANAPEPE

HAWAIIAN ISLANDS

Kauai

Oahu

PACIFIC OCEAN

Blowhole
Beach House

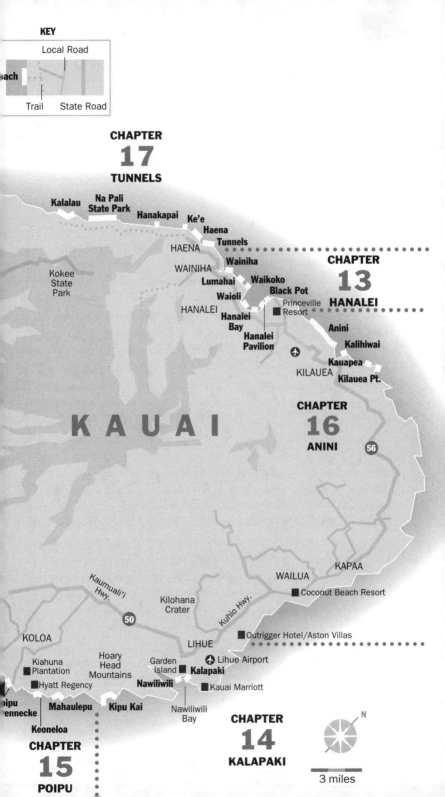

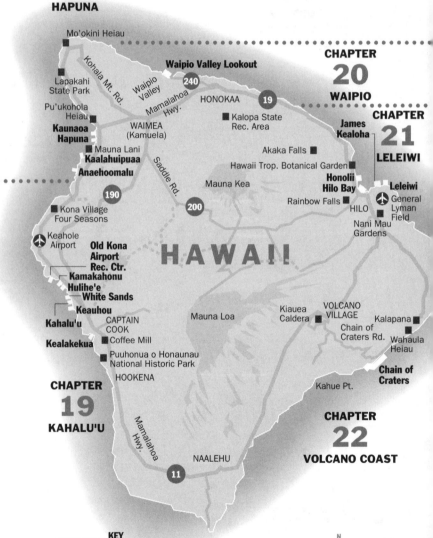

Big Island

Chapters 18–22

HAWAIIAN ISLANDS

PACIFIC OCEAN

Oahu

Hawaii

CHAPTER
18
HAPUNA

CHAPTER
20
WAIPIO

CHAPTER
21
LELEIWI

Mo'okini Heiau

Waipio Valley Lookout

Lapakahi
State Park

Kohala Mt. Rd.

Waipio
Valley

Mamalahoa Hwy.

240

HONOKAA

19

Pu'ukohola
Heiau

Kaunaoa
Hapuna

Mauna Lani

Kaalahuipuaa

Anaehoomalu

WAIMEA
(Kamuela)

Kalopa State
Rec. Area

James
Kealoha

Akaka Falls

Hawaii Trop. Botanical Garden

Honolii
Hilo Bay

Leleiwi

Mauna Kea

Rainbow Falls

General
Lyman
Field

190

Saddle Rd.

200

HILO

Kona Village
Four Seasons

Nani Mau
Gardens

Keahole
Airport

HAWAII

Old Kona
Airport
Rec. Ctr.

Kamakahonu

Hulihe'e
White Sands

Keauhou

Kahalu'u

CAPTAIN
COOK

Coffee Mill

Mauna Loa

Kiauea
Caldera

VOLCANO
VILLAGE

Kalapana

Kealakekua

Puuhonua o Honaunau
National Historic Park

Chain of
Craters Rd.

Wahaula
Heiau

HOOKENA

Chain of
Craters

CHAPTER
19
KAHALU'U

Kahue Pt.

CHAPTER
22
VOLCANO COAST

Mamalahoa
Hwy.

NAALEHU

11

KEY

Local Road

Beach

4-wheel drive   State Road

N

XX

9 miles

Lanai

Chapter 23

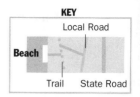

KEY
Local Road
Beach | Trail | State Road

Shipwreck Beach

Polihua Beach

Petroglyphs

LANAI

Garden of the Gods

Keomuku Rd.

430

Keomuku Village

Polihua Rd.

Lodge at Koele

LANAI CITY

Munro Trail

Mt. Lanaihale

440

Kaumalapau Hwy.

Manele Rd.

Palawai Basin

Petroglyphs

Lanai Airport

N

3 miles

440

Manele Bay Hotel

Sweetheart Rock

Kaunolu

Hulopoe

CHAPTER
23
HULOPOE

HAWAIIAN ISLANDS

Oahu

Lanai

PACIFIC OCEAN

Molokai

Chapters 24

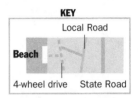

KEY

Local Road

Beach

4-wheel drive   State Road

CHAPTER
24
PAPOHAKU

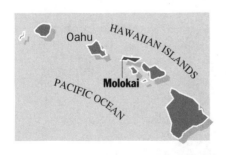

Kalaupapa Nat'l.
Historical Park

■ Kaluakoi
Kepuhi   Molokai   470   KALAUPAPA
Papohaku   Airport

Pelekunu
Bay   **Halawa**
                       HALAWA
Moaula Falls ■

MAUNALOA   **MOLOKAI**
                              ▲ Kamakou
Maunaloa Hwy.   **Sandy**
Palaau Rd.
           KAUNAKAKAI   Kamehameha V
                         Hwy.   Wavecrest ■
                              KAMALO

Oahu   HAWAIIAN ISLANDS

Molokai

PACIFIC OCEAN

N

3 miles

Niihau

Chapter 25

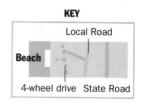

CHAPTER
25
KEAMANO

Keamano

▲ Pu'u Alaia

NIIHAU

PU'UWAI

HALAWELA

Pueo Pt.

Keanahaki

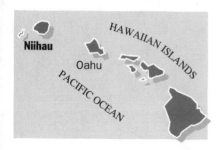

Niihau

Oahu

HAWAIIAN ISLANDS

PACIFIC OCEAN

N

3 miles

CHAPTER 1

Kailua

In all Hawaii, no beach town turns its back on the sea the way beautiful Kailua (*Kigh-LOO-ah*) does. Bordered by houses and shops, the beach is hardly noticeable from town, and no one seems interested in publicizing it. Everybody on Oahu knows how to find it, so tourists are left to their own devices. There's no information booth to welcome beachgoers, and no signs point the way.

Despite its spectacular setting at the foot of the sheer, green Koolau

Beauty	A
Swimming	A
Sand	A
Hotels/Inns/B&Bs	B
House rentals	A
Restaurants	B
Nightlife	C
Attractions	C
Shopping	D
Sports	A
Nature	A

Mountains, Kailua offers few clues that it's got one of the nation's top beaches or that other beautiful strands, such as Lanikai, Mokulua Island, and Waimanalo, are nearby. Only the string of stores renting kayaks, windsurfing equipment, and other water toys hint at what's up.

Well, now the secret's out. A two-mile crescent of golden sand, Kailua Beach has large dunes, a colonnade of palm trees, and inspiring views. On most days, the azure waters of Kailua Bay are dotted with the Technicolor sails of Windsurfers and Hobie Cats scooting by on the breeze.

A windsurfing center since the sport took off in the 1970s, Kailua is home to world champion Robbie Naish, and weather conditions make the bay an ideal place to master the art. Although some tourists prefer the baking sun of Waikiki, people on the Windward Coast believe they have

Oahu's best side: cool trade winds, lush foliage, ample sun, and miles of open beach.

For those who can't resist the lure of a great beach, Kailua exerts a strong pull. For day-trips, it's a scenic bus ride of about an hour from Waikiki, and visitors from many countries are beginning to find it. The annual Great Aloha Games, an Olympic-style event for amateur athletes, are held in Kailua.

A word of advice: To make your trip as enjoyable as possible, avoid rush hour when driving to or from Kailua. Many of its 50,000 citizens commute over the Pali Highway to Honolulu for work and school.

KAILUA BEACH PARK

Stepping onto the sand at Kailua Beach Park, visitors find themselves in one of Hawaii's most scenic panoramas. Just to the right is the imposing Alala Point. To the left, the wide beach curves toward Ulupau Crater on Mokapu Peninsula, site of a U.S.

Beauty	A
Swimming	A
Sand	A
Amenities	B

HOW TO GET THERE

◆ Kailua is a 40-minute drive, or a $45 taxi ride, from Honolulu International Airport. Take the H-1 Frwy. to Pali Hwy. (Hwy. 61) and drive east over the Koolau Mountains and through the tunnel to the windward side of Oahu. The Pali Hwy. changes its name to Kailua Rd. after the intersection with Hwy. 72 (also known as Castle Junction) and changes its name again, to Kuulei Rd., when it crosses the Kawainui Bridge and enters the town of Kailua. Drive straight through town on Kuulei Rd., until it ends at a T intersection by the beach. Turn right on Kalaheo Dr. and continue about 1 mi. After crossing Kaelepulu Stream, look for the entrance to Kailua Beach Park on the left.

Marine base. Offshore lie picturesque islets, home to seabirds.

The 35-acre public park is a pleasant expanse of green lawns meeting golden dunes, shaded by palm trees, ironwoods, and monkeypods. The wide beach is seldom crowded, except on weekends and holidays, and the water is warm and inviting. *Off Kalaheo Dr. about 1 mi. south of downtown Kailua. If the parking lot is full, you may also reach the beach by several public accessways dotting the shoreline north of the park off Kalaheo Dr.*

Swimming: Excellent. A sandy ocean bottom deepens gradually. Waves break gently. The water temperature is mid-70s and up.

Sand: Fine and golden on a wide beach with gentle dunes.

Amenities: Picnic facilities and pavilions with rest rooms, changing rooms, and outside showers. No food stand. Bring your own refreshments or patronize a nearby store or restaurant. Lifeguards on duty.

Sports: Kailua is Oahu's top beach destination for kayaking, windsurfing, and scuba diving. It also has a beach volleyball court and fitness equipment. Shops in town rent and sell water toys.

Parking: Free parking for 220 cars.

LANIKAI BEACH

Immediately south of Kailua Beach Park is one of Hawaii's best swimming spots, scenic Lanikai (*Lah-nee-KIGH*) Beach. If it seems too gorgeous to be real, there's a reason. Along with the twin Mokulua Islands that lie offshore, it has served as a backdrop

Beauty	A
Swimming	A
Sand	A
Amenities	NA

for numerous films, TV dramas, commercials, and photo shoots. The water is unusually calm, a turquoise lagoon protected by the islands and a coral reef about three-quarters of a mile offshore. It's like a giant swimming pool with a sandy bottom punctuated by coral "heads" that attract fish and the snorkelers who like to spy on them. The reef is popular with local surfers, even though they have to paddle a long way to get there.

Lanikai is narrower than Kailua Beach and is fronted entirely by homes, a small neighborhood spilling down the face of Kaiwa Ridge onto the beach. Residents include baseball's Sid Fernandez and actors Timothy Dalton and Gardner McKay. *From Kailua Beach Park, continue on Kalaheo to Aalapapa Dr., the entry road to the*

Lanikai community. Turn left at Kaiolena and find a parking space there or on another side street. Accessways lead to the beach from Mokulua Dr., which runs along the beach and leads back toward Kailua.

Swimming: The clear, calm water gets no deeper than 20 feet, and swimmers are particularly buoyant in the salty sea here. Close to the beach, it's shallow enough for tots to learn to swim.

Sand: The fine, soft sand is packed hard at the water's edge.

Amenities: None. No lifeguard.

Parking: Limited to what's available along the streets. If you park on the bike path, you're likely to get a ticket.

MOKULUA ISLAND BEACH

The two Mokulua (*Mo-koo-LOO-ah*) Islands poke like pyramids out of the Pacific, three-quarters of a mile off Lanikai Beach. The beach on the leeward side of the larger island is wide enough to land kayaks, surf-boards, or small sailboats, then have a beach

Beauty	A
Swimming	A
Sand	A
Amenities	NA

party. This is a popular spot for weddings, overnight fishing expeditions, and Robinson Crusoe-like escapes. A good way to reach it is by launching a kayak from Lanikai Beach on a calm morning.

Both of the Mokulua Islands are bird preserves and are off-limits above the sandy beach or the rocky shoreline. *Reached from Lanikai Beach by boat, surfboard, or vigorous swimming.*

Swimming: The strong waves at Mokulua can be disconcerting, but strong swimmers cross the Lanikai lagoon to the island and back, usually with fins and mask. Don't swim outside the reef, where the denizens of the deep hang out in aptly named Shark's Cove.

Sand: Same fine sand as Lanikai Beach, which it faces.

Amenities: None.

WAIMANALO BEACH

Nearly four miles long, Waimanalo (*Why-ma-NAH-lo*) Beach is Oahu's longest continuous sandy beach. The golden strand extends along the island's northeastern shore from Wailea Point to Kaiona Beach Park. On its northern end,

Beauty	A
Swimming	B
Sand	A
Amenities	B

the sand dunes and forests of Bellows Air Force Station make up one of Oahu's most popular beaches, open to the public on weekends and holidays, with campsites available by city permit. *From Kailua Beach Park, go north on Kalaheo Dr. to the first traffic light. Turn left on Kuulei Rd. and go through Kailua to the intersection of Hwys. 61 and 72. Turn left on Hwy. 72 (Kalanianaole Hwy.) and drive 3 mi. to the town of Waimanalo. Waimanalo Beach Park is on the southeast side of town.*

Swimming: Sandy bottom. Gentle waves are ideal for body-surfers of all ages. Safe, but watch toddlers closely.

Sand: Fine and golden.

Amenities: Public beach parks (Bellows, Sherwood Forest, Waimanalo Bay Recreation Area, Waimanalo Beach Park, and Kaiona) have pavilions with rest rooms, changing rooms, and outside showers. Lifeguards on duty at Waimanalo Bay Recreation Area and Waimanalo Beach Park.

Sports: Baseball fields and other park recreational facilities.

Parking: Free at public beach parks.

HOTELS/INNS/B&Bs

Kailua has no hotels and few condos, but it has become the bed-and-breakfast capital of Hawaii, with some 100 rooms to rent.

♦ **Halekai—House of the Sea** (moderate). Kailua Beach is just a few steps from this B&B, a one-bedroom cottage in a tropical garden. *41 Kaumana Pl., Kailua, HI 96734; tel. 800-258-7895.*

♦ **Lanikai Hale Mahina—House of the Moon** (moderate). This B&B on Lanikai Beach is a two-bedroom bungalow with koa-wood furniture and old Hawaii decor. *1277 Mokulua Dr., Kailua, HI 96734; tel. 808-261-1059.*

♦ **Hawaiian Islands Bed & Breakfast and Vacation Rentals** (inexpensive to very expensive). Offers a variety of options. *572 Kailua Rd., Suite 201, Kailua, HI 96734; tel. 808-261-7895, 800-258-7895.*

HOUSE RENTALS

Vacation cottages and homes in the area are available for rent, usually for a minimum of three days. Rates range from $60 to $350 a day.

♦ **John Walker's Beach House** (very expensive). This vintage beach house on Lanikai Beach has high ceilings, big rooms, and a picture window on the Pacific. Modern appliances. Sleeps six. *Tel. 808-261-7895.*

♦ **Kailua Beachside Cottages** (moderate to very expensive). Overlooking Kailua Beach Park but behind a wire-mesh fence that impedes the view, these tidy cottages are only a few steps from the sand. *204 S. Kalaheo Ave., Kailua, HI 96734; tel. 808-261-1653.*

RESTAURANTS

♦ **Buzz's Original Steak House** (moderate). This Polynesian-style hut across from Kailua Beach Park is renowned for its Buzz Burgers and grilled steaks, chops, and fresh fish. President Clinton once ducked out of a banquet in Waikiki to grab a bite at Buzz's. The salad bar is ample and fresh, and the four-inch slices of homemade ice-cream pie are outrageous. Reservations advised for dinner. No credit cards. *413 Kawailoa Rd., Kailua, HI 96734; tel. 808-261-4661. Open daily for lunch and dinner.*

♦ **El Charro Avitia** (moderate). Direct from Durango, Mexico, Antonio Avitia came for a vacation and stayed. The Avitia family serves regional specialties from the homeland, as well as fish and seafood fajitas, burritos, and tacos. *14 Oneawa St., Kailua, HI 96734; tel. 808-263-3943. Open Tue.-Sun. for lunch and dinner.*

♦ **Old World Bistro** (moderate). Arguably Kailua's best cuisine, created by chef Alfred Mueller, who left a major Waikiki hotel to start his own place a decade ago. *20 Kainehe St., Kailua, HI 96734; tel. 808-261-1987. Open Tue.-Sun. for dinner.*

♦ **Boston's North End Pizza Bakery** (inexpensive). An Italian family from Boston serves pizza just the way they did back home: huge, tasty, and well priced. *29 Hoolai St., Kailua, HI 96734; tel. 808-263-7757. Open daily for lunch and dinner.*

♦ **Cinnamon's Restaurant** (inexpensive). After dawn patrol, hungry surfers chow down at Cinnamon's, a home-style restaurant that serves heaping breakfast platters of fresh fish or Portuguese sausage, eggs, and rice. *Kailua Square, 315 Uluniu St., Kailua, HI 96734; tel. 808-261-8724. Open daily for breakfast and lunch, and Thu.-Sat. for dinner.*

NIGHTLIFE

Kailua's streets are dark by 10 p.m. The brightest lights in town belong to Blockbuster Video. Those who search may find an open bar.

SHOPPING

♦ **Elizabeth's Fancy.** One of Oahu's better gift shops, Elizabeth's sells authentic Hawaiian heirloom quilts, quilted pillow patterns, and items decorated with distinctive Hawaiian appliqué designs. *767B Kailua Rd., Kailua, HI 96734; tel. 808-262-7513. Open daily except Sun.*

♦ **Mahalo Mona.** Bright aloha-wear patterns are the hallmark of the casual women's clothing sold here. Along with the shorts, pants, sundresses, and tops, there are also drink holders, visors, and other clever gifts from the neighboring Kahala Creations factory. *767 Kailua Rd., Kailua, HI 96734; tel. 808-262-6366. Open daily.*

♦ **Tusitala Bookshop.** A second-hand book store with a stellar collection of Hawaiian books and old-fashioned Hawaiian song-sheets and menu covers that collectors seek for framing. Also many out-of-print books and autographed first editions. *116 Hekili St., Kailua, HI 96734; tel. 808-262-6343. Open daily.*

BEST FOOD SHOPS

SANDWICHES: ♦ **Ba-Le.** A Vietnamese sandwich shop with fresh-baked crusty rolls and croissants. *345 Hahani St., Kailua, HI 96734; tel. 808-261-2193. Open daily.*

SEAFOOD: ♦ **Kailua Safeway.** *200 Hamakua Dr., Kailua, HI 96734; tel. 808-263-8871. Open 24 hours daily.*

FRESH PRODUCE: ♦ **Kailua Safeway.** *200 Hamakua Dr., Kailua, HI 96734; tel. 808-263-8871. Open 24 hours daily.*

BAKERY: ♦ **Agnes Portuguese Bake Shop.** Specializes in fresh-baked *malassadas* (Portuguese donuts). *35 Kainehe St., Kailua, HI 96734; tel. 808-262-5367. Open daily except Mon.*

ICE CREAM: ♦ **Kalapawai Market.** *306 S. Kalaheo Ave., Kailua, HI 96734; tel. 808-262-4359. Open daily.*

BEVERAGES: ♦ **First Stop Grocery Store.** *130 Kailua Rd., Kailua, HI 96734; tel. 808-262-0408. Open 24 hours daily.*
WINE: ♦ **Michael's Liquor.** *515 Kailua Rd., Kailua, HI 96734; tel. 808-261-3433. Open daily.*

SPORTS

Kailua Beach gained an international reputation in the late 1970s as a windsurfing capital when surfers fitted sails to surfboards and began ripping across Kailua Bay to pioneer the sport. Although many of the daredevils have moved to windier Maui, Kailua Bay is an excellent place to show off speed and wave-jumping skills on a windy day. It's also a favorite spot to sail catamarans, bodysurf, or paddle a kayak or outrigger canoe.

BOATING

♦ **Bob Twogood Kayaks.** *171B Hamakua Dr., Kailua, HI 96734; tel. 808-262-5656. Open daily.*
♦ **Karel's Kayaks.** Karel Tresnak, the world-champion paddler from Czechoslovakia, sells and rents kayaks and other craft at his factory. *789 Kailua Rd., Kailua, HI 96734; tel. 808-261-8424. Open daily.*

SURFING

♦ **Naish Hawaii.** Windsurfers from all over the world come here to get tips from world champion Robbie Naish and his crew. They make, sell, and rent Windsurfer boards, harnesses, sails, and other gear. *155A Hamakua Dr., Kailua, HI 96734; tel. 808-262-6068. Open daily.*

DIVING

♦ **Aarons Dive Shop.** Hawaii's oldest dive shop is staffed by experienced underwater experts who sell a full line of scuba gear and air. They give lessons to beginners and take experienced divers to sites in Hawaii and farther out in the Pacific. *602 Kailua Rd., Kailua, HI 96734; tel. 808-262-2333. Open daily.*

TENNIS

♦ **Kailua Community Center.** Free courts are in the center of town near the library. *21 S. Kainalu Dr., Kailua, HI 96734; tel. 808-266-7652. Open daily.*

NATURE

◆ **Kaiwa Ridge.** The 40-minute hike to the peak of this old, 603-foot-high crater yields panoramic views of the Pali Mountain range and the windward side of Oahu. *From the Kailua Beach Park parking lot, turn left on Aalapapa Dr. and go one block. Turn right on Kaelepulu St. and drive half a block, passing the entrance to the Mid-Pacific Country Club. The trailhead begins on the left, next to the chain-link fence at the Bluestone condos.*

◆ **Kawaianui Marsh.** This 1,000-acre swamp is a sanctuary for such endangered water birds as Hawaiian stilts and Koloa ducks. Hiking trails lead into the marsh, a great spot to go birding at sunset. *From town, head west for about 1.5 mi. on Kailua Rd. (Hwy. 61). The trailhead is on the right at the Ulo Po Heiau monument. Look for the footpath to an earthen dike. Open sunrise to sunset.*

SAFETY TIPS

When the big waves come up, usually in January, they toss Portuguese man-of-war jellyfish over the reef. Tangling with one of these is like sitting on a bees' nest. If it happens, rub the sting with a papaya, Adolph's Meat Tenderizer, or urine, the ancient Hawaiian treatment.

TOURIST INFORMATION

◆ **Hawaii Visitors Bureau.** Brochures, maps, and guides available free. *2270 Kalakaua Ave., Suite 801, Honolulu, HI 96815; tel. 808-923-1811. Open Mon.-Fri. 8-4:30.*

CHAPTER 2

Ala Moana

An aquatic version of New York City's Central Park, Ala Moana is probably the best urban beach in the United States. Stretching for more than a mile between downtown Honolulu and Waikiki, it's the only beach with a world-class shopping mall (Ala Moana Center) right across the street. This 76-acre park, with spreading lawns shaded by banyans and palms, is one of the most popular playgrounds on Oahu, frequented each year by four million surfers, swimmers, fishermen, and picnickers, plus countless joggers.

Beauty	A
Swimming	A
Sand	A
Hotels/Inns/B&Bs	C
House rentals	NA
Restaurants	A
Nightlife	B
Attractions	A
Shopping	A
Sports	A
Nature	D

Ala Moana, which means, "By the Sea," has two harbors, one for yachts and the other for fishing and tour boats. Besides surfing and other water sports, it offers many activities ashore. Model-boat fanciers race their craft on park lagoons. Crafts fairs are held periodically under the trees. At McCoy Pavilion, crowds enjoy free ukulele and slack-key guitar concerts and other cultural events. On the Diamond Head side of the park, there's even a park within the park known as Magic Island. A man-made peninsula jutting out into Mamala Bay, it has a protected lagoon at the end, bordered by a swimming beach designed for children.

Ala Moana Park recently underwent a $5 million facelift. Tennis courts were renovated, two bathhouses were improved, and another comfort station was added to the facilities. A path was paved through the park for bikers, skaters, joggers, and walkers. Sometimes it seems as if everybody in Honolulu has come to the park to play. To avoid getting lost in the crowd, arrive early in the day.

ALA MOANA BEACH PARK

One hint that regulars at Ala Moana Park take swimming seriously is the number of swimmers churning out laps in the lagoon. There's also plenty of snorkeling, fishing, and general ocean recreation done on this mile-long beach.

Beauty	A
Swimming	A
Sand	A
Amenities	A

Offshore, the surfing is good, especially when a south swell is rising. Picnic, sports, and entertainment facilities on the lawns complete the picture.

Swimming: The water is calm and protected by an offshore reef.
Sand: Soft and golden, much of it imported.
Amenities: Rest rooms, showers, food concessions, pavilion, and stage. Lifeguards on duty.
Sports: Surfing, snorkeling. Tennis courts, softball fields, bowling green.
Parking: The 1,100 parking places fill up fast on weekends.

HOW TO GET THERE

◆ Ala Moana Beach Park is about 20 minutes by taxi or car from Honolulu International Airport. Take H-1 toward Honolulu and get off at the Waikiki exit, which puts you on Nimitz Hwy. (Hwy. 92). After you pass the Aloha Tower on the right, Ala Moana Beach Park will appear on the right in about a mile. From Waikiki, the nearest park entrance is across the Ala Wai Canal Bridge and to the left, through the Art Deco gate.

◆ Buses on Ala Moana Blvd. stop at any of the park's four bus stops. For people in hotels closest to the downtown border of Waikiki, it's a walk.

AINA MOANA STATE RECREATION AREA (MAGIC ISLAND BEACH)

When plans for a resort on a man-made island failed in 1964, Honolulu transformed the broken dream into a people's park. This great scoop of beach was created from imported sand covering 30 acres of shallow reef

Beauty	A
Swimming	A
Sand	A
Amenities	A

and coral fill dredged up from the sea bottom. Officially known as Aina Moana (literally, "Land from the Ocean") State Recreation Area, it is popularly called Magic Island. The beach offers a great view of Diamond Head and is popular with fishermen, including many who throw-cast their nets in the old Hawaiian way.

Swimming: Excellent, protected, and safe for children.
Sand: Golden and soft.
Amenities: Rest rooms. Lifeguards on duty.
Sports: None.
Parking: Served by the same 1,100 space lot as Ala Moana Beach.

KAKAAKO WATERFRONT STATE PARK

Not exactly a beach, Kakaako is a sea-side park for those who dislike getting sand on their feet. But it's too good to miss, especially if you like to watch bodysurfers and boardsurfers ride the summer swells at sundown.

Beauty	A
Swimming	NA
Sand	NA
Amenities	A

Kakaako is a waterfront park that opened a new view of Waikiki. Part of the city's continuing efforts to reclaim waterfront for public enjoyment, it's a series of grassy knolls with picnic and barbecue facilities.

Swimming: None.
Sand: None.
Amenities: Rest rooms, picnic area, waterfront promenade with benches.
Sports: None.
Parking: Ample and free.

HOTELS/INNS/B&Bs

♦ **Hawaii Prince Hotel & Golf Club** (very expensive). Just across the Ala Wai Canal Bridge from Ala Moana Beach Park, this pink granite, 33-story twin-tower hotel has terrific sunset views of the boat harbor, Magic Island, and the Pacific. All 521 rooms are ocean front, but only a few luxury suites have a lanai. Room 2917 has the best panoramic ocean view, if you don't mind paying $1,100 per night. In addition to the hotel's world-class restaurant, it has an informal bar and eatery outdoors, around the fifth-floor pool. *100 Holomoana St., Honolulu, HI 96815; tel. 808-956-1111, 800-321-6248.*

♦ **Ala Moana Hotel** (moderate to expensive). Only a block from the beach and next to Ala Moana Center, this newly remodeled 36-story brass-and-glass hotel is centrally located, away from the maze of Waikiki traffic. Some of Hawaii's best Chinese dim sum is served in the Royal Garden restaurant, near a pool with a commanding view of the ocean. *410 Atkinson Dr., Honolulu, HI 96814; tel. 808-955-4811, 800-367-6025.*

♦ **Pagoda Hotel** (inexpensive). This 360-room, Japanese-style hotel sits in a garden setting with open-air dining pavilions over koi carp ponds. The rooms are small and well kept. *1525 Rycroft St., Honolulu, HI 96814; tel. 808-941-6611, 800-472-4632. Located several blocks inland, behind Ala Moana Center.*

RESTAURANTS

The Ala Moana area of Honolulu's waterfront has many restaurants and eateries, ranging from the budget-conscious international food court at Ala Moana Center to top-notch fine dining.

♦ **John Domini's** (very expensive). You'll find outstanding ocean and sunset views from this high-ticket seafood restaurant on the water in an industrial zone at Kawalo Basin. Lobsters crawl around in an indoor stream prior to being selected for the table, and whole opakapaka, golden mahimahi, and red snapper stare blankly from crushed-ice bins. The tables are too close together, and some food critics complain that the place is a tourist rip-off, but sooner or later everyone comes for the view. *43 Ahui St., Honolulu, HI 96813; tel. 808-523-0955. Open daily for lunch and dinner.*

♦ **Andrew's** (expensive). One of Honolulu's best Italian restaurants, it earned its reputation by cooking tasty pastas, particularly ravioli and a cheesy cannelloni. The ink-black lounge near the entrance is a popular hangout for Hawaiian singers and dancers, who often crowd the piano bar to sing traditional songs. *1200 Ala Moana Blvd., Honolulu, HI 96814; tel. 808-591-8677. Open daily for lunch and dinner.*

♦ **Nicholas Nickolas** (expensive). With a glittery view of other high-rise buildings and a tiny glimpse of the ocean, this continental fine-dining establishment on the 36th floor of the Ala Moana Hotel is an old-fashioned supper club that originated in Chicago and washed ashore in Honolulu. It attracts a huge following of out-of-towners and local guys who wear gold neck chains. Black-tie waiters in dress shirts and tuxedo pants provide brisk service to diners in intimate booths facing Waikiki's skyline. Guests can listen to live music, and there's a dance floor. *410 Atkinson Dr., Honolulu, HI 96814; tel. 808-955-4466. Open daily for dinner.*

♦ **Prince Court** (expensive). With sunset views over the Ala Wai Yacht Harbor, this waterfront room glows as chef Gary Strehl presents dishes exemplifying Hawaii regional cuisine. One of the best: grilled Kona abalone with lime and macadamia nut butter. A sumptuous daily brunch features fresh juices and custom omelets. The best seat in the house is Table 95, overlooking the harbor. It's where jazzman Dizzy Gillespie once ordered catfish but settled for opakapaka. *In the Hawaii Prince Hotel & Golf Club, 100 Holomoana St., Honolulu, HI 96815; tel. 808-956-1111, ext. 61. Open daily for breakfast, lunch, and dinner.*

♦ **Scott's Seafood** (expensive). An indoor-outdoor seafood restaurant on the waterfront, done San Franciso-diner style with chrome and glass. Try the Moroccan-style local swordfish, the seared ahi tuna, or Manila clams in black-bean sauce. The catch of the day is displayed on ice behind the reservations desk. Grab a table outside on the lanai and watch cruise ships, cargo vessels, and tugboats entering and leaving Honolulu Harbor. Or sit inside and watch the chefs prepare your meal at the performance kitchen. *Aloha Tower Marketplace, 1 Aloha Tower Dr., Honolulu, HI 96813; tel. 808-537-6800. Open daily for lunch and dinner.*

♦ **Sunset Grill** (moderate to expensive). This California-style grill is often noisy and doesn't have a good sunset view, but nobody complains. Customers are immediately intoxicated by the mouth-watering smokehouse aroma and then completely won over by the grilled meat and fish. Try the grilled chicken gorgonzola salad with apples or the smoked marinated salmon. The walls are decorated with crayon art on placemats by talented doodlers. The booths are popular for power lunches. *500 Ala Moana Blvd., Honolulu, HI 96813; tel. 808-521-4409. Open daily for lunch and dinner.*

♦ **Gordon Biersch** (moderate). Honolulu's first brew-pub is an open-air harborfront bistro with three types of fresh beer and tasty informal dishes by a local chef. Expect such choices as fried calamari, chicken satay, garlic-heavy *pupus* (appetizers), and other foods that encourage customers to drink more beer. The outdoor bar is a popular gathering place every afternoon. *Aloha Tower Marketplace, 1 Aloha Tower Dr., Honolulu, HI 96813; tel. 808-599-4877. Open daily for lunch and dinner.*

♦ **Scoozee's** (inexpensive). A great bargain, this bright, crowded bistro serves good salads, pasta, pizza, and other Italian fare. There's a full bar with a selection of imported beers. You come here to eat—not for the view (of an asphalt parking lot at Ward Centre). Local folks like to eat inside in air-conditioned comfort, while tourists head to the outdoor patio for a table under an umbrella. *1200 Ala Moana Blvd., Honolulu, HI 96814; tel. 808-597-1777. Open daily for lunch and dinner.*

NIGHTLIFE

Hottest spots in Aloha Tower's new arcade are pubs, such as the Sloppy Joe's/Fat Tuesday combination and the Gordon Biersch brew-pub (*see* Restaurants).

♦ **Sloppy Joe's/Fat Tuesday.** *Aloha Tower Marketplace, 1 Aloha Tower Dr., Honolulu, HI 96813; tel. 808-528-0007. Open daily.*

♦ **Rumours Nightclub.** Strobe lights and hard rock for dancing the night away. *In the Ala Moana Hotel, 410 Atkinson Dr.,*

Honolulu, HI 96814; tel. 808-955-4811. Open Tue.-Sun.
♦ **World Cafe.** Food, drinks, and a pool combine for a good time. *500 Ala Moana Blvd., Honolulu, HI 96813; tel. 808-599-4450. Open nightly.*
♦ **Blue Zebra Cafe.** This popular dance club occasionally has live bands. *500 Ala Moana Blvd., Honolulu, HI 96813; tel. 808-538-0409. Open nightly.*

ATTRACTIONS

♦ **Aloha Tower Marketplace.** Aloha Tower, the beacon that welcomed visitors to Hawaii when they all came by ship, is the centerpiece of this shopping-eating-entertainment complex. You'll find good restaurants at various budget levels, interesting wares at shops and stalls, and free entertainment at stages built on working docks in the harbor. Ships are often tied up here. Visit the refurbished Art Deco clock tower. Take a ride on the fireboat *Abner T. Longley* and let off a little spray. *1 Aloha Tower Dr., Honolulu, HI 96813, tel. 808-528-5700. Open daily. On Pier 10 at the foot of Bishop St.*
♦ **Honolulu Fish Auction.** The scene at the United Fishing Agency is fascinating for those who care enough to get there at 6 a.m. Much of Hawaii's daily catch from local boats is arranged on icy pallets here and rolled through the auction house. The bounty is colorful. The auctioneer works in a sing-song blend of English, Japanese, and pidgin. Buyers include brokers, restaurants, and markets. Visitors can watch, if they stay out of the way. *117 Ahui St., Honolulu, HI 06813; tel. 808-536-2148. Open Mon.-Sat. From Ala Moana Beach, drive 1 mi. on Ala Moana Blvd. in the opposite direction from Diamond Head. Turn left on Ahui St. and drive half a block through the warehouse district. Look for the Fish Auction on the left.*

SHOPPING

♦ **Ala Moana Center.** One of the nation's largest shopping centers, this open-air mall across the street from Ala Moana Beach attracts 56 million visitors a year. The 200-shop international mall includes several large department stores and numerous

European designer boutiques. Island music and dance is performed on an outdoor stage. You can dine at Makai Market Food Court or other restaurants and snack shops. *1450 Ala Moana Blvd., Honolulu, HI 96814; tel. 808-946-2811. Open daily. Between Atkinson Dr. and Piikoi St.*

♦ **Ward Centre/Ward Warehouse.** A mecca for shoppers and diners, Ward Centre houses popular restaurants and specialty shops, including the Honolulu Chocolate Co. More shops are found in Ward Warehouse, including Nohea Gallery, with arts, crafts, jewelry, ceramics, and photography by local artists. *Centre: 1200 Ala Moana Blvd., Honolulu, HI 96814; tel. 808-591-8411. Warehouse: 1050 Ala Moana Blvd. Open daily. Between Ala Moana Center and downtown Honolulu.*

♦ **Aloha Flea Market.** It's worth the half-hour trip to the greatest outdoor bazaar in the Pacific, which takes place in the parking lot of Aloha Stadium, home of the University of Hawaii Rainbow football team and the annual Pro Bowl. Sundays are the busiest for this superbowl of shopping, with hundreds of vendors selling exotic produce, T-shirts, clothes, eel-skin bags, and seashells. *99500 Salt Lake Blvd., Aiea, HI 96701; Box 30666, Honolulu, HI 96820; tel. 808-486-1529. Open Wed., Sat., Sun. 6-3. Shuttles run from downtown hotels; call 808-988-9293 for reservations.*

BEST FOOD SHOPS

SANDWICHES: ♦ **Ba-Le Sandwich Shop.** Ba-Le Shops throughout Honolulu sell Vietnamese sandwiches on fresh rolls and croissants, with drinks and other dishes. *1450 Ala Moana Blvd., Honolulu, HI 96814; tel. 808-944-4752.*

SEAFOOD: ♦ **Bob's Fish Market.** *Ala Moana Farmers Market, 1020 Avahi St., Honolulu, HI 96814; tel. 808-596-8220. Open daily.*

FRESH PRODUCE: ♦ **Tropic Fish & Vegetable Center.** *Ala Moana Farmers Market, 1020 Avahi St., Honolulu, HI 96814; tel. 808-591-2936. Open daily.*

BAKERY: ♦ **Mary Catherine's Bakery.** *Ward Warehouse, 1050 Ala Moana Blvd., Honolulu, HI 96814; tel. 808-591-8525. Open daily.*

ICE CREAM: ♦ **Lapperts Royal Hawaiian Ice Cream Co.** *2005 Kalia Rd., Honolulu, HI 96815; tel. 808-943-0256. Open daily. In Hilton Hawaiian Village.*

BEVERAGES: ♦ **The Liquor Collection.** *Ward Warehouse, 1050 Ala Moana Blvd., Honolulu, HI 96814; tel. 808-524-8808. Open daily.*
WINE: ♦ **R. Field Wine Co.** *Ward Centre, 1200 Ala Moana Blvd., Honolulu, HI 96814; tel. 808-596-9463. Open daily.*

SPORTS
FISHING

Kewalo Basin is the fishing harbor for Honolulu's fleet, which includes several charter fishing boats.

♦ **Island Charters.** Full- and half-day shares or exclusive charters on 15 boats. *1089-A Ala Moana Blvd., Honolulu, HI 96814; tel. 808-593-9455. Open daily.*

♦ **Elo Sportsfishing.** Full- or part-day charters. Overnight fishing off other islands. *350 Ward Ave., Suite 106, Honolulu, HI 96814; tel. 808-947-5208. Open daily.*

BOATING

Ala Wai Yacht Harbor, next to Ala Moana Beach Park, provides anchorage for more than 400 pleasure craft of every size and type. Tour boats, ranging from giant motorized vessels to small sailboats, are moored at Kewalo Basin and near Aloha Tower Marketplace. Budget-conscious passengers can skip the on-board meals and just go for the sunset, which is the best part anyway.

♦ **Ali'i Kai Catamaran.** Sunset cruises are $48 for adults, $28 for children ages 5 to 11. Dinner sails are $140 for adults, $120 for children. *680 Iwilei Rd., Suite 700, Honolulu, HI 96817; tel. 808-524-6694. Open daily.*

♦ **Manu Kai.** One-hour sails on a 48-foot catamaran. Also sails to watch the sunset and private charters. *Box 8181, Honolulu, HI, 96830; tel. 808-946-7490, 800-281-1748. Open daily.*

♦ **Navatek.** Royal Hawaiian Cruises operates this 380-passenger high-tech cruiser, which is built to reduce seasickness. Various day cruise options and private charters. Whale-watching in winter. *841 Bishop St., Suite 1880, Honolulu, HI 96813; tel. 808-531-7001, 800-852-4183. Open daily.*

♦ **Tradewind Charters.** Three-hour sunset cruises on 40- to 70-foot yachts include dinner and drinks for $65. Also snorkeling, whale-watching, and interisland cruises. *1833 Kalakaua Ave., Suite 612, Honolulu, HI 96815; tel. 808-973-0311, 800-829-4899.*

SURFING
♦ **Hawaiian Islands Creations.** *Ala Moana Center, 1450 Ala Moana Blvd., Honolulu, HI 96814; tel. 808-973-6780. Open daily.*

DIVING
♦ **Dive Authority.** Equipment rentals, instruction, boat charters. *333 Ward Ave., Honolulu, HI 96813; tel. 808-596-7234. Open daily.*

TENNIS
♦ **Ala Moana Beach Park.** There are public courts at the McCoy Pavilion.

HISTORY
♦ **Hawaii Maritime Museum.** Hawaii's seafaring past comes to life in the artifact-packed Kalakaua Boat House. Outside, the *Hokulea*, a double-hulled sailing canoe used for reenacting Polynesian voyages of discovery, is moored next to the *Falls of Clyde*, a four-masted schooner. Inside, 30 exhibits include Matson cruise ships, which brought the first tourists to Waikiki, and seaplanes that delivered the mail. *Pier 7, Honolulu Harbor, Honolulu, HI 96813; tel. 808-536-6373. Next to Aloha Tower Marketplace.*

SAFETY TIPS
The greatest potential danger along this stretch of beach is from automobiles on Ala Moana Boulevard.

TOURIST INFORMATION
♦ **Hawaii Visitors Bureau.** Brochures, maps, and guides available free. *2270 Kalakaua Ave., Suite 801, Honolulu, HI 96815; tel. 808-923-1811. Open Mon.-Fri. 8-4:30.*

CHAPTER 3

Haleiwa

H aleiwa (*Haw-LAY-ee-vah*) is the ultimate beach town. Named for the mighty frigate bird (*iwa*), this funky clapboard village survived the demise of local sugar plantations to emerge as the undisputed surf capital of the world. It is home to the legendary beaches of Oahu's North Shore, where the world's most spectacular waves thunder ashore in winter, attracting big-wave surfers from around the globe.

Beauty	A
Swimming	B
Sand	A
Hotels/Inns/B&Bs	C
House rentals	C
Restaurants	B
Nightlife	C
Attractions	B
Shopping	B
Sports	A
Nature	A

When the top surfers are in town to compete in the annual professional surf meets, it seems every spectator whose car can fit on the two-lane Kamehameha Highway is here, too. They scramble to see nature's mesmerizing show of force and the daring young men who risk their lives trying to best it on slivers of Fiberglas.

In summer, when seas are flat, the town relaxes. Sun-bleached golden boys ride bicycles with surfboards tucked under their arms and jump off the old Anahulu River Bridge. Fashion photographers shoot women in skimpy swimsuits. Strangers from around the world stand in line for shave ice, a cooling kind of tropical snowcone. And everyone goes to the beach.

On any weekend, regardless of the season, the main drag is a slow parade of day-trippers bound for the beach. There's an abundance of choice along the 12-mile stretch of the North Shore, and the names are legend: Haleiwa, Waimea, Banzai Pipeline, Sunset.

An array of enterprises stands ready to sustain the throng. Arts-and-crafts folk, water-sports shops, boutiques, coffee shops, and burger stands line both sides of the highway. Roadside stands sell coconuts, bananas, papayas, mangoes, and "conch shells for blowing." Reminiscent of the 1960s, when the town was "discovered" by hippies from the mainland, a whiff of patchouli oil still mingles with the scent of plumeria.

HALEIWA BEACH

This beach has something for everyone, except avid surfers. It arcs around Waialua Bay with Haleiwa Beach Park on the northeast shore, the picturesque Haleiwa Small Boat Harbor in the center, and Alii Beach Park at the other end. Lifeguard

Beauty	B
Swimming	B
Sand	C
Amenities	A

Reggie Adric claims Alii is the best place for beginners to learn to surf. *In the town of Haleiwa, turn left off Hwy. 83 (Kamehameha Hwy.) onto Kahalewai Pl.*

Swimming: A sandy bottom and gentle waves protected by the harbor jetty combine to make this a safe place for youngsters to play in the surf, subject to seasonal conditions.

Sand: Coarse, golden with a tinge of red.

Amenities: Rest rooms, showers, beach park pavilion, food concession, trailer and tent camping. Lifeguard on duty.

Sports: Off to the left of the beach, a 60-foot-deep fish-filled trench in the coral reef attracts snorkelers and scuba divers.

HOW TO GET THERE

◆ From Honolulu International Airport (a 50-minute drive from Haleiwa), take I-H1 west (opposite from the Honolulu direction), then merge onto I-H2. When I-H2 ends at the edge of Wahiawa and Schofield Barracks, pick up Hwy. 99. Bear right at the Y intersection in about 2 mi., staying with Hwy. 99 toward the North Shore. Turn right on Hwy. 83 to reach the town of Haleiwa and its beach park.

There are also basketball and volleyball courts and baseball and softball fields.

Parking: Off-street lot.

WAIMEA BAY

A deep, sandy bowl with gentle summer waves excellent for swimming and other water sports. To one side of the bay is a huge rock that local kids like to dive from. But what a difference a season makes. Remember the huge wave that introduced

Beauty	A
Swimming	B
Sand	A
Amenities	B

the *Hawaii Five-0* TV show? That's Waimea (*Why-MAY-ah*) Bay. In summer, the only clue of what's to come are those evacuation whistles on poles beside the road. Winter waves pounding the narrow bay can rise 50 feet high, sweeping the bay and causing nearby areas to be evacuated. *4 mi. north of Haleiwa on Hwy. 83 (Kamehameha Hwy.). Turn left into the parking lot.*
Swimming: Safe when it's calm, life-threatening when it's not.
Sand: Golden, soft, and there's plenty of it.
Amenities: Rest rooms, showers. Lifeguard on duty.
Sports: Snorkeling, bodysurfing.
Parking: There's an off-street lot.

PUPUKEA BEACH PARK

An 80-acre park named for the tiny scallop shells that once littered the beach. Pupukea (*Poo-poo-KAY-ah*), which means "white shell," is a long, narrow strand with a rocky shoreline and booming surf in winter. The park has two popular summertime swim-

Beauty	A
Swimming	B
Sand	B
Amenities	B

ming sites: Shark's Cove on the south end and Three Tables on the north. Shark's Cove, one of the most beautiful tide pools in the state, is naturally formed by lava walls that sank into the sea. Despite its name, it's no more shark-prone than the waters off the other beaches throughout Oahu. *5 mi. north of Haleiwa on the north side of Waimea Bay Beach Park.*
Swimming: Good when waves are calm.
Sand: Golden, sometimes coarse, with shells on the stretch

north of the reef.
Amenities: Rest rooms, showers, recreation building, children's play area, camping facilities.
Sports: Basketball and volleyball courts. Shark's Cove is great for snorkeling in calm conditions.
Parking: Off-street lot.

EHUKAI BEACH (BANZAI PIPELINE)

Ehukai (*Ay-HOO-kigh*) Beach is the home of Banzai Pipeline, the world's most famous surfing break, which is aptly named. In winter, the big swells hit a shallow coral shelf just offshore and form waves so steep that the tops fall over

Beauty	A
Swimming	D
Sand	B
Amenities	D

before they break, curling to form a perfect tube. Naturally, the death-defying challenge of surfing through this attracts surfers from around the world.

The wide stretch of sand is also an ideal place for walking, sun-tanning, hanging out, or watching surfers, including bodysurfers, ride the waves. The beach slopes down to the edge of the water to create a natural, sandy amphitheater, seasonally occupied by film crews with long camera lenses and by spectators squinting through binoculars. *Reached by Ke Nui Rd., off Hwy. 83 (Kamehameha Hwy.).*
Swimming: Currents are dangerous, even in summer. Pick another spot.
Sand: Golden, soft, grainy, almost pebblelike.
Amenities: Rest rooms, showers. Lifeguard on duty.
Sports: Surfing, bodysurfing.
Parking: Roadside.

SUNSET BEACH

Renowned as a gathering spot for world-class surfers, Sunset Beach offers winter surfing for experts only. Its currents are extremely dangerous when the surf is up. One current even has a name, the Sunset Rip, which is said to deliver lost surf-

Beauty	A
Swimming	B
Sand	B
Amenities	B

boards all the way to Kauai.

Stretching for more than two miles, this is Oahu's longest expanse of wide beach, with an average width of 200 feet. It rolls gently down to the water's edge. They don't call it Sunset for nothing, either. The sunsets here are incredible. *2 mi. north of Pupukea Beach Park, just off Hwy. 83 (Kamehameha Hwy.) at Paumalu Pl.*
Swimming: Summer only. Winter waves are big, bad, and shifty.
Sand: Golden, soft, grainy.
Amenities: Lifeguard on duty.
Sports: Surfing.
Parking: Roadside and a small lot.

HOTELS/INNS/B&Bs

♦ **Turtle Bay Hilton Golf & Tennis Resort** (expensive). The only resort on the North Shore, this once-sparkling, Y-shaped hostelry shows signs of neglect inside and outside. Nevertheless, the 485-room hotel enjoys an awesome site on Kuilima Point, surrounded by five miles of secluded coves and beaches with spectacular ocean and mountain views. Big waves come rolling across Kawela Bay and often create spouts of water in lava tubes to the delight of hotel guests. Rooms are comfortable but nothing to write home about. Activities include golf, tennis, and horseback riding. There's a small sheltered public beach here, but you have to pay to park in the hotel lot. *57-091 Kamehameha Hwy., Kahuku, HI 96731; tel. 808-293-8811, 800-HILTONS.*

♦ **Kuilima Estates** (moderate). Inland from the Hilton, 100 Turtle Bay vacation condominium units (from studio to three-bedroom) represent one of the best alternatives for lodging. The brown, two-story condos are located near the beach and are just a short drive from Haleiwa. *Box 248, Kahuku, HI 96731; tel. 808-293-2800.*

♦ **Backpackers Vacation Inn & Plantation Village** (inexpensive). A low-budget port of entry, almost a crash pad. Its 25 units include cottages, double rooms, and hostel-style beds—all on the beach by a great snorkeling site. Kitchens available; also bicycles and snorkel gear. Airport pickup at Honolulu International. *59-788 Kamehameha Hwy., Haleiwa, HI 96712; tel. 808-638-7838.*

HOUSE RENTALS

Vacation rental homes on the beach are expensive. If you find one, book it fast.

♦ **Ke Iki Hale** (moderate). Alice Tracy's Pupukea beach front compound is a favorite of surfers, including Bruce Jenkins, whose *North Shore Chronicles* recalls how a monster wave wiped out Cottage No. 9 in 1986, while he lay sleeping inside. The layout includes a dozen one- and two-bedroom cottages. *59-579 Ke Iki Rd., Haleiwa, HI 96712; tel. 808-638-8229.*

RESTAURANTS

North Shore restaurants are limited in number and variety, but the food is good.

♦ **Chart House** (moderate to expensive). This harborside restaurant provides patrons with a good view of boats in the marina. If your appetite is bigger than your budget, hit the salad bar (avocados, mushrooms, and sprouts are abundant). Save room for the mud pie dessert. *66-011 Kamehameha Hwy., Haleiwa, HI 96712; tel. 808-637-8005. Open daily for lunch and dinner; Sun. for brunch. Located just before the bridge, looking out to the marina.*

♦ **Coffee Gallery** (moderate). Nestled among tropical plants at the North Shore Marketplace, this outdoor coffee bar that's a favorite of surfers sells Hawaii's own Kona coffee and flavored coffees ranging from mango to coconut cream. It serves only vegetarian meals, sandwiches, and hearty breakfasts. Service isn't speedy. *66-250 Kamehameha Hwy., Haleiwa, HI 96712; tel. 808-637-5571, 800-621-9614. Open daily for breakfast, lunch, and dinner.*

♦ **Jameson's by the Sea** (moderate). This pleasant roadside steak-and-seafood restaurant is the best bet for lunch and dinner. Jameson's broad lanai faces the harbor and, at sunset, is usually full of people sipping mai tais. The best seat in the house for two is Table 4, on the sunset corner of the lanai. *62-540 Kamehameha Hwy., Haleiwa, HI 96712; tel. 808-637-4336. Open daily for lunch and dinner; Sat.-Sun. for breakfast.*

♦ **Cafe Haleiwa** (inexpensive). Noted for its "Dawn Patrol" breakfast (three pancakes, two eggs, and fruit), this favorite of surfers opens at 6 a.m., when chefs start flipping the whole-wheat banana pancakes.

66-460 Kamehameha Hwy., Haleiwa, HI 96712; tel. 808-637-5516. Open daily for breakfast and lunch.

♦ **Kua Aina Sandwich** (inexpensive). Best hamburgers around, served with homemade lemonade and thin-strip French fries. The mahi burger is also recommended. You must stand in line to order; eat on the roadside lanai. *66-214 Kamehameha Hwy., Haleiwa, HI 96712; tel. 808-637-6067. Open daily for lunch and dinner.*

NIGHTLIFE

Not much. The town goes to bed at 8 p.m. to rise at dawn, with roosters crowing and surfers paddling.

♦ **Turtle Bay Hilton Golf & Tennis Resort.** Live entertainment on weekends. *57-091 Kamehameha Hwy., Kahuku, HI 96731; tel. 808-293-8811, 800-HILTONS.*

♦ **Coffee Gallery.** Live local bands at night. *66-250 Kamehameha Hwy., Haleiwa, HI 96712; tel. 808-637-5571.*

ATTRACTIONS

♦ **Waimea Falls Park.** Cliff divers, Hawaiian games, nature walks, moonlight walks, and archaeological sites are featured in a long river valley with tropical gardens. You can see remnants of old settlements, watch authentic hula, kayak the Waimea River, or ride an ATV into the 1,800-acre valley. Nighttime show spotlights valley history. *59-864 Kamehameha Hwy., Haleiwa, HI 96712; tel. 808-638-8511, 800-767-8046. Open daily. Across from Waimea Beach Park.*

♦ **Haleiwa Surf Museum.** Surfers like to visit this small shrine. Exhibits include old surfboards, 1950s surf-meet posters, 1960s album covers, and photos by legendary LeRoy Grannis (who's in his late 70s and still surfing daily). *66-250 Kamehameha Hwy., C-103, Haleiwa, HI 96712; tel. 808-637-3406. Open daily. At North Shore Marketplace.*

SHOPPING

Haleiwa's quaint buildings are jammed with galleries, boutiques, and surf shops. The old general stores sell shave-ice, a cooling local treat (try such refreshing flavors as coconut, mango, and *lilikoi*). North Shore Marketplace, a cluster of shops open daily, is located at 66-250 Kamehameha Highway and has ample parking and shade.

♦ **Plantation Gallery.** This historic plantation house specializes in textiles, pottery, and bowls of rare Hawaiian hardwood. There are also Hawaiian books, food, and live entertainment. *66-521 Kamehameha Hwy., Haleiwa, HI 96712; tel. 808-637-2343. Open daily. At the west end of town.*

♦ **Pomegranates in the Sun.** Imported women's clothes to suit the climate and style of Hawaii: colorful, light, and filmy. *66-250 Kamehameha Hwy., Haleiwa, HI 96712; tel. 808-637-9260. Open daily.*

♦ **Kaala Tropical Farms.** Where to find macadamia nuts, dried tropical fruit, and jams and jellies, including Lilikoi Gold, a passion-fruit-butter spread. Free Kona coffee. *66-250 Kamehameha Hwy., Haleiwa, HI 96712; tel. 808-637-1688. Open daily.*

BEST FOOD SHOPS

SANDWICHES: ♦ **Chun Store & Market.** *66-412 Haleiwa Rd., Haleiwa, HI 96712; tel. 808-637-4375. Open daily.*

SEAFOOD: ♦ **Haleiwa Super Market-IGA.** *66-1907 Kamehameha Hwy., Haleiwa, HI 96712; tel. 808-637-5004. Open daily.*

FRESH PRODUCE: ♦ **Haleiwa Super Market-IGA.** *66-1907 Kamehameha Hwy., Haleiwa, HI 96712; tel. 808-637-5004. Open daily.*

BAKERY: ♦ **Sunset Beach Store.** *59-026 Kamehameha Hwy., Haleiwa, HI 96712; tel. 808-638-8207. Open daily.*

ICE CREAM: ♦ **Flavormania Exotic Gourmet Ice Cream.** *Haleiwa Shopping Plaza, 66-145 Kamehameha Hwy., Haleiwa, HI 96712; tel. 808-637-9362. Open daily.*

BEVERAGES: ♦ **Chun Store & Market.** *66-412 Haleiwa Rd., Haleiwa, HI 96712; tel. 808-637-4375. Open daily.*

WINE: ♦ **Haleiwa Super Market-IGA.** *66-1907 Kamehameha Hwy., Haleiwa, HI 96712; tel. 808-637-5004. Open daily.*

SPORTS
FISHING

Anyone with a pole and a line can walk out on the jetty at the

Haleiwa Small Boat Harbor and catch a fish, but serious anglers charter a boat, hire a captain, and go in search of marlin, mahimahi, and tuna.

♦ **Capt. Greg Matney.** The master of the *Chupu* will take you to where the big ones bite. *59619 Maulukua Pl., Haleiwa, HI 96712; tel. 808-638-7655.*

BOATING
No boat rentals in the area.

BICYCLING
Cane-hauling roads, mountain trails, and a coastal bicycle path all add up to mountain biking, a new North Shore sport for landlubbers. Haleiwa's new 3.5-mile bike-and-hike path, which runs along the old Haleiwa Railway right-of-way, links three beaches: Pupukea, Ehukai, and Sunset.

♦ **Raging Isle Sports.** Surfboard designer Billy Barnfield opened the North Shore's first full-blown bike shop, with bicycles for sale or rent, plus repairs, parts, gear, and clothing. *66-250 Kamehameha Hwy., Haleiwa, HI 96712; tel. 808-637-7700.*

GOLF
♦ **Links at Kuilima.** An 18-hole course designed by Arnold Palmer. *Turtle Bay Hilton Golf & Tennis Resort, 57-091 Kamehameha Hwy., Kahuku, HI 96731; tel. 808-293-8811, 800-HILTONS. Open daily.*

♦ **Turtle Bay Country Club.** An attractive nine-hole course. *Turtle Bay Hilton Golf & Tennis Resort, 57-091 Kamehameha Hwy., Kahuku, HI 96731; tel. 808-293-8811, 800-HILTONS. Open daily.*

TENNIS
♦ **Turtle Bay Court & Pro Shop.** *Turtle Bay Hilton Golf & Tennis Resort, 57-091 Kamehameha Hwy., Kahuku, HI 96731; tel. 808-293-8811, 800-HILTONS. Open daily.*

HORSEBACK RIDING
♦ **Turtle Bay Hilton Golf & Tennis Resort.** Sunset rides on Kuilima Point by special arrangement on weekends. Daily

trail rides along the coast. *57-091 Kamehameha Hwy., Kahuku, HI 96731; tel. 808-293-8811, 800-HILTONS.*

HISTORY

◆ **Pu'u O Mahuka Heiau.** One of the largest ancient Hawaiian sacrificial temples (heiau) on Oahu, this five-acre site on a bluff overlooking Waimea Bay and the North Shore coastline has been preserved as a National Historical Landmark. *Open daily sunrise-sunset. Driving east on Hwy. 83 (Kamehameha Hwy.), go 1 mi. past Waimea Bay. Turn right at Foodland, turn right again at the heiau sign, and drive 0.7 mi. up a switchback road.*

◆ **Queen Liliuokalani's Church.** Haleiwa is a Historic Cultural and Scenic District that was founded by successful sugar magnate Benjamin Dillingham, who built a railroad to link his Honolulu and North Shore plantations at the end of the 19th century. He constructed a Victorian hotel on the coast and then named it Haleiwa ("House of the Iwa"). If you do not see an *iwa* (frigate bird) on the wing, look for the brass replica on the steeple of this church. *66-090 Kamehameha Hwy., Haleiwa, HI 96712; tel. 808-637-9364. Open daily.*

SAFETY TIPS

North Shore surf is wild and dangerous in winter. Even in summer, strong currents, high surf, and turbulent water can affect every beach. Before entering the water, look for the warning flags and check with lifeguards on surf and weather conditions. Let them know your level of experience in heavy surf. Don't fake it; people die here. Lifeguards are posted in orange towers equipped with radio telephones, binoculars, and rescue equipment.

TOURIST INFORMATION

◆ **Hawaii Visitors Bureau.** Brochures, maps, and guides available free. *2270 Kalakaua Ave., Suite 801, Honolulu, HI 96815; tel. 808-923-1811. Open Mon.-Fri. 8-4:30.*

CHAPTER 4

Malaekahana

G reen as Tahiti, steepled like Moorea, Oahu's spectacular northeastern Windward Coast resembles storied South Sea islands, with one notable exception: The beaches are better—and underpopulated. From Kahuku Point, the island's northern tip, the scenic coast, dotted with beaches and bays, stretches for 30 miles, paralleling the rugged peaks and cliffs of the Koolau Range. The green, spiky mountains are often wreathed in clouds.

Beauty	A
Swimming	A
Sand	A
Hotels/Inns/B&Bs	C
House rentals	C
Restaurants	B
Nightlife	NA
Attractions	B
Shopping	C
Sports	A
Nature	A

Each spot has its special appeal (one was even sacred to Hawaiians of old), but the best beach of all is Malaekahana (*Mah-ligh-KAH-haw-nah*), a little-known strand that's part state park and part private enclave. This is where wealthy Honolulu city folks years ago escaped to spend a week or a month at the beach. A number of private homes are still nestled on the forested shoreline.

On your way there, you will take in scenic Kaneohe Bay and its islets, one of which was used in filming TV's *Gilligan's Island*. You'll pass through such little beach towns as Kaaawa, Hauula, Punaluu, and Kahaluu, with their shell shops and art galleries. Along the way, there are working cattle ranches, fishermen's wharfs, and roadside stands selling ice-cold coconuts (to drink) and tree-ripened mangoes, papayas, and bananas. The tiny bays and inshore reef are full of fish.

Sugar, once the sole industry, is gone. But Kahuku, the old plantation town, has new life as an aquaculture community with prawn and clam farms that supply restaurants. The mill itself lives on as a small shopping center.

MALAEKAHANA STATE PARK

With more than a mile of golden coral sand, Malaekahana is one of Oahu's best-kept secrets, a beautiful, little-visited beach that meets almost everyone's expectations of the perfect tropical beach in Hawaii. The long, curving strand sits between a forest of

Beauty	A
Swimming	A
Sand	A
Amenities	B

dark green ironwood (casuarina) trees and the green-blue waters of Malaekahana Bay. Best of all, it's virtually empty during the week. On weekends, it attracts plenty of beachgoers and campers. The campground, protected by the ironwoods, is the best on the Windward Coast.

Malaekahana Bay is guarded by an outer reef marked by two islands. The nearer, Mokuauia, known locally as Goat Island because it was once populated by banished goats, now serves as a seabird preserve. It has a great little sandy beach on the lee-

HOW TO GET THERE

◆ To reach the Windward Coast from Honolulu International Airport (an hour's drive from Malaekahana State Park), go toward Honolulu, taking the lefthand exit, and then stay right to get on Likelike Hwy. (Hwy. 63). Follow the highway across the mountains and through a tunnel toward the town of Kaneohe. At an intersection after the tunnel, take Kahekili Hwy. (Hwy. 83) north. (You will proceed 25 mi. up the coast to reach Malaekahana.) At Kahuluu Fishpond, the road joins Kamahameha Hwy. Continue north through a number of villages. After Laie Bay, slow down until you see the entry sign for Malaekahana State Park, on the right in a grove of ironwood trees.

ward side, which many reach by wading across the reef from Malaekahana Beach in the waist-deep water at low tide. Wear sneakers to avoid cutting your feet on the coral. *Heading north on Kamehameha Hwy., slow down after Laie Bay. The park entrance is on the right in a grove of ironwood trees.*

Swimming: Excellent and safe year-round inside the reef, except during winter storms. Gradually sloping sand bottom. A light surf breaks gently ashore when trade winds blow.

Sand: Golden, soft, and fine. The beach slopes gradually to the surf, spiked by beach rock.

Amenities: Rest rooms and showers. Camping. No lifeguard.

Sports: Snorkeling.

Parking: Ample lot in the park.

POUNDERS BEACH

This popular bodysurfing beach ostensibly was named by local college students because of the pounding they took here. Long and wide, Pounders is ideal for beachcombing, but the only good swimming is in the long, protected pool along

Beauty	A
Swimming	C
Sand	C
Amenities	C

the shore to the left of the beach park, the site of an old boat landing. *About 4 mi. south of Malaekahana State Park on Kamehameha Hwy. There's no sign, just a wide, sandy clearing on the left side of the road.*

Swimming: Waves are rough, and there's a sharp drop-off, so stay in the protected pool.

Sand: Golden and grainy.

Amenities: Rest rooms. No lifeguard.

Sports: Bodysurfing.

Parking: Off-road lot.

KAHANA BAY BEACH PARK

This small, U-shaped bay has a beauty all its own. The eight-acre beach park is set in a forest of ironwood trees that line the golden sand. The steady, small waves that wash ashore (and the lack of spectators) make Kahana one of the best places outside Waikiki to learn how to surf.

Beauty	A
Swimming	A
Sand	B
Amenities	B

About 10 mi. south of Malaekahana State Park on Kamehameha Hwy. Turn left into the parking area.

Swimming: Great beach for swimming, with a gently sloping sand bottom. Small waves near shore.

Sand: Golden and soft. The attractive beach is flat and wide. Ironwood trees drop tiny cones, so watch your step when walking barefoot.

Amenities: Rest rooms, picnic tables, boat-launching ramp. Lifeguards on duty.

Sports: Surfing, snorkeling.

Parking: Ample lot in the park.

KUALOA REGIONAL BEACH PARK

Windward Oahu's most beautiful beach park, Kualoa (*Koo-ah-LO-ah*) is a great, green peninsula jutting into Kaneohe Bay. In the background are the spectac-ular 2,000-foot Koolau ridges. The warm, inviting sea is green to blue,

Beauty	A
Swimming	A
Sand	B
Amenities	A

depending on depth. The long, narrow beach is perfect for walking, beachcombing, or just enjoying the natural beauty of this shore, which was held sacred by Hawaiians of old. Just offshore is the much-photographed islet of Mokolii, otherwise known as Chinaman's Hat. At low tide, it's easy to wade there. Kualoa is also one of Oahu's premier beachside picnic sites, carpeted with well-kept lawns and fringed by coco palms at the water's edge. *About 15 mi. south of Malaekahana State Park on Kamehameha Hwy. Turn left into the parking area.*

Swimming: Considered safe year-round, but currents can be strong in winter. The bottom is gently sloping and sandy, with coral reef in spots.

Sand: Golden.

Amenities: Rest rooms, showers, picnic facilities, and camping areas. Facilities for group activities and games. Lifeguards on duty.

Sports: Tag football and kite-flying, especially when the trade winds blow.

Parking: Ample lot in the park.

HOTELS/INNS/B&Bs

Cottages are for rent all along the Windward Coast. A private organization rents cabins in Malaekahana State Park. There are also public campsites there and at Kualoa Regional Beach Park.

♦ **Rodeway Inn Hukilau Resort** (moderate). This motellike lodge (formerly Laniloa Lodge) next to the Polynesian Cultural Center has 48 units, a pool, and complimentary continental breakfast. *55-109 Laniloa St., Laie, HI 96762; tel. 808-293-9282 or 800-LANILOA.*

♦ **Malaekahana State Park** (moderate). Malaekahana is the only state park with beach-front cabins for rent. Six fully equipped cabins are managed by a nonprofit group. *Friends of Malaekahana, Malaekahana State Beach Park, Kahuku Section, Box 305, Laie, HI 96762; tel. 808-293-1736.*

♦ **Malaekahana State Park** (inexpensive). Camping is considered safe at this state park, where the gates are locked at night, but stays are limited to Friday night through Wednesday morning. Write or call ahead for permits. *Division of State Parks, Box 621, Honolulu, HI 96809; tel. 808-587-0300.*

♦ **Hawaiian Islands Bed & Breakfast and Vacation Rentals.** Offers a free brochure with many Windward/Oahu listings. *572 Kailua Rd., Suite 201, Kailua, HI 96734; tel. 808-261-7895, 800-258-7895.*

HOUSE RENTALS

Vacation rentals usually require a minimum stay of three days. Nearly all beach-front houses are booked well in advance by the same people who've been renting them for years. Rates range from $60 a day for cottages to $2,000 a day for a seaside estate.

♦ **Hawaiian Islands Bed & Breakfast and Vacation Rentals.** Its listings on the Windward Coast range from rustic to luxurious. *572 Kailua Rd., Suite 201, Kailua, HI 96734; tel. 808-261-7895, 800-258-7895.*

RESTAURANTS

♦ **Charthouse at Haiku Gardens** (expensive). Haiku Gardens is a bowllike botanical garden with towering mountains behind it. The restaurant is on the rim, in a lush garden setting. The salad bar even has caviar, and there are steaks, fresh seafood, and decadent desserts. *46-336 Haiku Rd., Kaneohe, HI 96744; tel. 808-247-6671. Open Mon.-Sat. for dinner; Sun. for brunch.*

♦ **Ahi's Kahuku Restaurant** (inexpensive). This old plantation house is packed nightly with hungry diners who come for fresh, farm-raised clams, freshly caught fish, and homemade macadamia nut cream pies. On Friday nights, there's live Hawaiian music. *Box 427, Laie, HI 96762; tel. 808-293-5650. Open Tue.-Sat. On Kamehameha Hwy., next to the Kahuku Sugar Mill.*

♦ **Deli on Heeia Kea Pier** (inexpensive). Fishermen, sailors, and kayakers come to this spot on Kaneohe Bay for Ernie Choy's sandwiches and plate lunches. His popular early-bird special is the Mahalo Kai ("Thank You, Sea") Breakfast of fried saimin noodles, Portuguese sausage, and two eggs, served on a paper plate. He also sells beer to take out. *46-499 Kamehameha Hwy., Kaneohe, HI 96744; tel. 808-235-2192. Open daily for breakfast, lunch, and dinner.*

NIGHTLIFE

Nightlife is virtually nonexistent on this sleepy shore. There are no spots that feature entertainment, and even the restaurants close early. Bring good books and great wine.

ATTRACTIONS

♦ **Sen. Fong's Plantation Gardens.** Hiram Fong, the first Chinese-American elected to the U.S. Senate, retired and took up tropical gardening. His 200-acre botanical garden, which may be viewed on open-air tram tours, also offers horseback riding, freshwater fishing, and archery. Lunch is included in the full-day adventure. *47-285 Pulama Rd., Kaneohe, HI 96744; tel. 808-239-6775. Open daily 10-3.*

♦ **Kualoa Ranch.** At this 4,000-acre working cattle ranch, you can ride on horseback or in a helicopter. It also has mountain bike trails, canoe paddling, volleyball, badminton, snorkeling, and barbecues on Secret Beach. *Box 650, Kaaawa, HI 96730; tel. 808-237-8515. Open daily 7-5.*

SHOPPING

♦ **Kahuku Sugar Mill.** Bank, florist, medical clinic, gasoline station, bar, jewelry store, video-rental shop, lawyer's office, and post office are all located in this old sugar mill. *56-565 Kamehameha Hwy., Kahuku, HI 96731; tel. 808-293-8747. Open daily.*

BEST FOOD SHOPS

SANDWICHES: ♦ **Foodland Super Market.** *55-510 Kamehameha Hwy., Laie, HI 96762; tel. 808-293-4443. Open daily. In Laie Village Shopping Center.*

SEAFOOD: ♦ **Seafoodland.** *55-510 Kamehameha Hwy., Laie, HI 96762; tel. 808-293-4443. Open daily. In Laie Village Shopping Center.*

FRESH PRODUCE: ♦ Treat yourself to tree-ripened tropical fruits and vegetables at roadside stands.

BAKERY: ♦ **Foodland Super Market.** *55-510 Kamehameha Hwy., Laie, HI 96762; tel. 808-293-4443. Open daily. In Laie Village Shopping Center.*

ICE CREAM: ♦ **Baskin Robbins.** *46-056 Kamehameha Hwy., Kaneohe, HI 96744; tel. 808-235-0231. In the Windward Mall Shopping Center.*

BEVERAGES: ♦ **Kahuku Superette.** *56-505 Kamehameha Hwy., Kahuku, HI 96731; tel. 808-293-9878. Open daily.*

WINE: ♦ **Kahuku Superette.** *56-505 Kamehameha Hwy., Kahuku, HI 96731; tel. 808-293-9878. Open daily.*

SPORTS

Scenic Kaneohe Bay is the center for sailing, boating, snorkeling, and other water sports.

FISHING

No charters or fishing excursion boats operate in this part of Oahu.

BOATING

♦ **Dreamer Yacht Charters.** Sail around Kaneohe Bay's eight-mile shoreline aboard a 35-foot Erickson yacht. *Box 8209, Honolulu, HI 96830; tel. 808-947-1373. Departures daily.*

♦ **Capt. Bob's Picnic Sail.** If you don't have your own 42-foot catamaran with a glass bottom, this is the best way to see Kaneohe Bay's barrier reef on a snorkel cruise. *1860 Ala Moana Blvd., Suite 414, Honolulu, HI 96815; tel. 808-942-5077. Departures daily.*

BICYCLING

This surf-oriented area is not the best for cycling, so there are no bike shops around (*see* Chapter 3, Haleiwa).

GOLF

You can't go anywhere in Hawaii without finding a golf course or two. These are the best on the Windward Coast.

♦ **Koolau Golf Course.** Ranked among the nation's most difficult, it is surely one of the most beautiful. Ravines, jungle, and a devilish mango tree are just some of the hazards. *45-550 Kionaole Rd., Kaneohe, HI 96744; tel. 808-236-4653. Open daily.*

♦ **Bayview Golf Course.** A pleasant 18-hole layout by Kaneohe Bay. *45-285 Kaneohe Bay Dr., Kaneohe, HI 96744; tel. 808-247-0451. Open daily.*

TENNIS

Nothing local (*see* Chapter 1, Kailua).

HISTORY

♦ **Polynesian Cultural Center.** In 1864, Mormons settled in Laie and established a sugar plantation. On the 42-acre site today is a theme park that re-creates village life from seven Pacific island cultures. Visitors tour on foot and by boat to see art and architecture and to take in Polynesian dances and costumes. Dinner show and IMAX theater. *55-370 Kamehameha Hwy., Laie, HI 96762; tel. 808-923-2911, 800-367-7060. Open daily 10-5. Dinner show 5-10.*

NATURE

The best way to see the natural wonders surrounding Kaneohe Bay is from a sandbar known as Ahu O Laka, which means "Altar of Hula Goddess Laka." By any name, this three acres of sand in the middle of the bay makes a terrific beach, even if it does disappear at high tide. It's accessible by kayak, sailboat, or motor launch. At low tide on a weekend, it's a busy little sandbar.

SAFETY TIPS

Most beaches on Oahu's northeastern coast are protected by reefs and considered safe for swimming, especially in summer when the ocean is calm. Few have lifeguards on duty, however, so always check with others at the beach if you are uncertain about wave and weather conditions. Trade winds usually blow onshore on the Windward Coast, but when they reverse, unsuspecting swimmers and boaters may be blown out to sea and perish.

TOURIST INFORMATION

◆ **Hawaii Visitors Bureau.** Brochures, maps, and guides available free. *2270 Kalakaua Ave., Suite 801, Honolulu, HI 96815; tel. 808-923-1811. Open Mon.-Fri. 8-4:30.*

CHAPTER 5

Makaha

On Oahu's very Hawaiian west coast, beaches not only provide recreation but help perpetuate a way of life. Tide pools, golden sand beaches, pocket coves, bays, and a harbor punctuate the coast. At the end of the coastal highway, a wilderness known as Kaena Point Natural Area Reserve has empty beaches, sand dunes, and rocky headlands. It's a world quite removed from Waikiki.

Beauty	A
Swimming	B
Sand	B
Hotels/Inns/B&Bs	B
House rentals	C
Restaurants	B
Nightlife	C
Attractions	A
Shopping	D
Sports	B-
Nature	A

Known as the Waianae Coast, this barren shore is one of Oahu's last enclaves of native Hawaiians, the other being Waimanalo on the Windward side. They reside in the ancestral fishing villages of Nanakuli, Waianae, and Makaha on the reef-fringed 20-mile coast between Barbers Point and Kaena Point, Oahu's needle-nosed, westernmost headland.

Not many tourists venture into this Hawaiian coastal community, but those who do discover a real place, seldom advertised or touted in travel magazines. Here, many people still depend on the ocean as their main source of both food and fun. The coast is known for offshore fishing spots, and fishing and diving charters can be arranged at Waianae Boat Harbor.

Every serious surfer knows about Makaha (*MOCK-a-ha*). This crescent beach is the home of Buffalo's Big Board Surfing Classic, a springtime competition where surfers ride massive waves on long wooden boards that encourage a graceful, fluid style in the old tradition of Hawaiian surfing.

The Waianae Coast is hot and dry, especially in summer. Each town along Farrington Highway has a beach park in its front yard. Each is watched over by lifeguards who sit on bright signal-orange stands and know each beach intimately and most of the regular surfers' names as well. Visitors, especially first-timers, should check with the lifeguard before entering the water.

Sunsets at Kaena Point are often dramatic and always toasty. *Kaena* means "heat" in Hawaiian, and according to a chant, this lonely point "throbs with the blaze of the sun." On the low, rocky shore at the foot of 768-foot Pu'u Pueo is Leinaakauhane, or Ghost's Leap, where legend has it that the souls of ancient Hawaiians departed for the netherworld.

Rocky, bare ridges of the Waianae Mountain range run down to the sea. Deep, green valleys shelter homes and the lone resort on this coast. Almost every mile of shoreline reveals another great beach.

MAKAHA BEACH PARK

Some of Oahu's biggest winter surfing waves break on Makaha, the best beach on the northwest coast. This nearly mile-long half-moon of coarse golden sand is a dent in the coast between Lahilahi Point, a 231-foot high rock that locals call Black

Beauty	A
Swimming	B
Sand	B
Amenities	C

Rock, and Kepuhi Point, a toe of the Waianae Mountain range.

Depending on how you accent the word in Hawaiian, *maka-*

HOW TO GET THERE

◆ From Honolulu International Airport (a 45-min. drive from Makaha Beach), head west on the H-1, veering left on the sky ramp after leaving the airport. Drive west 16 mi. across the Ewa Plain to the Waianae Coast. The H-1 merges into Farrington Hwy. (Hwy. 93) at Ko Olina Resort. Drive north-west on Farrington Hwy. for 14 mi., to the town of Makaha. The beach is on the left side of the road.

ha can mean either "sluice gate for a fish pond" or "fierce." Since a big fishpond known as Makaha once stood here, the name is probably derived from that, but it may also refer to a notorious community of bandits who once terrorized anyone unfortunate enough to pass by.

Swimming: Good, but use caution according to wave conditions. Hazards include a dangerous shore break in the middle of the beach, a backwash when the surf is big, and rocks on the right side of the park. Runaway surfboards can also pose a serious threat to swimmers. The safest place to swim, especially for children, is the sandy north side of the beach in the lee of Kepuhi Point. That's near the lifeguard station, which is usually staffed by Pua Mokuau, one of the few female lifeguards in Hawaii.

Sand: Coarse, golden, and soft.

Amenities: Rest rooms, camping, and showers. Lifeguard on duty.

Sports: Besides surfing, popular sports include snorkeling, skin diving, bodysurfing, and fishing from the rocky ledge around Kepuhi Point. Offshore, a deep trench may be explored by divers who join charters at Waianae Boat Harbor.

Parking: Roadside apron by the beach is often crowded. There's an unpaved lot across the highway.

MAKUA BEACH

This long, wild beach with sand dunes is backed by rugged ridges of the Waianae Mountains, which reach their summit on 4,020-foot Mount Kaala, Oahu's tallest peak. In the inland valley, off-limits to civilians, military forces conduct target

Beauty	**A**
Swimming	**B**
Sand	**B**
Amenities	**NA**

practice. In 1965, a film crew shot part of James Michener's *Hawaii* here. *From Makaha Beach, go 5 mi. north on Farrington Hwy. (Hwy. 93).*

Swimming: Safe when conditions are calm.

Sand: Golden and soft.

Amenities: None. No lifeguard.

Sports: Surfing, snorkeling, shore fishing.

Parking: Roadside.

KEAWA'ULA BEACH (YOKOHAMA BAY)

Where the paved road comes to an end and the 2 1/2-mile foot trail to Kaena Point begins is a big, wide, beautiful sandy beach made for beachcombers, daring surfers and bodysurfers, and fair-weather swimmers. Lifeguards patrol the seashore

Beauty	A
Swimming	C
Sand	A
Amenities	B

on Honda ATV motorbikes and hit the water with wave skis. This final sandy stretch of Oahu's northwest shore is known locally as Yokohama Beach because it's where immigrant Japanese pole fishermen used to cast their lines in the general direction of their home port. *From Makua Beach, go 4 mi. north on Hwy. 93. Paved road ends at the entrance to the beach park.*
Swimming: Best in summer but only when the water is calm.
Sand: Golden, soft, fine.
Amenities: Rest rooms, showers. Lifeguard on duty.
Sports: Surfing, bodysurfing.
Parking: Dirt lot to the right of highway, next to the rest rooms.

HOTELS/INNS/B&Bs

Closing of the Sheraton Makaha hotel leaves just one resort on the west coast of Oahu, plus some condominium rentals.
◆ **Ihilani Resort and Spa** (very expensive). Oahu's newest beach destination, for now it's the only hotel in the 640-acre Ko Olina Resort. The 387-room luxury hotel created by Japan Air Lines is on a man-made lagoon with a gold-sand beach and a lava reef. The standard rooms, the island's largest at 640 square feet, are nearly all ocean-front; they're equipped with compact disc and video players and six-language computer telephones. With its own lanai, spa, and tropical garden, the best room is the beach-front suite. *92-1001 Olani St., Kapolei, HI 96707; tel. 808-679-0079. In Ko Olina Resort, on the lagoon.*

HOUSE RENTALS

◆ **Hawaiian Princess.** Vacation rental units within the 16-story condo tower that is the tallest building on the Waianae Coast.

84-1021 Lahilahi St., Waianae, HI 96792; tel. 808-696-6400. From Makaha Beach, drive south 1 mi. on Farrington Hwy. and turn right on Lahilahi St.

◆ **Makaha Beach Cabanas.** Six plain beachfront units with a three-night minimum. *84-965 Farrington Hwy., Waianae, HI 96792; tel. 808-696-6400. Beachfront in Waianae.*

◆ **Makaha Shores Condominium.** Six-story condo on the headland at Makaha Beach. Mostly residential, with some vacation-rental units. Moderately priced studios and two-bedrooms are seldom empty in winter. *84-265 Farrington Hwy., Waianae, HI 96792; tel. 808-696-6400.*

RESTAURANTS

◆ **Azul** (very expensive). With its old-world look, deeply stocked wine cellar, and European-trained chef, this establishment makes many customers feel like they're in the Mediterranean. Chef Katsuo Sugiura, who planned to open a French restaurant in Japan but came to Hawaii instead, whips up such delightful entrées as sautéed island chicken with eggplant and smoked mozzaarella in a light cream of white truffle butter and porcini mushrooms. Also look for sautéed tiger-tail shrimp with crispy herb gnocchi and light cream of curry tomato. The best seats are in semiprivate booths; the table closest to the French doors provides a view of the torch-lit ponds. *92-1001 Olani St., Kapolei, HI 96707; tel. 808-679-0079. Open daily for dinner. In Ihilani hotel.*

◆ **Naupaka Terrace** (expensive). An open-air cafe overlooking the pool, beach, and lagoon, Naupaka (a white-flower Hawaiian beach plant) offers casual dining in an earth-tone room with Hawaiian murals on the wall and Hawaiian fish on a menu that goes beyond the usual opakapaka. Try such local favorites as grilled opah with tiny shrimp, calamari, and artichoke, or marinated, lightly smoked rack of lamb with oolong tea. *92-1001 Olani St., Kapolei, HI 96707; tel. 808-679-0079. Open daily for breakfast, lunch, and dinner. In Ihilani hotel.*

◆ **Makaha Drive-In** (inexpensive). Surfers stock up on teriyaki plate lunches at this popular Waianae Coast stop. Best-selling take-out specialty is the Japanese-style bento, a box lunch with rice, teri chicken or other entrée, turnip pickles, and maybe a slice of Spam. *84-1150 Farrington Hwy., Waianae, HI 96792; tel. 808-696-4811. Open daily.*

◆ **Masago's Drive Inn** (inexpensive). This family-owned landmark has served local food to hungry diners since 1955, making it one of the oldest roadside diners on the Waianae Coast. Founder Masako Aona created specials like pork tofu and pork eggplant. Now, son Walter runs the restaurant. *85-956 Farrington Hwy., Waianae, HI 96792; tel. 808-696-7833. Open daily for breakfast, lunch, and dinner.*

NIGHTLIFE

Surf towns are ordinarily early to bed and early to rise for dawn patrol, and the Makaha-Waianae area is no exception. Except for occasional concerts of live Hawaiian music or private luaus, the nightlife tends to involve the latest release at the video store.

◆ **Hokulea Lounge.** Library-style piano bar with comfortable seating. *92-1001 Olani St., Kapolei, HI 96707; tel. 808-679-0079. Open daily. In Ihilani hotel.*

◆ **Paradise Cove Luau.** Commercial luau at fabulous 12-acre seaside site in West Oahu puts on a good show for visitors, although it may not bear much resemblance to private family luaus farther up the Waianae Coast. Polynesian show and feast. *Cove Marketing, 1580 Makaloa St., Suite 1200, Honolulu, HI 96814; tel. 808-945-3571. Open nightly. Admission. Next to Ihilani hotel.*

ATTRACTIONS

◆ **Makaha Beach Park.** Buffalo's Big Board Surfing Classic brings aging beachboys home for an annual competition on three weekends in February or March. They strike heroic poses on vintage boards as the winter surf rolls in. Stunts, tandem surfing, entertainment, and food. *Waianae, HI 96792; no park telephone. For information about the surfing classic, call 808-696-2487.*

SHOPPING

◆ **Waianae Mall.** Several small, ethnic take-out restaurants save this shopping center from being bland. *86-120 Farrington Hwy., Waianae, HI 96792; tel. 808-696-2690. Open daily.*

◆ **Waikele Center.** Stop here on your way to the Waianae Coast for a huge assortment of factory-outlet and national chain stores, including a large Borders bookstore. *H1 Freeway and Kunia Rd., 94-790 Lumiaina St., #100, Waipahu, HI 96797; tel. 808-676-5656. Open daily. Take exit 7 from H1 Frwy. at Waipahu. Turn right at first stop, then right or left into parking lots. The No. 48 bus stops there.*

BEST FOOD SHOPS

For large grocery buying, there's a Big Way Super Market in the Waianae Mall Shopping Center. *86-120 Farrington Hwy., Waianae, HI 96792; tel. 808-696-2690. Open daily.*

SANDWICHES: ◆ **Subway Sandwiches and Salads.** *Waianae Mall, 86-120 Farrington Hwy., Waianae, HI 96792; tel. 808-696-5858. Open daily.*

SEAFOOD: ◆ **Toshi's Fish Market.** *87-1784 Farrington Hwy., Waianae, HI 96792; tel. 808-668-8670. Open daily.*

FRESH PRODUCE: ◆ **Waianae Store.** *85-863 Farrington Hwy., Waianae, HI 96792; tel. 808-696-3131. Open daily.*

BAKERY: ◆ **Waianae Bakery.** *85-888 Farrington Hwy., Waianae, HI 96792; tel. 808-696-3959. Open daily.*

ICE CREAM: ◆ **Dave's Ice Cream.** *94-050 Farrington Hwy., Waianae, HI 96792; tel. 808-677-5016. Open daily.*

BEVERAGES: ◆ **Waianae Store.** *85-863 Farrington Hwy., Waianae, HI 96792; tel. 808-696-3131. Open daily.*

WINE: ◆ **Waianae Store.** *85-863 Farrington Hwy., Waianae, HI 96792; tel. 808-696-3131; fax 808-696-7411. Open daily.*

SPORTS

FISHING

◆ **Miss Makaha Charters.** Charter fishing with Captain Jim

Hodges. *95-273 Waikalani Dr., 703D, Mililani, HI 96789; tel. 808-623-4450. Open daily. Departs Waianae Boat Harbor.*

◆ **Summerhawk Fishing Charters.** Fishing charters on 40-foot *Summerhawk* with Captain Rod Bartlett. *91-341 Ewa Beach Rd., Ewa Beach, HI 96706; tel. 808-689-0214, 808-574-1552. Open daily. Departs Waianae Boat Harbor.*

SURFING
◆ **Makaha Planet Surf.** Surfboard rentals and sales; snorkeling gear rentals. *85-876 Farrington Hwy., Waianae, HI 96792; tel. 808-696-5897. Open daily.*

DIVING
◆ **Ocean Concepts.** Daily dive tours on a sunken ship and sunset cruises aboard a 38-foot boat. Diving-equipment rentals and certification instruction. *94-547 Ukee St., Waipahu, HI 96797; tel. 808-677-7975, 800-808-DIVE. Open daily. Boats leave from Waianae Boat Harbor.*

BICYCLING
No bikes for rent in the area.

GOLF
◆ **Ko Olina Golf Club.** Par-72 18-hole seaside resort course with imaginative water hazards. Restaurant and clubhouse, lessons, rentals, driving range. *92-1220 Aliinui Dr., Kapolei, HI 96707; tel. 808-676-5300. Open daily. Admission. Ko Olina Resort in West Oahu.*

◆ **Makaha Country Club West.** Par-72 18-hole championship course designed by William Bell. Driving range, pro shop, restaurant, clubhouse. *84-626 Makaha Valley Rd., Waianae, HI 96792; tel. 808-695-9544. Open daily. Admission. From Farrington Hwy. in Makaha, take Makaha Valley Rd. inland 3 mi. and turn right at the Y in the road.*

◆ **Makaha Valley Country Club.** Par-71 18-hole public course designed by William Bell. *84-627 Makaha Valley Rd., Waianae, HI 96792; tel. 808-695-7111. Open daily. Admission. From Farrington Hwy. in Makaha, take Makaha Valley Rd. inland 3 mi. and turn left at the Y in the road.*

HISTORY

◆ **Kaneaki Heiau.** This 700-year-old stone temple, restored in 1969, is an excellent example of an early religious site honoring gods of agriculture and war. A guard will escort you to the site or provide a parking sign for your car. You will be asked for your driver's license and car documents. *84-880 Maunaolu, Maunaolu Estates Security, Waianae, HI 96792; tel. 808-695-8174. Open Tue.-Sun. 10-2. Up Makaha Valley Rd. to Maunaolu Estates guard shack.*

NATURE

◆ **Kaena Point Natural Area Preserve.** Native plants flourish on a 12-acre preserve of sand dunes at the foot of towering sea cliffs. Albatross nest in the dunes, endangered Hawaiian monk seals bask onshore, and humpback whales cruise by in winter. Hike in on the 2-1/2-mile trail. Bring food and water. *State Division of Forestry, 1151 Punchbowl St., Honolulu, HI 96813; tel. 808-587-0166. Open daily. At the end of the road on the Waianae Coast.*

SAFETY TIPS

The Waianae Coast's rocky ledges attract beachcombers, surf casters, and wave watchers. Large waves often break on the ledges and can claim the unwary. Heed the posted high-surf warnings. Also be aware that on this coast, the most remote part of Oahu, parked cars tend to attract thieves. Don't leave valuables in your vehicle at beaches or scenic lookouts.

TOURIST INFORMATION

◆ **Hawaii Visitors Bureau.** *2270 Kalakaua Ave. Suite 801, Honolulu, HI 96815; tel. 808-923-1811; fax 808-922-8991. Open Mon.-Fri 8-4:30.*

CHAPTER 6
Waikiki

With 50 miles of sandy beaches, Oahu is Hawaii's premier beach destination, but a two-mile stretch on Mamala Bay attracts all the attention and most of the visitors. It is Waikiki Beach, the most famous beach resort in the world. Waikiki is a round-the-clock beach party every day of the year, and it's big-bucks business, with sunburns and fireworks, surfers and hookers, hawkers and haute-couture boutiques. It basks by day, boogies by night, and attracts nearly five million visitors a year from every corner of the planet.

Beauty	B+
Swimming	B+
Sand	B+
Hotels/Inns/B&Bs	B
House rentals	B
Restaurants	B+
Nightlife	A
Attractions	B+
Shopping	A+
Sports	B
Nature	C

Somehow, everyone manages to find a place in the sun, often elbow to elbow with nearly naked strangers of every age, shape, gender, and nationality.

Waikiki is the center of Pacific tourism, Hawaii's major hotel and convention district, and the state's most densely populated neighborhood, with some 50,000 residents. It's actually a city within a city. Packed into a one-square-mile area are 33,000 visitor rooms in 175 hotel and condominium properties, as well as restaurants, night spots, fast-food stands, movie theaters, and shops of every description. Visitors throng the sidewalks along Kalakaua Avenue, by the beach, and a block back on Kuhio Avenue, too.

A century or two ago, Waikiki was the favorite playground of Hawaii's kings, who invented surfing and had a royal good time. Much of the area was swampy (*Waikiki* means "spouting water,"

48

apparently referring to freshwater springs), and rice, ducks, and taro were farmed here. Construction of the Ala Wai Canal drained the swamp in 1926 and turned Waikiki into a peninsula. From then on, developers have steadily decorated it with concrete, steel, and glass.

No beach's sand is more lavishly tended than Waikiki's. It is groomed, raked, combed, and cleaned daily, then swept by a cadre of folks with metal detectors looking for lost rings, hotel room keys, and enough spare change to make their sundown rounds worthwhile. Much of the sand is actually imported, from Molokai and elsewhere, because Waikiki's sands are constantly slipping out to sea. If progress has sapped Waikiki of old-fashioned Hawaiian charm, the city can still be enjoyed for what it is: high-rise and international, corny and chic, worldly and wacky, and warm every day of the year. And no matter what goes on around it, the beautiful beach survives, sheltered by the famous Diamond Head crater. Its offshore reefs are home to colorful fish, whales still come cruising by, and old-timers grab their boards to catch a few waves.

So step over the bodies basting cheek to cheek and grab some of that well-tended sand in front of a landmark hotel. Or pick a quiet spot in the shade of a rustling coco palm and watch the kids sand-slide or surf on their Boogie boards. To get the best spot, go early or late, after the sun and the crowds cool down. Basically, though, anytime is the right time to be on the beach at Waikiki.

HOW TO GET THERE

◆ **From Honolulu International Airport (25 minutes from Waikiki), veer right on the sky ramp after leaving the airport and take the Waikiki exit, which puts you on the H-1 Fwy. Take the Nimitz Hwy. exit and drive southeast through an industrial zone along the Honolulu harbor front. The highway becomes Ala Moana and goes along the shore past Ala Moana Beach to the bridge over Ala Wai Canal, which marks the entrance to Waikiki.**

SANS SOUCI BEACH

"If anyone desires such old-fashioned things as lovely scenery, quiet, pure air, clear sea water, good food, and heavenly sunsets hung out before his eyes over the Pacific and the distant hills of Waianae, I recommend him cordially to the Sans

Beauty	A
Swimming	A
Sand	A
Amenities	A

Souci." That's how Robert Louis Stevenson put it in 1889, after spending quality time under a shady tree making friends with a Hawaiian princess. He might be pleased to know that the essential qualities of Sans Souci (*Sahn-soo-ZEE*) Beach and the tree (still shady at the Hau Tree Lanai Restaurant) survived him by 100 years.

This beach, at the Diamond Head end of Waikiki's crescent, is a favorite because it is separated from all the Waikiki commotion by peaceful, green Kapiolani Park, the newly renovated Waikiki Aquarium, and the funky War Memorial Natatorium, a relic that remains the nation's largest saltwater pool. The few buildings at the foot of Diamond Head, including the New Otani Kaimana Beach Hotel and the Colony Surf, enjoy direct beach access in a quiet atmosphere.

Beachgoers staying in the heart of Waikiki can walk or drive to Sans Souci, locally nicknamed Dig Me Beach. Neighboring Queen's Surf Beach, between the aquarium and the Natatorium, is also a good choice, especially for picnicking. *From the Ala Wai Canal entry to Waikiki, go east on Kalakaua Ave. about 3 mi. (passing the Waikiki Aquarium) to the New Otani Kaimana Beach Hotel, which is between Kapiolani Park and Sans Souci Beach.*

Swimming: Excellent, and safe for children. Calm waters or gentle waves, with sandy access to the water, which is clear enough to see through.

Sand: Fine, soft, golden sand, bordered by a shaded lawn at the public end (near the Natatorium) and by hotel restaurants at the other.

Amenities: Showers, dressing rooms, and some shade. Lifeguard on duty.

Sports: Snorkeling, kayaking, outrigger canoeing, surfing.

Parking: A small, off-street area has limited spots; more are around the edges of Kapiolani Park.

KUHIO BEACH

Kuhio Beach is the best place to sample Waikiki without crossing a hotel lobby to reach the beach. Even while you're driving, it's easy to spot Kuhio stretching toward Diamond Head because it's separated from the sidewalk along Kalakaua Avenue by a

Beauty	B
Swimming	B
Sand	B
Amenities	A

low concrete wall. The beach is named for Prince Jonah Kalanianaole Kuhio, to whom every Hawaii beachgoer owes thanks. On July 22, 1918, he knocked down the fence around his beach-front property and opened it to the public. As a result, all of Hawaii's beaches are accessible to the public.

A bronze statue of Duke Kahanamoku, Hawaii's beloved early-1900s Olympian swimmer and world-famous surfer, greets visitors. Four large rocks nearby commemorate four ancient kahuna who left their power in the stones. Open pavilions give old-timers a cool place to sit and play chess or swap tales. At sunset, palms on the upper beach frame one of Waikiki's most famous silhouette vistas: people strolling along the walk with the sunset and sailboats in the background. *From the Ala Wai Canal entry to Waikiki, drive about 2 mi. east on Kalakaua Ave. to the open beach on the Diamond Head side of the Sheraton Moana Surfrider hotel.*
Swimming: Good, with sandy bottom. Excellent bodysurfing.
Sand: Golden, fine, soft, and resilient throughout but better at the Diamond Head end.
Amenities: Full city park facilities, including rest rooms, outdoor showers, and a police substation built in the sand. Lifeguard on duty.
Sports: Volleyball court, canoe and surfboard rentals.
Parking: None.

WAIKIKI BEACH

"Action Central," the heart of Waikiki Beach stretches for two miles from the Moana Surfrider hotel to the Sheraton Waikiki. The golden beach that fronts the line of big hotels is wide, inviting, and rarely empty. At night, it beckons to the

Beauty	B
Swimming	B
Sand	B
Amenities	A

51

romantic to shed shoes and go for a stroll to watch the moon rise over Diamond Head. A public walkway runs along the hotel grounds. Beach bars and live music are conveniently close by. *Waikiki Beach extends from the Ala Wai Canal to Kapahulu Ave. There are 16 streets that lead from Kalakaua Ave. to the beach.*

Swimming: It gets congested, but the water is warm and shallow for a long way out. Watch for toe-stubbing coral heads underwater and the catamarans and outrigger canoes for hire that pull right up on the sand.

Sand: Soft, golden, fine, well used, and well kept.

Amenities: Concessions for food and beach equipment. Restaurants, shops, and entertainment are just across the street. Lifeguards on duty.

Sports: Canoe, sailboat, snorkeling, and surfboard rentals.

Parking: In hotel facilities, which are expensive.

HOTELS/INNS/B&Bs

◆ **Halekulani** (very expensive). Waikiki's best hotel lacks its neighbors' broad strand, but it more than compensates for its sliver of beach with a pool featuring an orchid mosaic on the bottom and a large sun deck lanai offering a spectacular view of Diamond Head. The Halekulani's 456 rooms are the biggest and best-appointed in Waikiki, decorated in seven shades of white. The hotel has two open-air, seaside restaurants that are excellent. *2199 Kalia Rd., Honolulu, HI 96815; tel. 808-923-2311, 800-367-2343. Beach front at Waikiki.*

◆ **Sheraton Moana Surfrider** (very expensive). The venerable Moana, a restored Victorian masterpiece that was the brainstorm of New Orleans gambler William Peacock, has welcomed guests since 1901. Ask for Room 661 at the end of the Diamond Head-Makai wing; it has a classic Waikiki Beach and Diamond Head view. Sip tea in the afternoon on the veranda next to the old banyan tree where Robert Louis Stevenson recited poems to a Hawaiian princess. Don't miss the history exhibits in the lobby. *2365 Kalakaua Ave., Honolulu, HI 96815; tel. 808-922-3111, 800-325-3535. Beach front at Waikiki.*

◆ **Alana Waikiki** (expensive). A boutique jewel with a modern art gallery and Picasso ceramics in the bar. The fabulous decorator suites justify having to walk a short way to the beach. Get the one with the wraparound penthouse deck and throw a party. Good location for business trips. *1956 Ala Moana Blvd., Honolulu, HI 96815; tel. 808-941-7275, 800-367-6070. A two-block walk from Ft. DeRussy Beach.*

◆ **Outrigger Waikiki on the Beach** (expensive). One of the best Waikiki Beach locations, with less glamour and relatively reasonable rates. *2335 Kalakaua Ave., Honolulu, HI 96815; tel. 808-923-0711, 800-822-4282. Beach front between the Royal Hawaiian and Moana hotels.*

◆ **New Otani Kaimana Beach Hotel** (moderate). The best deal in town, this little hotel is away from the crowds and enjoys great views of city, sea, and Diamond Head. Enjoy the less traveled beach. Ask for an Art Deco-style junior suite. *2863 Kalakaua Ave., Honolulu, HI 96815; tel. 808-923-1555, 800-421-8795. On Sans Souci Beach at the Diamond Head end of Waikiki.*

◆ **Royal Garden at Waikiki** (moderate). One of the best values among the expensively redone boutique hotels, it's way off the beach but has a notable restaurant and is beautifully appointed. *440 Olohana St., Honolulu, HI 96815; tel. 808-943-0202, 800-367-5666. Between Kuhio Ave. and Ala Wai Blvd., about a 5-minute bus ride from the beach.*

◆ **Waikiki Beachcomber** (moderate). Shop till you drop and then walk a block to the beach. Affordable and of adequate quality, with shops all around and lively entertainment handy. *2300 Kalakaua Ave., Honolulu, HI 96815; tel. 808-922-4646, 800-622-4646. Off-beach, mid-Waikiki.*

◆ **Malahini Hotel** (inexpensive). The cheapest rooms in Waikiki: no frills, but clean and friendly. Short walk to Ft. DeRussy Beach. *217 Saratoga Rd., Honolulu, HI 96815; tel. 808-923-9644. Off-beach, across from Ft. DeRussy Beach.*

◆ **Waikikian on the Beach** (inexpensive). Certainly not the Ritz, but the price is right at this relic of old Hawaii that was described as the most beautiful hotel in the state when it opened in 1959. A 132-room oasis amid high-rises, it has a loyal following that once rallied to help save it from demolition. Hurry, if you want to enjoy one of the last of the old Hawaiian hangouts.

1811 Ala Moana Blvd., Honolulu, HI 96815; tel. 808-949-5331, 800-922-7866. On Duke Kahanamoku Lagoon by the beach.

RESTAURANTS

◆ **La Mer** (very expensive). If price is no object, go directly here: French-born chef George Mavrothalassitis serves the town's best (and most expensive) food in a teak-paneled open-air dining room. He finds the freshest seafood, herbs, and produce—essential ingredients for Hawaii regional cuisine. Ask for Table 25, overlooking the sea. Jackets required for men (they have some to lend). After dinner, stop at the Lewers Lounge, a tavern with a live jazz trio. *2199 Kalia Rd., Honolulu, HI 96815; tel. 808-923-2311. Open daily for dinner. Beach front at Halekulani.*

◆ **Alan Wong's** (expensive). Pacific Rim cuisine with fresh Hawaiian ingredients by chef Alan Wong, who left Mauna Lani in 1995 to start his own place in a neighborhood setting. *1857 S. King St., Honolulu, HI 96815; tel. 808-949-2526. Open daily for dinner. Inland, about 1 mi. from Waikiki.*

◆ **Hanatei Bistro** (expensive). Japanese and French seafood served in a beautiful room fashioned like a Japanese inn, with a built-in garden and stream. Chef On Jin Kim, a petite Korean woman whose operatic voice is good enough to entertain guests with an aria, adds a personal touch to her creations, including signature bouillabaisse with Hawaiian fish and shellfish. *6650 Kalanianaole Hwy., Honolulu, HI 96825; tel. 808-395-0777. Open daily for lunch and dinner. In Hawaii Kai, a half-hour drive from Waikiki.*

◆ **Hy's Steak House** (expensive). Sooner or later in this fish-and-rice city, you may want a steak. Hy's delivers the beef perfectly grilled, in an elegant room with Art Deco touches. The grill master works in a smoke-free glass house as tuxedoed waiters serve patrons in leather banquettes or at tables. The wine list is heavy with cabernets and also offers velvet-smooth pinot noirs and exquisite ports. *2440 Kuhio Ave., Honolulu, HI 96815; tel. 808-922-5555. Open daily for dinner. Off-beach 1 block.*

◆ **Roy's Restaurant** (expensive). Chef Roy Yamaguchi, who has a TV cooking show, made Hawaii Kai a culinary destination worth the drive. His 140-seat second-floor restaurant with sunset views is noisy, but the Hawaii regional cuisine is worth shouting about. Half the menu is daily specials, the other half inexpensive and equally wonderful. *6600 Kalanianaole Hwy., Honolulu, HI 96825; tel. 808-396-7697. Open daily for dinner. In Hawaii Kai, 30 minutes from Waikiki.*

◆ **Keo's Thai Cuisine** (moderate). An ethnic eatery raised to celebrity status by Laotian owner Keo Sananikone, who has a following among the Hollywood set as well as local devotees. Not only is the northern Thai food excellent and steamy but the tropical decor is spectacular. Try the Evil Jungle Prince with chicken, shrimp, or scallops. *625 Kapahulu Ave., Honolulu, HI 96815; tel. 808-737-8240. Open daily for dinner. 1 mi. inland from Diamond Head.*

◆ **Kirin** (moderate). Seafood so fresh that the huge prawns, crabs, and lobsters are swimming nervously in a tank by the door, ready to be prepared Hong Kong style for your dinner. Try the house special—minced spiced meat and greens served with steaming, flaky sesame pocket buns—and don't miss the salt-and-pepper baked fresh prawns. *2518 S. Beretania, Honolulu, HI 96826; tel. 808-942-1888. Open daily for dinner. 1 mi. from Waikiki, near the university.*

◆ **Shore Bird Restaurant** (moderate). Cook your own fish, chicken, or steak on huge grills, then eat it in this open-air restaurant on the beach. *2169 Kalia Rd., Honolulu, HI 96815; tel. 808-922-2887. Open daily for breakfast, lunch, and dinner. Beach front in the Outrigger Reef Hotel.*

NIGHTLIFE

◆ **Duke's Canoe Club.** Open-air restaurant and bar overlooking the beach, with live Hawaiian music on weekends. Watch hula from the sand for free or come on up and have a tall cool one. *2335 Kalakaua Ave., Suite 116, Honolulu, HI 96815; tel. 808-922-2268. Open daily. In the Outrigger Waikiki on the Beach hotel.*

◆ **Hanohano Room.** Saturday-night live jazz with local sax man Gabe Balthazar and others in the dining room high atop Waikiki. Fine view of Diamond Head and the beach. *2255 Kalakaua Ave., Honolulu, HI 96815; tel. 808-922-4422. Late-*

night entertainment Sat. Admission. Atop the Sheraton Waikiki.

◆ **Moose McGillycuddy's Pub and Cafe.** Dance spot, bar, and restaurant with Honolulu's best burgers. *310 Lewers St., Honolulu, HI 96815; tel. 808-923-0751. Open daily. Off-beach in mid-Waikiki.*

◆ **Paradise Lounge.** Olomana, a contemporary Hawaiian group, performs weekend nights in an open-air room, one of several lounges in the complex. *2005 Kalia Rd., Honolulu, HI 96815; tel. 808-949-4321. Open daily. In the Hilton Hawaiian Village.*

◆ **Waikiki Shell, Kapiolani Park.** For a special evening in Honolulu, check newspapers for the entertainment schedule at this outdoor venue. Go early and bring a picnic supper or Japanese bentos (boxed meals with rice) and a beach blanket to spread on the grassy knoll. Then enjoy a concert under the stars, hopefully with hula and Hawaiian music. *2805 Monsarrat Ave., Honolulu, HI 96815; tel. 808-591-2211. Admission. In Kapiolani Park, by Diamond Head.*

◆ **Wave Waikiki.** A favorite of the under-30 set. Live rock music and DJs for dancing. Go before 10 p.m. or pay a small cover charge. *1877 Kalakaua Ave., Honolulu, HI 96815; tel. 808-941-0424. Open daily. On the downtown edge of Waikiki.*

ATTRACTIONS

◆ **Honolulu Time Walks.** Historian/actor Glen Grant helps visitors visualize Waikiki's past in a lively walking tour, sharing such secrets as where the beautiful Hawaiian princess Kaiulani lived by the sea and where the ghost of Jane Stanford walks. Program includes 22 different walks. *2634 S. King St., Suite 3, Honolulu, HI 96826; tel. 808-943-0371. Office open Mon.-Fri. 8:30-5. Admission.*

◆ **Waikiki Aquarium.** One of America's oldest public aquariums, it features more than 1,000 tropical sea creatures from Hawaii and the Pacific, including giant clams, live chambered nautilus shells, sharks, and the endangered monk seal. Exhibits help snorkelers understand what they see underwater in the wild. *2777 Kalakaua Ave., Honolulu, HI 96815; tel. 808-923-9741. Open daily 9-5. Admission. Beach front in Kapiolani Park at Waikiki.*

SHOPPING

Honolulu, especially Waikiki, is the shopping center of the Pacific, with wares ranging from *très chic* threads at pricey European and American boutiques to cheap T-shirts on the streets. In Duke's Alley, the Kuhio Mall, and the International Market Place, sellers hawk their goods from mobile carts, where you can to try to bargain. (For other shopping nearby, *see* Chapter 2, Ala Moana.)

◆ **Avanti Fashion.** Designer John Hui re-creates old-fashioned aloha shirt patterns on modern washable silk at a fraction of the price collectors pay for the originals. *2229 Kuhio Ave., Honolulu, HI 96815; tel. 808-926-6886.*

◆ **International Market Place.** Giant banyan trees festooned with lanterns shade this shopper's carnival teeming with buyers and vendors. Browsers can "dive" for pearls at oyster stands, have palm trees painted on their fingernails, and search for trinkets in 150 shops and kiosks. *2330 Kalakaua Ave., Honolulu, HI 96815; tel. 808-923-9871. Open daily. In central Waikiki.*

◆ **Kilohana Square.** This mall complex has stores with Western and Asian antiques, art galleries, Hawaiian clothing, and handi-crafts. *1022 Kapahulu Ave., Honolulu, HI 96815. Open Mon.-Sat. On Kapahulu, 1 1/2 mi. inland from Waikiki.*

◆ **Royal Hawaiian Shopping Center.** This conglomeration of glitz and gewgaws includes fine imported clothing, Asian art, aloha wear, souvenirs, and good jewelry. Hawaiian arts and crafts are sold at the Little Hawaiian Craft Shop. *2201 Kalakaua Ave., Honolulu, HI 96815; tel. 808-922-0588. Open daily. Central Waikiki.*

BEST FOOD SHOPS

SANDWICHES: ◆ **The Patisserie.** *2330 Kuhio Ave., Honolulu, HI 96815; tel. 808-922-9752. Open daily.*

SEAFOOD: ◆ **Ala Moana Farmers Market.** Several fish and veggie markets under one roof. *1020 Auahi, Honolulu, HI 96814; tel. 808-591-2936. Open daily. 2 mi. toward downtown from Waikiki, behind Ward Warehouse.*

FRESH PRODUCE: ◆ **Henry's Place.** *210 Beach Walk, Honolulu, HI 96815; tel. 808-926-0213. Open daily.*

BAKERY: ◆ **Paradise Bakery.** *Ala Moana Center, 1450 Ala Moana Blvd., Honolulu, HI 96814; tel. 808-946-0205; fax 808-949-7876. Open daily.*

ICE CREAM: ◆ **Dave's Ice Cream.** *2330 Kalakaua Ave., Honolulu, HI 96815; tel. 808-926-6104. Open daily.*

BEVERAGES: ◆ **ABC Discount Stores.** Cold drinks, film, beach mats, souvenirs, snacks. *Main store: 766 Pohukaina St., Honolulu, HI 96813; tel. 808-591-2550. Open daily. 35 stores in Waikiki.*

WINE: ◆ **R. Field Wine Co.** Excellent wine cellar, plus gourmet foods, Hawaiian chocolate, deli items. *1200 Ala Moana Blvd., Honolulu, HI 96814; tel. 808-596-9463. Open daily. In Ward Centre on Ala Moana, 2 mi. toward downtown from Waikiki.*

SPORTS
FISHING

◆ **Tradewind Charters.** Sport- and bottom fishing, charters, and party boats that hold up to 25. Call for reservations. *1833 Kalakaua Ave., Suite 612, Honolulu, HI 96815; tel. 808-973-0311; fax 808-973-0310. Open daily.*

BOATING

The booze-cruise fleet leaves every afternoon for sunset sails in a giant lazy loop along the Honolulu shoreline, from the harbor to just short of Diamond Head. It's a fine way to get a little sea air and ponder the shoreline from the water. Many cruises offer dinner, but it's often disappointing and overpriced. Just the boat trip, drinks, and entertainment make a pleasant evening.

◆ **Leahi Catamaran.** A green-sailed 45-foot catamaran for short sails and private parties, including weddings. *Box 8193, Honolulu, HI 96830; tel. 808-922-5665, 800-462-7975. Open daily. On the beach near Halekulani.*

◆ **Manu Kai.** A 48-foot sailing catamaran for brief rides or longer private charters. *Box 8181, Honolulu, HI 96830; tel. 808-946-7490, 800-281-1748. Open daily. On Kuhio Beach right behind the statue of Duke Kahanamoku.*

◆ **Star Beachboys.** Catch a wave while riding a 30-foot outrigger canoe for a memorable thrill. *c/o Outrigger Waikiki, Honolulu, HI 96815. Open daily. By the Outrigger Waikiki on the Beach hotel.*

SURFING

Surfing is a way of life for people of all ages in Hawaii, especially in Waikiki, where the kings invented it. From beginners to pros, surfers ride the perfect waves here every day. It's a great place to learn, so rent a board at Kuhio Beach and take a lesson from a beach boy. The best beginner's surf lane is Canoes, near the Royal Hawaiian hotel.

◆ **Local Motion.** Surfing gear, surfboard rentals and sales. *1714 Kapiolani Blvd., Honolulu, HI 96814; tel. 808-955-7873. Open daily. Just outside Waikiki, toward downtown.*

◆ **Nancy Emerson School of Surfing.** The acclaimed world surfing champion and certified instructors give group and private lessons at Diamond Head and Ala Wai. *Box 463, Lahaina, HI 96767; tel. 808-244-7873. Open daily.*

DIVING

◆ **Dive Waikiki.** Scuba and snorkel tours. Scuba gear rentals and sales. Group and private classes. *2055 Kalia Rd., Honolulu, HI 96815; tel. 808-949-3483. Open daily. At the Hale Koa Hotel.*

BICYCLING

◆ **Wiki Wiki Wheels.** Bike rentals. *2310 Kuhio Ave., Honolulu, HI 96815; tel. 808-923-5544. Open daily.*

GOLF

The only course close to Waikiki is the Ala Wai Golf Course, a public layout that the Guinness book says is the busiest in the world. Few tourists attempt to play here. The Hawaii Prince Hotel has a golf course in west Oahu. (For other courses, *see* Chapter 5, Makaha, and Chapter 3, Haleiwa.)

TENNIS

Land is at a premium in Waikiki, so the few tennis courts here, other than the public courts in Kapiolani Park, are mostly atop buildings.

◆ **Ilikai Hotel Nikko Waikiki.** Five courts and a ball machine. Pro shop, rentals, lessons, lighted courts. *1777 Ala Moana Blvd., Honolulu, HI 96815; tel. 808-949-3811. Admission.*

NATURE

◆ **Diamond Head.** For a big-picture view of Waikiki and the downtown Honolulu area, climb this 760-foot landmark. Go early in the morning, before it gets hot. It's a 45-minute hike, with steep stairs and tunnels as well as an outdoor path. *Start at Monsarrat and 18th Ave. Bus 58 stops here.*

◆ **Kapiolani Park.** A shady 200-acre green with lawns, flowers, tennis courts, and a zoo. Kite-fliers compete here, and families picnic. Many special events are staged in the park. *In the shadow of Diamond Head.*

SAFETY TIPS

Waikiki is one of Hawaii's safest beaches, which is one reason it draws nearly 8 million beachgoers a year. There are plenty of lifeguards, but you may still find a few dangers: currents and sharp coral, seasonal stinging jellyfish, surfers, canoes, and too much sun. The most prevalent beach crime is theft from parked automobiles. Take all valuables with you, and don't leave them unguarded on the beach while you swim or stroll on the sand.

TOURIST INFORMATION

◆ **Hawaii Visitors Bureau.** *2270 Kalakaua Ave., Suite 801, Honolulu, HI 96815; tel. 808-923-1811; fax 808-922-8991. Open Mon.-Fri. 8-4:30.*

CHAPTER 7

Hamoa

Hana, often called "heavenly" because of its hard-to-attain location at the end of a narrow, winding road, is not usually thought of as a beach town, even though its beaches are some of the loveliest on the island of Maui, if not in the entire Pacific.

Beauty	A
Swimming	B-
Sand	B
Hotels/Inns/B&Bs	B
House rentals	C
Restaurants	B
Nightlife	NA
Attractions	C
Shopping	D
Sports	B
Nature	A

Such names as Waianapapa and Kaihalulu are not on the tip of anyone's tongue except Polynesians, but anyone who's laid eyes on, say, Hamoa Beach, will never forget its stunning beauty. It so inspired James Michener that the inveterate beachgoer wrote: "Paradoxically, the only beach I have ever seen that looks like the South Pacific was in the North Pacific—Hamoa Beach, on Maui Island in Hawaii, a beach so perfectly formed that I wonder at its comparative obscurity."

Although many have tried, no artist is likely to capture the subtle colors of the Hana shore. Beaches black as coal lapped by turquoise waves and white foam simply do not look real. Offshore, such islets as Alau look like Japanese brush paintings. To complete the picture, Hana's sands also come in gold, gray, and even a rare red.

The outside world discovered Hana in 1926, when the Hana Highway, a narrow, twisting coastal road with 65 bridges that skirt the tails of waterfalls, first opened. That year, the Hana Bus Line began twice weekly shuttle service between Hana and Kahului.

The road was paved in 1962, when tourist traffic increased to record levels. Now, an estimated 80,000 to 100,000 people a year drive to Hana in a bumper-to-bumper rental-car parade.

Relatively few of them stay overnight, however. Accommodations are scarce and expensive, so day-trippers race up and down the 30-mile highway in a mad attempt to savor the lush landscape, splash in the seven pools at Ohe'o Gulch, and pay an obligatory visit to Hasegawa's General Store. Some come to pay homage to aviator Charles Lindbergh, who died here in 1974 and lies buried in a church graveyard under river rocks.

They miss a lot. In their rush to "do" Hana in a day, most visitors find they have no time to enjoy the beach, the essential element of this old Hawaiian place.

HAMOA BEACH

Who's to argue with Michener? Hamoa is one of Hawaii's most beautiful beaches, right up there with Kauai's Lumahai, Oahu's Lanikai, Lanai's Hulupoe, and the Big Island's Kaunaoa.

Beauty	A
Swimming	B
Sand	B
Amenities	A

Half-moon-shaped Hamoa Beach is a crescent of gray sand (a mix of coral and lava), but it's a true postcard beach, with tall volcanic needles, lush pandanus trees,

HOW TO GET THERE

◆ From Kahului Airport (two hours from Hana), turn right on Hana Hwy. (Hwy. 36) and drive southeast along the coast to Hana. Bear in mind that this is a scenic road with some 600 hairpin turns, so allow another hour or so for splashing in waterfall pools, visiting tropical flower gardens, or picnicking.

◆ There's an airstrip at Hana where small planes come in from Honolulu International Airport (a 35-minute flight on Mahalo Airlines, IslandAir, or Hawaiian Air) and from Kahului.

tropical flowers, and a sprinkling of VIPs, including Lady Di and Hilary Rodham Clinton.

The dark sand doesn't appeal to everyone, but the waves are just right and the tropical setting is truly exotic. This 100-foot-wide beach is about three football fields long and sits in a bowl of 30-foot-high cliffs that is open to the sea. The surf breaks offshore and rolls up on the beach.

The beach park is public, but facilities, including a snack bar, rest rooms, and a lifeguard, are maintained by Hotel Hana-Maui, which has created the illusion of a private beach reserved for its high-ticket guests. Don't be fooled. Act like you're somebody and hit the beach. *Turn left on the coastal road 3 mi. south of Hotel Hana-Maui.*

Swimming: Excellent in warm, clear water. Good bodysurfing waves; choppy when surf's up.

Sand: Coarse black-and-gold sand.

Amenities: Rest rooms, shower, snack bar, benches, lounges. Shuttle van for hotel guests. Lifeguard on duty.

Sports: Swimming, snorkeling, bodysurfing.

Parking: Roadside.

HANA BAY BEACH PARK

Another perfect tropical beach, Hana Bay is about a half mile in diameter and open to the east, which makes for great sunrises and moonscapes over the water. The half-moon bay is guarded by Nanu'alele Point and Kauiki Head, a

Beauty	A
Swimming	A
Sand	B
Amenities	B

390-foot extinct crater that is the easternmost point of Maui. *Turn left off Hana Hwy. (Hwy. 36) at Keawa Pl.*

Swimming: Safest place to swim in Hana; shallow, protected with gentle waves, ideal for children.

Sand: Gray, gravelly sand.

Amenities: One-acre beach park with rest rooms, showers, picnic tables, barbecue grills. No lifeguard.

Sports: Swimming, skin diving, fishing. Good snorkeling on south side of bay, toward the lighthouse.

Parking: Ample lot in the park.

WAIANAPANAPA STATE BEACH PARK

This unusual horseshoe-shaped black-sand beach on Pailoa Bay is in a beautiful jungle setting. Waianapanapa (*Why-AH-napa-napa*), which means "Glistening Water" in Hawaiian, is one of the state's most popular beach campgrounds (*see*

Beauty	A
Swimming	C
Sand	A
Amenities	NA

Hotels/Inns/B&Bs). *Driving north on Hana Hwy. (Hwy. 36) from Hana, look for a sign on the right after about 4 mi.*
Swimming: Dangerous because of strong waves breaking offshore, rip currents at the edge, and a pounding shore break. Unsafe for nonswimmers.
Sand: Black volcanic sand, coarse and hot in the sun.
Amenities: A 120-acre state park with 12 lodging units, rest rooms, showers, picnic tables, historical sites, and a caretaker. No lifeguard.
Sports: Shore fishing, hiking along shoreline trails.
Parking: Ample lot.

KAIHALULU

A rare red-sand beach set in a lush tropical cove with lava rocks offshore, Kaihalulu (*Kigh-HA-loo-loo*), which means "Roaring Sea" in Hawaiian, is exotic but daunting. It's in a wild setting on the *makai* ("sea") side of Kauiki Head south of

Beauty	A
Swimming	C
Sand	A
Amenities	NA

Hana Bay. Here, thousands of years ago, a now-extinct 390-foot-high crater blew out its seawall, spilling tons of red cinders to make this weird beach. In this paradisiacal setting, some beachgoers can't keep their clothes on—expect nudity. *Walk south on Uakea Rd. to the Hotel Hana Maui beach units. Turn left across an open field and go past the cemetery to a short, precipitous trail leading to the beach.*
Swimming: For experts only. Rough, turbulent water swirls between offshore rocks, then out to sea.
Sand: Volcanic cinder beach with heavy iron deposits, which create redness.
Amenities: None. No lifeguard.

KOKI BEACH PARK

Koki is a rock-strewn pocket beach with killer rip currents and a rocky bottom that creates swirling eddies. Offshore, boulders still drop at the base of Ka Iwa o Pele, a crumbling cinder cone. Why should anyone bother with this precinct of mortal danger?

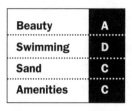

Beauty	A
Swimming	D
Sand	C
Amenities	C

It's the view.

A half-mile offshore stands Alau Island, a 150-foot-high black rock decked out in ferns and two coconut trees. It's a seabird sanctuary and a prime subject for every photographer who visits Hana. Closer by are two fishponds with tide pools near Mokai Cove. In the distance, the north shore of the Big Island of Hawaii may be seen 30 miles across Alenuihaha Channel. *Turn left off Hana Hwy. (Hwy. 36) onto the coastal road to Hamoa Bay, about 2 mi. south of Hana.*

Swimming: Extremely dangerous. Only for the experienced.

Sand: Pockets of gold sand between exposed boulders.

Amenities: Roadside park with picnic tables and barbecue grills. No lifeguard.

Sports: Bodysurfing for experts only.

Parking: Ample parking in lot.

HOTELS/INNS/B&Bs

◆ **Hotel Hana-Maui** (very expensive). Low, slow, and blissfully old-Hawaii, this is a jewel of a place to relax and forget the rest of the world. Rooms, suites, and cottages are exceptional. The 96 units are arranged in one-story clusters around serene lawns, gardens, and pools. The oceanfront Sea Ranch Cottages have hot tubs. Rates include bicycles, beach gear, and tennis. Ranch trails for hiking and riding. *Box 8, Hana, HI 96713; tel. 808-248-8211, 800-321-4264; fax 808-248-7202.*

◆ **Heavenly Hana Inn** (expensive). Peaceful garden setting for Japanese-style inn with four two-bedroom units that have futon beds on platforms. Continental breakfast served in tea room. No smoking *Box 790, 4155 Hana Hwy., Hana, HI 96713; tel. 808-*

248-8442. On the ocean side of Hana Hwy. just past the high school.

◆ **Aloha Cottages** (inexpensive). Mrs. Zenzo Nakamura operates five units, ranging from a studio to a three-bedroom house, in a residential area near Hana Bay. It's an affordable alternative to an expensive resort, but there's one near enough to walk to for breakfast if you don't want to fix your own. *Box 205, Hana, HI 96713; tel. 808-248-8420. In the center of town on Keawa St., across from the Hotel Hana-Maui.*

◆ **Waianapanapa State Beach Park** (inexpensive). Popular campground with tent sites and 12 cabins, all with ocean views. Cabins house six people and have kitchens, utensils, and linens. Reservations are taken a year in advance. Check-in time will be noted on your confirmed reservation. *State Division of Parks, 54 S. High St., Rm. 101 Wailuku, HI 96793; tel. 808-243-5354. Coming from Kahului Airport on Hwy. 36, look for a sign on the left 1 mi. after the town of Kaeleku.*

HOUSE RENTALS

◆ **Hana Alii Holidays.** This agency handles some 20 vacation rentals in the Hana area, from seaside cottages to large villas. Rates range from moderate to very expensive. *Box 536, Hana, HI 96713; tel. 808-248-7742, 800-548-0478. Open daily. Check-in office is at 103 Keawa Pl., by the entrance to Hana Bay Beach Park.*

◆ **Hana Kai Maui Resort.** A dozen studio and one-bedroom units right on the beach at Hana Bay. Rates are expensive, but it's worth the price to be lulled to sleep by the sound of the surf. *Box 38, Hana, HI 96713; tel. 808-248-7506, 800-346-2772. Open daily. On Hana Bay Beach.*

RESTAURANTS

◆ **Hana Gardenland Cafe** (moderate). It's a celebration of Hana's bounty of fresh, healthy foods, plus espressos, fruit smoothies, and fresh juices. Hilary Clinton ate lunch here every day when she visited. Try the Hanamole (guacamole made from football-sized local avocadoes) with taro chips. Gift shop, gallery, and nursery on premises. *Box 248, Hana, HI 96713; tel. 808-248-*

7340. *Open daily for breakfast and lunch. As you enter town on Hana Hwy., at the Kalo Rd. intersection.*

◆ **Hana Ranch Restaurant & Takeout** (moderate). Hearty steaks, ribs, seafood platters, and notable mahimahi for dinner. Lunch includes onion rings, burgers, sandwiches, salads, and plate lunches. *Hana Town Center, Hana, HI 96713; tel. 808-248-8255. Open daily for lunch and takeout service, Fri.-Sat. for dinner, Wed. night for pizza. Across Hana Hwy. from the Hotel Hana-Maui, in Hana Town Center.*

◆ **Tutu's Snack Shop** (inexpensive). Beach basics: hotdogs, teriyaki burgers, veggie sandwiches. *Hana, HI 96713; tel. 808-248-8224. Open daily for breakfast and lunch. At Hana Bay.*

NIGHTLIFE

In Hana, life after dark is up to you. Nobody comes here for the nightlife. The splash of waves and the lowing of cattle are the dominant noises of the night. The rural seaside tranquillity is ideal for newlyweds, incurable romantics, and all who prefer a good book, intelligent conversation, and congenial company.

ATTRACTIONS

◆ **Hana Cultural Center.** Cultural Center and courthouse building dating from 1871 display old photographs and artifacts of Hana's historic past. *Box 27, Hana, HI 96713; tel. 808-248-8622. Open daily 10-4. On Uakea St. past the police station.*

SHOPPING

◆ **Hana Coast Art Gallery.** Local artists' paintings, sculpture, wood and stone carvings. *Hotel Hana-Maui, Hana, HI 96713; tel. 808-248-8636. Open daily 9-5.*

◆ **Hana Ranch Store.** Drinks, food, and other necessities of Hana life. *Hana Town Center, Hana, HI 96713; tel. 808-248-8261. Open daily. In Hana Town Center, across from the Hotel Hana-Maui.*

◆ **Hasegawa General Store.** Such a famous institution that a Hawaiian song was written about it. It's a place to get nearly anything: food, clothing, souvenirs, necessities, even gasoline. *Hana Hwy., Hana, HI 96713; tel. 808-248-8231, 808-248-7079. Open daily. Across from the Hotel Hana-Maui stables.*

BEST FOOD SHOPS

SANDWICHES: ◆ **Hana Gardenland Cafe.** *Hana, HI 96713; tel. 808-248-7340. Open daily. As you enter town on Hana Hwy., at the Kalo Rd. intersection.*

SEAFOOD: ◆ **Hana Ranch Store.** Fresh fish sometimes available. *Hana, HI 96713; tel. 808-248-8261. Open daily. In Hana Town Center, across from the Hotel Hana-Maui.*

FRESH PRODUCE: ◆ **Hasegawa General Store.** *Hana Hwy., Hana, HI 96713; tel. 808-248-8231. Open daily. Across from the Hotel Hana-Maui stables.*

BAKERY: ◆ **Hana Ranch Restaurant & Takeout.** Hana's only bakery is in the Hotel Hana-Maui, its goods available through the Hana Ranch Restaurant takeout stand. *Hana Town Center, Hana, HI 96713; tel. 808-248-8255. Open daily. Across from the Hotel Hana-Maui.*

ICE CREAM: ◆ **Hasegawa General Store.** *Hana Hwy., Hana, HI 96713; tel. 808-248-8231. Open daily.*

BEVERAGES: ◆ **Hasegawa General Store.** *Hana Hwy., Hana, HI 96713; tel. 808-248-8231. Open daily.*

WINE: ◆ **Hasegawa General Store.** Carries a limited wine selection. *Hana Hwy., Hana, HI 96713; tel. 808-248-8231. Open daily.*

SPORTS

In addition to water sports, hiking and horseback riding are popular around Hana. No golf is available except on the Hotel Hana-Maui's practice course. The hotel has two tennis courts for guests.

◆ **Hotel Hana-Maui Stables.** Guided trail rides on 4,500-acre cattle ranch, from mountains to shoreline. Custom rides available on request. Reservations required. *Box 8, Hana, HI 96713; tel. 808-248-8211. Open daily. Across the road from the Hotel Hana-Maui.*

◆ **Oheo Stables.** Three-hour guided trail rides go high into rain forest above Seven Pools. Call for reservations. *Box 280, Hana,*

HI 96713; tel. 808-667-2222. Open daily. By the ranger station at Oheo Gulch (Seven Pools).

FISHING
Although there are no charters or party boats in the Hana area, many people fish from the shore.

SURFING
There are no surf shops in the area. Most of the surfing done here is bodysurfing, and that's so risky it's best left to the experts.

BICYCLING
The only bikes are those that the Hotel Hana-Maui provides for guests.

HISTORY

◆ **Palapala Hoomau Church.** Lovers of flight will find the way to pioneering aviator Charles Lindbergh's grave in the tiny cemetery of this historic church, built in 1857. The Lindberghs moved here to escape the world's relentless attention. He died in 1974. One wall of the church features a Hawaiian Jesus painted on glass, wearing a traditional Hawaiian chief's feather robe. *Kipahulu, HI 96713. Open daily. A rough 1 1/2 mi. down the road from Oheo Gulch.*

NATURE

◆ **Oheo Gulch/Seven Pools.** An enchanting set of waterfalls and pools along Palikea Stream drains Kipahulu Valley from high on Haleakala down to the sea. It's a dream for hiking, swimming in the pools, and camping on the coastal meadow nearby. Ask a park ranger about features and hazards. As with any Hawaiian mountain stream, hikers must be alert to the danger of flash floods caused by sudden showers. *Haleakala National Park, Kipahulu, HI 96713; tel. 808-248-7375. Open daily. 10 mi. of bad road and slow going on the highway beyond Hana town. Look for a large, arched concrete bridge with a grassy parking lot.*

SAFETY TIPS

Observe signs that say, "No Swimming—Bad Undertow." Hana's coast is largely unprotected from ocean currents that course through the Alenuihaha Channel between Maui and the Big Island of Hawaii. In winter, use extreme caution no matter where you are contemplating swimming. In summer, check conditions and observe others in the water before you enter. Currents and conditions can change dramatically while you're in the ocean. On coastal trails, watch out for falling boulders, especially around Kauiki Head at Hana Bay and Ka Iwa o Pele, the red cinder cone at Koki Beach Park.

TOURIST INFORMATION

◆ **Hawaii Visitors Bureau.** *2270 Kalakaua Ave., Suite 801, Honolulu, HI 96815; tel. 808-923-1811; fax 808-922-8991. Open Mon.-Fri. 8-4:30.*

◆ **Maui Visitors Bureau.** *1727 Wili Pa Loop, Wailuku, HI 96793; tel. 808-244-3530. Open Mon.-Fri. 8-4:30.*

CHAPTER 8

Kapalua

On Maui there are nude beaches, windsurfing beaches, and whale-watching beaches. There are black-sand beaches and rare red-sand beaches. There's even a beach named for Admiral Jean Francois Galapu, Comte de La Perouse, the French explorer who anchored off southern Maui in 1786. Had he sailed around to the island's northwest coast, he might have discovered one of America's best beaches.

Beauty	**A**
Swimming	**B+**
Sand	**A**
Hotels/Inns/B&Bs	**A**
House rentals	**A**
Restaurants	**B**
Nightlife	**C**
Attractions	**B**
Shopping	**C**
Sports	**A**
Nature	**A**

It's Kapalua Beach.

Fans of this small crescent beach on Maui's northwest shore won't hesitate to tell you that it has the softest sand, warmest water, mildest breezes, smallest crowds, least crime, and most scenic vistas of any beach, not just on Maui but maybe even in the world.

You decide. You'll find the beach by the Kapalua Bay Hotel at the end of a country lane framed by towering Norfolk Island pines. From the water's edge, the beach slopes gradually to a depth of 12 feet near the outlying reef. Underwater, coral heads and lava rocks attract schools of blue needle-nose fish, yellow butterfly fish, and pink, blue, and green wrasses.

Kapalua is one of many great golden-sand beaches on this rocky coast, which massive lava peninsulas have divided into six bays. In the 16th century, the bays were favorites of Hawaiian royalty, who erected fishing shrines and temples on the headlands. Today, they serve as underwater parks, marine-life conservation districts, and beach playgrounds for all.

That the natural beauty of the coastland remains largely unspoiled is a tribute to the late Colin Cameron, a fifth-generation islander who developed the Kapalua Bay Resort showing sensitivity to both the environment and Hawaiian culture. The resort's two hotels, the Kapalua Bay Hotel & Villas and the Ritz-Carlton, Kapalua, were built in that spirit and, as a result, preside over one of Maui's finest resorts, known for its beauty, seclusion, and nearly faultless beaches.

Some 23,000 acres of surrounding pineapple fields, owned by the Kapalua Land Co., ensure the resort's serenity. The land extends from the coastal bays, across rolling meadows and the green hills of the West Maui Mountains, through a rain forest, and on to the 5,788-foot peak of Pu'u Kukui, the second wettest place on earth. In 1982, rain gauges collected a record 654.83 inches there.

All that rain keeps the mountains green and lush, but it seldom dampens the fun along the windswept coast, where the sun shines reliably on a community that refuses to be hurried.

HOW TO GET THERE

◆ Maui is a 35-minute jet flight from Honolulu International Airport. Most arrivals on Maui, including many nonstop flights from the mainland, land at Kahului Airport. From Kahului Airport (45 minutes from Kapalua Bay Resort), drive southwest 8 1/4 mi. on Kuihelani Hwy. (Hwy. 38) to Honoapiilani Hwy. (Hwy. 30) and continue on Hwy. 30 as it heads north up the coast. Pass through Lahaina and drive 10 mi. to Kapalua. Turn right at the entrance to the resort or, to reach the beach park, keep going and follow "Shoreline Access" signs.

◆ Kapalua is also served by West Maui Airport, which handles interisland flights by Mahalo Airlines, IslandAir, and Hawaiian Air. From there, it's a 10-minute shuttle ride to the resort.

Authentic plantation houses serve as stores and restaurants, and a New England-style church dominates a fairway.

KAPALUA BAY BEACH

Palm-fringed Kapalua Beach is a crescent of golden sand that extends approximately 700 feet along the shore of Kapalua Bay and offers fine views of Molokai, across the Pailolo Channel. *Kapalua* means "Arms Embracing the Sea," and in fact,

Beauty	**A**
Swimming	**A**
Sand	**A**
Amenities	**A**

the beach is tucked in the embrace of two black lava rock points (Hokuanui and Kaekaha) that protect the bay.

Snorkeling is exceptional here, thanks to small, scattered coral colonies along the flanks of the bay that attract an abundance of tropical fish. Waves are good for bodysurfing. Kayakers explore the area by heading east for Honolua Bay, a marine preserve up the coast. *The public right-of-way is at the southern end of the beach, by the Bay Club. You reach it from Lower Honoapiilani Rd., by the Napili Kai Beach Club.*

Swimming: Sheltered from currents and riptides, the beach is considered one of the area's safest for swimming and snorkeling.

Sand: The sandy bottom has a gentle slope to deep water offshore.

Amenities: Rest rooms, showers, landscaped path to beach. Lifeguard on duty.

Sports: The beach activities center rents body boards, tubes, kayaks, snorkeling gear, and windsurfing rigs.

Parking: In the lot or along the roadside.

ONELOA BAY

Dramatic and very appealing, Oneloa Bay, whose Hawaiian name means "Long Sand," is just that: the longest (nearly one mile), widest, straightest sand beach in Kapalua. At the foot of the popular, lush Kapalua Bay Hotel, it stretches from the rocky bluff at

Beauty	**A**
Swimming	**C**
Sand	**A**
Amenities	**NA**

Hawea Point to the sand dunes at Makaluapuna Point.

The beach is quite popular for windsurfing, but boards can

scrape the reef in winter, when the sand washes away. Bodysurfing is good in winter, when there's a swell. Rough surf causes swimmers to look elsewhere much of the time. *Public access is at the Makaluapuna end of the beach. Reach it by driving down the main Kapalua entrance road to the sea and turning right at the Ironwoods development. The public parking lot is on the left.*
Swimming: Good in calm conditions, which are rare.
Sand: Golden and soft.
Amenities: None. No lifeguard.
Sports: Windsurfing, bodysurfing.
Parking: Off-road and ample.

D. T. FLEMING BEACH

After Kapalua Bay, this is the most popular beach in the area. Long and wide, it's backed by big dunes on the west shore and sheltered by ironwood trees inland. It is named for the rancher-turned-pineapple-grower who opened Kapalua's beaches to

Beauty	A
Swimming	B
Sand	B
Amenities	A

public use in the early 1900s. *Drive past the entrance to the Kapalua Bay Resort for 1 mi. Turn left and follow "Shoreline Access" signs.*
Swimming: A sandbar and a shallow reef dampen the waves, but the beach's sharp incline causes a backwash that can surprise beachgoers. It's safe for swimming in summer, but a winter swell can bring life-threatening rip currents.
Sand: Golden and grainy.
Amenities: Rest rooms, showers, barbecue grills, picnic tables. Lifeguard on duty.
Sports: Swimming, surfing, body boarding.
Parking: Ample lot.

HONOLUA BAY

When winter waves crease the Pailolo Channel, surfers catch them on the east side of this bay, which is considered Maui's best surf spot. For those who prefer under-water exploring, Honolua Bay also gets high marks in diving and snorkeling. In

Beauty	A
Swimming	A
Sand	A
Amenities	NA

fact, it is named for the endangered Hawaiian green sea turtle, which is protected in this Marine Life Conservation District, and more than 30 species of Hawaii and Pacific tropical fish are in residence. If that's not enough, you can try the sights in Mokuleia Bay, next door.

Not all of Honolua's beauty is under water, either. With cliffs, coves, and a boulder-strewn beach that edges the green-blue water, this is one of Maui's picture-postcard beaches. *Drive 2 mi. past the entrance to Kapalua Bay Resort and follow "Shoreline Access" signs to beach. Trails lead down the cliffs to pockets of sand at the shore. Swimming:* Generally safe and protected in the lee of Lipoa Point.
Sand: Patches of golden sand among rocks, boulders, and debris.
Amenities: None. No lifeguard.
Sports: Surfing is tops here, and diving and snorkeling are also excellent.
Parking: Roadside.

HOTELS/INNS/B&Bs

◆ **Kapalua Bay Hotel & Villas** (very expensive). Elegant but unpretentious, with open, soaring architecture and lots of trees and gardens. Hospitable Hawaiian spirit and a choice of outdoor party sites with memorable sunsets. One is Cliff House, a private home on the rocks over the bay, which also accommodates guests. Best room is No. 130, a ground-floor suite only steps from the beach. *1 Bay Dr., Kapalua, HI 96761; tel. 808-669-5656, 800-367-8000.*

◆ **Ritz-Carlton, Kapalua** (very expensive). Lavish in the way of Ritz-Carltons but geared to the cultural history of its 37-acre site, this 550-room luxury hotel is the northernmost on Maui's resort coast and offers a sense of seclusion. Built on a knoll overlooking Honokahua Bay, the Ritz has an ancient burial ground in its front yard that was unearthed—and preserved—during construction. *1 Ritz-Carlton Dr., Kapalua, HI 96761; tel. 808-669-6200, 800-262-8440.*

◆ **Kapalua Villas** (expensive). Palatial, spacious, fully equipped condos at various spots around the resort: ocean front, hillside, golf course, ridgetop. Ask for a unit by the sea and you'll have an excellent ocean view plus proximity to the hotels and their restaurants and lounges. *500 Office Rd., Kapalua, HI 96761; tel. 808-669-8088, 800-545-0018.*

◆ **Napili Kai Beach Club** (expensive). A beach-front complex whose guests have been returning for 25 years. Two-story wooden buildings with units ranging from studios to three-bedrooms, scattered over ten acres hugging a gorgeous beach. *5900 Honoapiilani Rd., Lahaina, HI 96761; tel. 808-669-6271, 800-367-5030; fax 808-669-5740. Next door to Kapalua Resort.*

◆ **Kahili Maui** (moderate). A small condominium complex (30 units) and pool next door to the Kapalua Bay Golf Course, with studios and one-bedrooms. *5500 Honoapiilani Rd., Kapalua, HI 96761; tel. 808-669-5635; fax 808-669-2561. Across the street from Napili Beach.*

HOUSE RENTALS

◆ **Kapalua Vacation Rentals.** *10 Hoohui Rd., Suite 301, Kapalua, HI 96761; tel. 808-669-4144.*

RESTAURANTS

◆ **The Grill** (expensive). Hawaii regional cuisine rules the dinner menu. Treat yourself to a whole new world of food with the likes of ahi tartare, charbroiled onaga topped with Pohole ferns, or wok-seared whole opakapaka. Unbelievable spread for Sunday brunch. *Ritz-Carlton, Kapalua, 1 Ritz-Carlton Dr., Kapalua, HI 96761; tel. 808-669-6200. Open daily for dinner, Sunday for brunch.*

◆ **Banyan Tree** (moderate). Poolside lunches with an international flavor. If you're not in the mood for the crispy salmon wonton with soy-ginger aioli, try the marinated, grilled eggplant pizza with tomato, onion, and sweet basil goat cheese. *Ritz-Carlton, Kapalua, 1 Ritz-Carlton Dr., Kapalua, HI 96761; tel. 808-669-6200. Open daily for lunch.*

◆ **Kapalua Grill & Bar** (moderate). Great view overlooking the golf course, resort, and sea in a cool, open-air setting. Friendly, efficient staff. Delicious turkey sandwiches. *200 Kapalua Dr.,*

Kapalua, HI 96761; tel. 808-669-5653. Open daily for lunch and dinner. In Kapalua Bay Course clubhouse.

♦ **Plantation House** (moderate). A restaurant dedicated to the notion that golfers should be able to get something decent to eat at the clubhouse. Food is imaginative and tasty, and the hilltop view of Molokai across the channel is spectacular. *2000 Plantation Club Dr., Kapalua, HI 96761; tel. 808-669-6299. Open daily for lunch and dinner. In the clubhouse of the Kapalua Plantation Golf Course.*

♦ **The Bay Club** (moderate). The food is good, and the setting, overlooking Kapalua Beach, Molokai, Lanai, and Napili Bay, is inspiring in this newly renovated Hawaiian-style place. The bar features one of Maui's best mai tais. Fresh fish headline the menu. *1 Bay Dr., Kapalua, HI 96761; tel. 808-669-8008. Open daily for lunch and dinner. On the waterfront at the south end of Kapalua Bay beach.*

NIGHTLIFE

There's not a lot of nightlife in Kapalua. Hotel lounges feature live music at night, usually of the quiet dinner variety.

ATTRACTIONS

Kapalua Resort stages annual events, around which trips can be planned. On Easter, the Ritz-Carlton hosts a Hawaiian arts-and-crafts festival, in which artists show children and adults how to create their own leis or hats. In June, the Kapalua Music Festival celebrates chamber music. In July, the Kapalua Wine and Food Festival offers gourmet delights and a chance to taste wines from the world's great wine regions. In November, it's the Lincoln-Mercury Kapalua International Golf Tournament, a PGA post-season tour event.

SHOPPING

♦ **Honolua General Store.** A quaint plantation-days historic store with Kapalua logo wear, history books, gifts, and food—including coffee, Maui potato chips, groceries, and newspapers. *502 Office Rd., Kapalua, HI 96761; tel. 808-669-6128. Open daily. In* *the Kapalua Resort near the Ritz-Carlton.*

◆ **Kapalua Shops.** Upscale collection of 16 boutiques offering everything from Tahitian black pearls to souvenirs, flowers, and a deli. Thursday mornings, hula dancers perform here for free. *900 Kapalua Dr., Kapalua, HI 96761; tel. 808-669-1029. Open daily. Adjoining the Kapalua Bay Hotel.*

BEST FOOD SHOPS

SANDWICHES: ◆ **Market Cafe.** *115 Bay Dr., Kapalua, HI 96761; tel. 808-669-4888. Open daily. At Kapalua Shops.*

SEAFOOD: ◆ **Napili Market.** *5095 Napilihau, Napili, HI 96761; tel. 808-669-1600. Open daily. 1 mi. south of Kapalua Beach in a shopping center on the right side of Honoapiilani Hwy. (Hwy. 30).*

FRESH PRODUCE: ◆ **Napili Market.** *5095 Napilihau, Napili, HI 96761; tel. 808-669-1600. Open daily. 1 mi. south of Kapalua Beach in a shopping center on the right side of Honoapiilani Hwy. (Hwy. 30).*

BAKERY: ◆ **Cafe Kahana.** Serves muffins, cinnamon rolls, and other baked goods. *4405 Honoapiilani Hwy., Kahana, HI 96761; tel. 808-669-6699. Open daily. In Kahana Gateway Shopping Center, 1 mi. south of the Kapalua Resort.*

ICE CREAM: ◆ **Honolua General Store.** *502 Office Rd., Kapalua, HI 96761; tel. 808-669-6128. Open daily.*

BEVERAGES: ◆ **Honolua General Store.** *502 Office Rd., Kapalua, HI 96761; tel. 808-669-6128. Open daily.*

WINE: ◆ **Napili Market.** *5095 Napilihau, Napili, HI 96761; tel. 808-669-1600. Open daily. 1 mi. south of Kapalua Beach in a shopping center on the right side of Honoapiilani Hwy. (Hwy. 30).*

SPORTS

FISHING

Hotel beach activities centers book fishing charters out of Lahaina harbor for guests.

BOATING

Kayak rentals and boat trips can be arranged through hotel beach activities centers.

SURFING
Maui's best surfing is found in the Kapalua area, but there is no local surf shop. Body boards, "see" boards, and snorkeling equipment can be rented through the hotels.

DIVING
Diving activities for all levels, from introductory to experienced, can be arranged through the Ritz-Carlton and Kapalua Bay hotels.

◆ **Kapalua Dive Co.** Free clinics in the pool. Introductory dives as well as night dives, reef dives, kayak dive trips, and boat dives for experienced divers. Full certification course offered. *Beach Pavilion, Kapalua, HI 96761; tel. 808-669-4085. Open daily. At Kapalua Bay Hotel.*

BICYCLING
None available.

GOLF
◆ **Kapalua Golf Club.** Offers a choice of three spectacular top-ranked courses: Kapalua Bay, Kapalua Village, and Kapalua Plantation. Each of these 18-hole championship courses is laid out among the pineapple fields, by the sea, and over the rolling hills. *300 Kapalua Dr., Kapalua, HI 96761; tel. 808-669-8044. Open daily. Admission.*

TENNIS
◆ **Kapalua Tennis Club.** A tennis stadium plus a complex of 20 courts, 9 lighted. Rentals, pro shop, instruction. *100 Kapalua Dr., Kapalua, HI 96761; tel. 808-669-5677. Open daily. Admission. From the entrance to the Kapalua Bay Resort, drive 1 mi. toward the coast on Office Rd. Turn left on Kapalua Dr. and look for the club on the left.*

TOURIST INFORMATION
◆ **Maui Visitors Bureau.** *1727 Wili Pa Loop, Wailuku, HI 96793; tel. 808-244-3530; fax 808-244-1337. Open Mon.-Fri. 8-4:30.*

CHAPTER 9

Wailea

Wailea is Maui's newest luxury destination, carved out of coastal scrub on land thought to be too dry, hot, and dusty for anything but cattle and cactus. What once looked like Mexico now resembles an exclusive California suburb: wide boulevards lined with palm trees and cul-de-sacs of "statement" houses on championship golf courses. Multi-million-dollar resort hotels have sprung up along five great beaches on the palmy two-mile coast. Every waving palm, blooming hibiscus, and gushing

Beauty	B+
Swimming	B+
Sand	B
Hotels/Inns/B&Bs	A
House rentals	C
Restaurants	B
Nightlife	C
Attractions	C
Shopping	C
Sports	A
Nature	A

waterfall was plotted on the blueprints of this master-planned 1,500-acre resort. It transformed forever the coastal scrub lands of Alexander and Baldwin, one of territorial Hawaii's Big Five companies, and turned them into a dream neighborhood out of *Architectural Digest.*

If it starts to feel too perfect, the real Maui is just down the coast, where the black lava desert begins, or upcountry on the dimpled, rolling slopes of 10,023-foot Haleakala, which last went off in 1790. And nature in the raw is always near at hand out there in the deep blue waters of the Alalakeiki Channel, where humpback whales and tiger sharks roam.

Wailea boasts many pluses. Tennis enthusiasts can improve their game at a full-service complex modestly dubbed Wimbledon West. Kids staying at the Grand Wailea Resort

Hotel have their own restaurant and recreation facilities. Water temperatures are in the mid-70s year-round. Cane fires are the only source of air pollution. Oh, yes, and there's hardly any traffic, unless you count golf carts.

All the beaches are spectacular: Keawakapu, Mokapu, Ulua, Wailea, Polo. Because they are hidden by luxury resorts, they may seem off-limits, but these beaches are open and free to all. Big blue white-lettered "Shoreline Access" signs on Wailea Alanui, the resort's main boulevard, point the way.

WAILEA BEACH

Of all the strands on Maui's sun-baked Gold Coast, none is finer than Wailea Beach. Wailea (*WHY-lay-ah*), which means "Water of Lea," the Hawaiian goddess of canoemakers, is a big, wide golden-sand crescent that's one of Maui's best swimming locales, because it's protected on either side by lava points.

Beauty	A-
Swimming	A
Sand	B
Amenities	A

It also happens to be the front yard of the Four Seasons and

HOW TO GET THERE

◆ Maui is a 35-minute jet flight from Honolulu International Airport. Most arrivals on Maui, including many direct flights from the mainland, are at Kahului Airport. From Kahului Airport (45 minutes from Wailea Beach), drive south on Mokulele Hwy. (Hwy. 35) to Pi'ilani Hwy. (Hwy. 31), and contine on that, bypassing the town of Kihei. Turn right at Wailei Iki Dr., then left on Wailea Alanui. Just before the Four Seasons, look for "Shoreline Access" sign. Turn right and drive down to the beach park.

◆ On Maui, rental cars and small four-wheel-drive vehicles are available through the hotels. Wailea Resort is served by a free airport shuttle.

Grand Wailea resorts. Two of Maui's most elegant hotels, they're frequented by such celebrities as TV's David (*Baywatch*) Hasselhoff, syndicated *San Francisco Chronicle* humorist Art Hoppe, and other rich folks who aren't necessarily famous.

Offshore stands the popular snorkeling islet of Molokini, a submerged crater that's a tropical fish preserve, and beyond that the "target" island of Kahoolawe, which the U.S. Navy used for bombing practice. President George Bush called a halt to that, ending another chapter in the area's military history. During World War II, the Wailea Coast was a staging ground for more than 4,000 island-hopping American combat troops.

It's a peaceful spot now. There's a popular coastal walk featuring native plants (each identified with a name tag), panoramic island views, and spectacular Pacific sunsets. Early-morning joggers often see humpback whales breaching the calm blue waters. *From Wailea Alanui, look for "Shoreline Access" sign just before the Four Seasons. Turn right and drive down to the beach park.*
Swimming: Gentle waves and the lack of rip currents make this beach perfect for swimming. Slight undertow, sandy bottom.
Sand: Grainy golden sand flecked with black lava.
Amenities: Rest rooms, showers. Lifeguard on duty.
Sports: Snorkeling, especially around lava rocks at Wailea Point. Kayaking.
Parking: Ample free parking in paved lot.

ULUA BEACH

A popular pocket beach named for one of Hawaii's favorite food fish, Ulua (*OO-loo-ah*) is tucked between the Stouffer Wailea Beach Resort and the Maui Inter-Continental Resort. A grassy knoll with shade trees makes this a dandy coastal

Beauty	B
Swimming	A
Sand	B
Amenities	A

park for a picnic or sunset gazing. A paved trail leads down to the sands, often frequented by Hollywood stars working on their year-round tans. *From Wailea Beach, go north on Wailea Alanui to Hale Alii, where there's a "Shoreline Access" sign. Turn left and drive to the beach park.*
Swimming: Warm, clear, calm water excellent for swimming.

Sand: Grainy golden sand flecked with black lava.
Amenities: Rest rooms, water fountain. No lifeguard.
Sports: Great bodysurfing when the swell is running. Superb snorkeling beach—lots of tropical fish, few snorkelers.
Parking: Limited free parking in paved lot.

POLO BEACH

This sheltered cove, edged by a wide beach peppered with black lava rocks, was once known as Dead Horse Beach. It seems that horses from the Ulupalakua Ranch roamed wild here, and one apparently died. When the resort opened, the

Beauty	B
Swimming	B
Sand	B
Amenities	A

developer changed the name to something more upscale. Well, Polo is still pretty horsey. *From Wailea Beach, drive south on Wailea Alanui to the "Shoreline Access" sign at the Kea Lani Hotel. Turn right on Kauakahi and drive to the beach park.*
Swimming: Safe swimming on calm summer days. A dangerous shore break pounds the beach in winter, eroding sand and exposing beach rock and lava stacks.
Sand: Grainy golden sand flecked with black lava. Subject to erosion in winter.
Amenities: Rest rooms, showers, landscaped minipark, paved walkway to beach. No lifeguard.
Sports: Excellent snorkeling around black lava points.
Parking: Ample free parking in paved lot.

MOKAPU BEACH

Mokapu (*Mow-KAH-poo*), a short but wide pocket beach in front of the Stouffer Wailea Beach Resort, is a good place to experience the Pacific at its peaceful best, which is somewhat ironic. The beach takes its name, which means "Sacred

Beauty	B
Swimming	B
Sand	B
Amenities	A

Island" in Hawaiian, from an offshore islet that is no more. Volcanic action? Hardly. It was shelled to oblivion by U.S. forces during World War II combat exercises. *From Wailea Beach, drive north on Wailea Alanui to the intersection of Okolani, which connects with S. Kihei Rd. Turn left and double back on S. Kihei Rd. to Wailea Ekahi and the entrance to the beach park. Look for "Shoreline Access" sign on S. Kihei Rd.*

Swimming: Excellent in calm, clear, tropical water.

Sand: Grainy golden sand with flecks of black lava.

Amenities: Rest rooms, shower, landscaped beach park, paved walkway to beach. No lifeguard.

Sports: Snorkeling, kayaking.

Parking: Ample free parking in paved lot.

KEAWAKAPU BEACH

One of Maui's best-looking beaches, Keawakapu (*KAY-ah-va-ka-poo*) is a half-mile-long palm-fringed strand nestled between black lava points. Tropical fish congregate here, because several boat-loads of old car bodies were fashioned into a man-made reef in 80 feet of water 400 yards offshore.

Beauty	B
Swimming	B
Sand	B
Amenities	A

The beach has no protection from the open ocean, which is okay in summer when gentle waves make this beach tops for swimmers, snorkelers, and bodysurfers. Winter is another story. Big waves smash the shore and often cause damage to coastal houses. *From Wailea Beach, drive north on Wailea Alanui to Okolani and continue north on S. Kihei Rd. to Kilohana Dr. Turn left and go to beach. Look for "Shoreline Access" sign on S. Kihei Rd.*

Swimming: Good summer swimming, but heavy winter surf poses danger despite the artificial reef.

Sand: Gold, grainy sand with black lava flecks.

Amenities: Rest rooms, shower, boat ramp. No lifeguard.

Sports: Excellent snorkeling, with abundant tropical fish attracted to artificial reef.

Parking: Ample parking for cars and boat trailers.

HOTELS/INNS/B&Bs

Wailea Resort stretches along 1,500 acres of Haleakala Crater's lower slope, a planned community that enjoys five excellent beaches. Five hotels, mainly high in the luxury ranks, and a range of condominium complexes make up the accommodations. A resort shuttle links the properties, a shopping village, the Wimbledon West tennis complex, three highly rated golf courses, and a growing number of swank homes occupied by high-powered types, including some Hollywood stars and producers.

◆ **Four Seasons Wailea Resort** (very expensive). No other place on Maui feels so much like home, especially if you're from Malibu. The Four Seasons is the perfect beach resort: a quiet, sophisticated retreat on a crescent beach on Maui's sunny southern shores. Elegant, not stuffy—and, if you have an eye for celebrity-watching, you may see some famous faces here. *3900 Wailea Alanui, Wailea, HI 96753; tel. 808-874-8000, 800-334-6284; fax 808-874-2222.*

◆ **Grand Wailea Resort Hotel & Spa** (very expensive). At $600 million, it was the world's most expensive hotel project when it opened in 1991. What makes it grand? Large rooms, an elaborate spa, five restaurants, and commissioned sculpture and art, much of it by Hawaii artists. Then there's the kids' vacation "camp," with its own restaurant, computer center, and movie theater, plus a multilevel waterfall/pool/slide water playground complete with water-operated elevator. The beach is nice too. *3850 Wailea Alanui, Wailea, HI 96753; tel. 808-875-1234, 800-888-6100; fax 808-874-2411.*

◆ **Kea Lani Hotel** (very expensive). Arabian Nights reinterpreted, with luxurious suites throughout, all equipped with high-tech entertainment centers and plush appointments. Unless, of course, you'd rather have a villa with two or three bedrooms and individual plunge pools. In blinding white architecture with restaurants, lounges, and a good beach. *4100 Wailea Alanui, Wailea, HI 96753; tel. 808-875-4100, 800-659-4100; fax 808-875-1200.*

◆ **Maui Inter-Continental Resort** (expensive). Perched on a rugged point above two of Wailea's fine beaches, the Inter-Continental is a comfortable spot with all the usual resort amenities at lower rates than its neighbors. *3700 Wailea Alanui, Wailea, HI 96753; tel. 808-879-1922, 800-367-2960; fax 808-875-4878.*

HOUSE RENTALS

Destination Resorts books some 250 condo units at several of Wailea's condo villages, with a choice of beach, golf course, or hillside sites. The units have one, two, or three bedrooms, plus kitchens, laundries, and daily maid service. A concierge arranges babysitters, dinner reservations, or golf tee times. Other condos at Wailea are handled separately.

◆ **Destination Resorts' Villas at Wailea.** *3750 Wailea Alanui, Wailea, HI 96753; tel. 808-879-1595, 800-367-5246. Open daily.*

◆ **Palms at Wailea.** A 150-unit complex up a steep hill from the beach, with new, fully equipped one- and two-bedroom units. *3200 Wailea Alanui, Wailea, HI 96753; tel. 808-879-5800, 800-688-7444; fax 808-874-3723, 800-622-4852. Open daily.*

RESTAURANTS

Wailea's restaurants tend to have outstanding settings and sunset ocean views, fresh seafood, and moderate to very expensive prices.

◆ **Raffles** (very expensive). Newly renovated, featuring Pacific Rim cuisine with an emphasis on fresh fish. Try the island seafood paella. On Tuesdays and Wednesdays, Raffles moves the feast outdoors for dinner on the green beside the sea. *3550 Wailea Alanui, Wailea, HI 96753; tel. 808-879-4900. Open Mon.-Sat. for dinner, Sun. for brunch. In the Stouffer Wailea Beach Resort hotel.*

◆ **Seasons** (very expensive). Elegant open-air setting by the sea; Mediterranean cuisine. See what's playing in the "Seasons Dessert Symphony for Two." Great wine list. *3900 Wailea Alanui, Wailea, HI 96753; tel. 808-874-8000. Open daily for dinner. In the Four Seasons Wailea Resort.*

◆ **Chart House** (expensive). Standard Chart House fare, which is to say a terrific salad bar, steaks, fish, chicken, and prime rib, followed by mud pie for dessert. Fine sunset-watching spot. *100 Wailea Ike Dr., Wailea, HI 96753; tel. 808-879-2875. Open daily for dinner. On the 15th tee of the Wailea Golf Course, on the main approach road coming down to the resort from Wailea Alanui.*

◆ **Hula Moons** (moderate). Sea view, salads, and Pacific Rim cuisine: grilled steaks and chops as well as fresh fish. Arrive in time for sunset, when Hawaiian music and dance are featured, along with a torch-lighting ceremony. *3700 Wailea Alanui, Wailea, HI 96753; tel. 808-879-1922. Open daily for lunch and dinner. In the Maui Inter-Continental.*

◆ **Lobster Cove and Harry's Sushi Bar** (moderate). Specializes in fresh fish and international seafood dishes. *100 Wailea Ike Dr., Wailea, HI 96753; tel. 808-879-7677. Open daily for dinner. Next to the Chart House, on the road down to Wailea Resort from the main highway.*

◆ **Sandcastle at Wailea** (moderate). Everything from sandwiches to prime rib. American fare, informal setting. *3750 Wailea Alanui, Wailea, HI 96753; tel. 808-879-0606. Open daily for lunch and dinner. In Wailea Shopping Village.*

◆ **SeaWatch Restaurant** (moderate). Enjoy a fabulous hillside view while you dine. And this is your best bet for tasty, imaginative dishes at reasonable prices. Informal atmosphere. Chef Richard Matsumoto does a fine job of blending island ingredients with a bit of Asia. Sample: Chinese five-spice crab cakes with papaya-pineapple salsa. *100 Wailea Golf Club Dr., Wailea, HI 96753; tel. 808-875-8080. Open daily for breakfast, lunch, light appetizers, and dinner. In the Wailea Golf Clubhouse. At Wailea's south end, turn left off Wailea Alanui at the sign and proceed uphill to the clubhouse.*

NIGHTLIFE

◆ **Tsunami.** High-tech disco. The music thumps through the room, and it doesn't sound Hawaiian. *3850 Wailea Alanui, Wailea, HI 96753; tel. 808-875-1234. Open nightly. Cover charge Fri. and Sat. In the Grand Wailea Resort Hotel & Spa.*

ATTRACTIONS

◆ **Grand Wailea Hotel Art Tour.** Hawaii's most expensive art collection (at $30 million) is set among the gardens, lobby, and other public areas of the Grand Wailea Resort Hotel. It's worth a tour even without the art. Massive Botero bronzes are easy to spot. There are also works by Fernand Leger, Picasso, and Warhol. A group of lifesize bronzes by Hawaii artists is particularly noteworthy. Don't forget to look up, at the tropical murals on the domed ceilings. *3850 Wailea Alanui, Wailea, HI 96753; tel. 808-875-1234. Tours Tue. and Fri. at 10 a.m. from Na Pua Gallery. Contact hotel concierge for details.*

◆ **Grand Wailea Hotel Wedding Chapel.** This perfect little New England-style church, with stained glass murals by Hawaii artist Yvonne Cheng, is a popular site for weddings (an average of two per day, seven on Valentine's Day) and vow renewals. If you prefer an outdoor setting, the golden beach is close by. To use the chapel, reserve well ahead. *3850 Wailea Alanui, Wailea, HI 96753; tel. 808-875-1234. Open daily.*

SHOPPING

◆ **Coast Gallery Maui.** Gary Koeppel of the Coast Gallery in Big Sur came to Maui in 1984 and started the annual Maui Marine Art Expo, which exhibits marine artworks at the Inter-Con in March. This is his permanent gallery, featuring Maui artists and beautiful crafts such as baskets woven of native materials. *3700 Wailea Alanui, Wailea, HI 96753; tel. 808-879-2301. Open daily. In the lobby of the Wailea Inter-Continental Resort.*

◆ **Maui's Best.** Maui products: food, clothing, jewelry, and mementos. *3750 Wailea Alanui, Wailea, HI 96753; tel. 808-879-4734. Open daily. In Wailea Shopping Village.*

◆ **Su-Su's Boutique.** A bit of old-fashioned local charm amid the resort world. Women's wear, including muumuus (Hawaiian missionary legacy of granny dresses), Hawaiian wedding wear, swim and beach togs. *3750 Wailea Alanui, Wailea, HI 96753; tel. 808-879-2623. Open daily. In Wailea Shopping Village.*

BEST FOOD SHOPS

SANDWICHES: ◆ **Cafe Ciao.** Deli and bakery. *4100 Wailea Alanui, Wailea, HI 96753; tel. 808-875-4100. Open daily. In Kea Lani Hotel.*

SEAFOOD: ◆ **Fresh Island Fish Co.** *RR 1, Box 373B, Wailuku, HI 96793; tel. 808-244-9633. Open daily. 10 mi. north on Maalaea Rd. at Maalaea Harbor.*

FRESH PRODUCE: ◆ **Aloha Flea Market.** A collection of market stalls selling fresh produce and fruit. *S. Kihei Rd., Kihei, HI 96753. Open daily. In Kihei, on the ocean side of the road near Azeka Shopping Center.*

BAKERY: ◆ **Cafe Ciao.** Deli and bakery. Try the banana-nut muffins. *4100 Wailea Alanui, Wailea, HI 96753; tel. 808-875-4100. Open daily. In the Kea Lani Hotel.*

ICE CREAM: ◆ **Ed & Don's Candies and Ice Cream.** Roselani ice cream with tropical flavors. Try Kona Mud Pie or Wailea Sunset. *3750 Wailea Alanui, Suite C1, Wailea, HI 96753; tel. 808-879-1227. Open daily. In Wailea Shopping Village.*

SPORTS

Wailea excels at tennis and golf, and all water sports are available to guests: snorkeling, diving, sailing, windsurfing, kayaking, and fishing. Contact hotel or condo concierges to book trips. Operators will pick up and deliver Wailea guests.

BOATING

◆ **Maui Dive Shop.** Snorkeling, scuba, and private boat trips that depart from the nearby Kihei Boat Ramp make this the closest choice for cruises from Wailea to Molokini Crater. *2463 S. Kihei Rd., Kehei, HI 96753; tel. 808-879-1533. Operates daily.*

DIVING

◆ **Maui Dive Shop.** Scuba- and snorkel-gear rentals as well as Boogie boards. *3750 Wailea Alanui, Wailea, HI 96753; tel. 808-879-3166. Open daily. In Wailea Shopping Village.*

GOLF

Distractions, such as leaping whales and panoramic views, tend to interfere with the shots at Wailea's three renowned courses, named Emerald, Blue, and Gold. Other hazards include prehistoric rock walls and lava outcroppings. Robert Trent Jones, Jr., designed the Gold and Emerald links. Arthur Jack Snyder takes credit for the Blue.

◆ **Wailea Golf Club.** Wailea's three golf courses have two clubhouses with restaurants and pro shops. This one serves the Gold and Emerald courses (the Blue course clubhouse is located at 120 Kaukahi St.). *100 Wailea Golf Club Dr., Wailea, HI 96753; tel. 808-875-5111. Open daily. Admission.*

TENNIS

◆ **Wailea Tennis Club.** They call it Wimbledon West, a tennis complex with three grass courts among its 14 courts and a 1,000-seat stadium. *131 Wailea Ike Pl., Wailea, HI 96753; tel. 808-879-1958; fax 808-874-6295. Open daily. Admission.*

NATURE

Wailea's natural environment is hillside beach and ocean front on Haleakala Crater's southern slope. Tour it on foot along the 1 1/2-mile coastal beach walk. You'll pass a historic ruin near Wailea Point. At the Inter-Continental Resort, a telescope is set up to afford a closer view of the whales that cavort offshore all winter.

TOURIST INFORMATION

◆ **Wailea Destination Association.** *3750 Wailea Alanui, Wailea, HI 96753; tel. 808-879-4258. Open Mon.-Fri. 8-5.*

CHAPTER 10

Kamaole III

O n the sun-baked, almost desert side of Maui, where rain rarely falls and temperatures hit the mid-80s, the funky beach town of Kihei (*KEE-hay*) appears as a ten-mile strip of sand interrupted periodically by black points of lava and white stucco condominiums.

Beauty	B+
Swimming	B-
Sand	B
Hotels/Inns/B&Bs	A
House rentals	C
Restaurants	B
Nightlife	C
Attractions	B
Shopping	C
Sports	A
Nature	A

With beach-front condos, budget hotels, minimalls, and fast-food chains, Kihei is a slice of America set down in Polynesia-by-the-Sea. It may not be quaint or sophisticated, but Kihei, population 16,000 and growing, is where people on a budget find their place in the sun. It has developed a genuine small-town atmosphere. People actually live in new, "affordable" sub-urban houses that start at $200,000. For vacationers, Kihei is the best bargain in Hawaii.

On its coast there are eight beach parks. The best is Kamaole Beach III, which on weekends and holidays can be as packed as Waikiki, though a lot friendlier. The beach is one of the most popular on Maui because of its size, beauty, and accessibility.

French explorer Admiral Compte de la Perouse, who in 1786 became the first Westerner to set foot on Maui, described the "burning climate" of the leeward coast, and his description rings true. The coast is fanned by the hot wind that streaks across the isthmus of Maui, and there are fewer than six inches of rain a year. All that sunshine makes Kihei one of Maui's most popular beach resorts.

The water off Kihei (Hawaiian for "Cape") also attracts annual visitors from Alaska: 50-ton humpback whales. They spend the winter in Hawaii, calving, nursing, and mating in the warm water and, unwittingly, fostering a whale-watch industry.

From the harbor of Maalaea to the golden sands of Keawakapu, the beaches of Kihei stretch endless and varied. On the north by Kealia Pond, a 500-acre U.S. Fish and Wildlife bird preserve, they are long, broad, and flat. To the south, they become small pockets of golden sand defined by fingers of black lava that long ago ran to the sea.

And the best of them is almost exactly in the middle of Kihei.

KAMAOLE BEACH III

If every small town in America had a beach like this, nobody would ever come to Hawaii. Kihei's version of the town square is Kamaole Beach Park III. It's where everybody is when they're not at work, asleep, or otherwise occupied. Most

Beauty	A
Swimming	B
Sand	B
Amenities	A

of the time, Hawaiians call it K-3 or Kam 3, but officially it's Kamaole (*Kaw-ma-OH-lay*).

This long, wide roadside beach in the heart of Kihei has a tree-shaded grass park, great facilities, and views of the West Maui Mountains and the islands of Lanai and Kahoolawe. Popular with ancient Hawaiians, who established a fishing village nearby, the beach was "discovered" in the 1970s by

HOW TO GET THERE

◆ Maui is a 35-minute jet flight from Honolulu International Airport. Most arrivals on Maui, including many direct flights from the mainland, are at Kahului Airport. From Kahului Airport (30 minutes from Kamaole Beach III), drive south on Mokulele Hwy. (Hwy. 35) to Pi'ilani Hwy. (Hwy. 31), the inland highway. Turn right on Keonekai Rd. and head for the coast. Turn left on S. Kihei Rd. Kamaole Beach III is on the right.

Canadian snowbirds looking for a tropical beach on which to dodge winter. They came up with a winner. *On S. Kihei Rd. in the 2600 block of Kihei, across the street from Maui Parkshore condos.*
Swimming: Safe except in winter.
Sand: Golden sand with scattered black lava rocks at the surf line and on both the north and south shores. The beach rises to a steep ledge in the grassy park.
Amenities: Rest rooms, showers, picnic tables, barbecue grills, playground. Lifeguard on duty.
Sports: Good snorkeling around lava fingers, bodysurfing.
Parking: Ample free parking in lot.

KAMAOLE BEACH I

Another great roadside beach, Kamaole I is like a 7-Eleven: It's handy, it's always open, and it's got what you need. With gentle surf, golden sand, and views of distant islands, Kamaole I is tops when it comes to instant relaxation. Thanks to

Beauty	B
Swimming	B
Sand	B
Amenities	B

convenient parking, it has the shortest distance from street to sand of any beach on Maui. The north end, known as Young's Beach, has good bodysurfing waves. *On S. Kihei Rd. in the 2400 block of Kihei, across the street from the Dolphin Shopping Center.*
Swimming: Good swimming with a gentle surf break in summer. Dangerous in winter because of heavy surf.
Sand: Golden, mixed with grains of black lava.
Amenities: Rest rooms, outside showers, grassy park with picnic tables and barbecue grills. Lifeguard on duty.
Sports: Bodysurfing.
Parking: Ample parking in paved lot.

KALAMA BEACH

On the south side of Kihei's three shopping malls is a 36-acre beach park named for Samuel E. Kalama (*Kaw-LAH-ma*), the complete island politico. From 1893 until his death in 1933, he served Maui County in every possible capacity, from

Beauty	C
Swimming	A
Sand	B
Amenities	A

sheriff to senator, keeping himself so busy that he seldom had time to go to the beach.

Here, the coastline takes a jog inland and the coral fringing reef begins its long run down this rugged southern coast. The golden-sand beach lacks natural beauty because of a bouldered seawall and man-made revetment installed to save the sand from eroding in winter waves. *On S. Kihei Rd. in the 1800 block of Kihei, just south of Kihei Town Shopping Center and the Kukui Mall.*

Swimming: Safe for children.

Sand: Pockets of golden sand between lava rocks.

Amenities: Rest rooms, showers, 12 pavilions, picnic tables, barbecue grills and other equipment, playground. Lifeguard on duty.

Sports: Snorkeling. Soccer field, volleyball, basketball, and tennis courts.

Parking: Ample parking in paved lot.

MAALAEA BEACH

Popular with birders, this three-mile stretch of golden barrier beach curves along the southwest shore of Maui's isthmus and protects the few remaining endangered Hawaiian stilts and coots in Kealia Pond from Kihei's inevitable

Beauty	A
Swimming	B
Sand	B
Amenities	B

sprawl. Maalaea (*Maw-ah-LAY-ah*) is a tropical version of Florida's great beaches: an empty, flat strand that rises to low dunes inshore. Hot as a griddle, with no shade, it's a morning beach, ideal for jogging, walking, and beachcombing. Every afternoon, a hard, hot wind sweeps across the wide valley between the West Maui Mountains and Haleakala and scours the beach with airborne grit, unpleasant to all. *From town, drive north on N. Kihei Rd., passing the intersection with Mokulele Hwy. (Hwy. 35). The beach is between the junction and Honoapiilani Hwy. (Hwy. 30), the road to Lahaina.*

Swimming: Most of the time, there's a gentle shore break. There are no strong currents inshore except during the winter months, when the inexperienced should avoid swimming here. Gradually sloping sandy bottom.

Sand: Long, flat uninterrupted golden-sand beach with dunes inshore.

Amenities: On the west end, Maalea Boat Harbor has rest rooms, restaurants, a boat launching ramp, and other facilities. No lifeguard.

Sports: Canoeing, occasional surfing.

Parking: Off road.

HOTELS/INNS/B&Bs

Kihei is condo land, fueled by a loyal contingent of returning visitors who love Maui but can't afford hotel rooms and dining out three times a day. The 3,700 units between Maalaea and Wailea on Maui's southern shore are located mostly in 45 condominium complexes, generally low-rise clusters of units on the inland side of the road. There are also four small hotels, bed-and-breakfasts, and 20 private homes for rent.

◆ **Mana Kai Maui** (moderate). A terrific beach-front location plus good rates that include a car and breakfast make this the best hotel deal in Kihei. Some units have kitchens, and some have two bedrooms. At the quiet south end of resort area. Restaurants on site and next door. *2960 S. Kihei Rd., Kihei, HI 96753; tel. 808-879-1561, 800-525-2025; fax 808-874-5042.*

◆ **Maui Coast Hotel** (moderate). One of the few hotels recently built on Maui that is not luxury-priced. Located on a slight rise, back far enough from the busy main street for peace and quiet, it is half a block from the popular Kamaole Beach Park I. Tennis and an affordable restaurant are on the property. Great golf nearby. *2259 S. Kihei Rd., Kihei, HI 96753; tel. 808-874-6284, 800-895-6284; fax 808-875-4731.*

◆ **Maui Lu Resort** (moderate). Old-fashioned Hawaiian resort with some beach-front units and the rest across the road on a sweep of green lawn. Live Hawaiian music on weekends in the lounge. Pay extra and get a beach unit, one of the few spots on Maui where the access is this direct and the surroundings this natural. *575 S. Kihei Rd., Kihei, HI 96753; tel. 808-879-5881, 800-321-2558; fax 808-879-4627. Beach front at the north end of Kihei, before the commercial district.*

HOUSE RENTALS

◆ **Condominium Rentals Hawaii.** Wide variety of South Maui condos at reasonable prices. *362 Huku Lii Pl., Kihei, HI 96753; tel. 808-879-2778, 800-367-5242. Open daily.*

◆ **Hale Pau Hana.** An 80-unit beach-front complex of one- and two-bedroom moderately priced, well-located condominium units with pool. *2480 S. Kihei Rd., Kihei, HI 96753; tel. 808-879-2715, 800-367-6036; fax 808-875-0238. Open daily.*

◆ **Kamaole Nalu.** Small complex of two-bedroom, two-bath condo units with kitchens, laundries, pool, and barbecue areas. Located on Kamaole Beach, within walking distance of shops and restaurants. *2450 S. Kihei Rd., Kihei, HI 96753; tel. 808-879-1006, 800-767-1497; fax 808-879-8693. Open daily.*

◆ **Maui Beach Homes.** Private homes for vacation rental in Kihei area. *Box 1776, Kihei, HI 96753; tel. 808-879-3328, 800-541-3060. Open daily.*

RESTAURANTS

Kihei's 50 eateries range from must-taste Hawaii regional cuisine restaurants and beach-front celebrity hangouts to steak houses, fast-food chains, and neighborhood lunch counters serving local-style plate lunch specials.

◆ **Carelli's on the Beach** (very expensive). Charming, intimate, beach-front setting (ask for a table near the water). The fish is fresh, the pasta a bit dear, but the dishes are classic Italian and the theme, "Where the stars come out at night," refers, accurately enough, to the celebrities who like to eat here. *2980 S. Kihei Rd., Kihei, HI 96753; tel. 808-875-0001; fax 808-874-7571. Open daily for dinner. Between the Mana Kai Maui hotel and the uphill turn that defines Wailea.*

◆ **A Pacific Cafe** (expensive). Outstanding, and one of Maui's best dining choices. Chef Jean-Marie Josselin's second restaurant (the first is on Kauai) stars Hawaii regional cuisine as only a Provence-born genius can render it. His wife, Sophie, created the whimsical hand-painted plates and colorful interiors that set the stage for dishes combining Hawaiian, Mediterranean, and Indian influences. *1279 S. Kihei Rd., Suite B102, Kihei, HI 96753; tel. 808-879-0069. Open daily for dinner. In the Azeka Place Shopping Center in the middle of Kihei.*

◆ **Maalaea Waterfront Restaurant** (expensive). Fish and seafood Continental style by the sea. Eight different preparations for fresh Hawaiian fish. Also meats and game. *50 Haouli St., Maalaea, HI 96793; tel. 808-244-9028. Open daily for dinner. On the water at Maalaea Harbor.*

◆ **Five Palms Beach Grill** (moderate). Informal, open-air beach-front restaurant that shares Keawakapu Beach with Carelli's but serves basic fare and is less costly. *2960 S. Kihei Rd., Kihei, HI 96753; tel. 808-879-2607. Open daily for breakfast, lunch, and dinner. In the Mana Kai Maui hotel.*

◆ **Hamilton's Beach Cafe** (moderate). Panoramic ocean view and a good selection of American cuisine. Specialties include stuffed scampi and smoked prime rib. *760 S. Kihei Rd., Kihei, HI 96753; tel. 808-879-6399. Open daily for breakfast, lunch, and dinner. In the Menehune Shores condominium.*

NIGHTLIFE

◆ **The Sports Page Bar & Grill.** *2411 S. Kihei Rd., B-4, Kihei, HI 96753; tel. 808-879-0602. Open daily.*

SHOPPING

South Kihei Road is an endless string of shopping centers, restaurants, galleries, boutiques, and sporting-goods stores. The Akina Shopping Shuttle makes it easy to get around from shops to beaches in Wailea, Makena, and Kihei. Fare: $1.

◆ **Little Polynesians.** Kids' stuff. Irresistible swimsuits for little girls with hula skirts and lei tops built in. Toys, games, puppets, stuffed animals, aloha wear, and books. *1215 S. Kihei Rd., Kihei, HI 96753; tel. 808-874-3571. Open daily.*

◆ **Suda Kihei Store.** Old-fashioned plantation store with color-ful variety of goods, and patrons. Farmer's market sells fresh produce in the parking lot, and nearby roadside vendors sell fresh fish, lobsters, flowers, fruit, fresh coconut juice, and hand-painted coconut "postcards" to sign, stamp, and mail home. *61 S. Kihei Rd., Kihei, HI 96753; tel. 808-879-2668. Open daily.*

◆ **The Coffee Store.** Coffee to drink or by the bag, plus sandwiches, soups, and salads for lunch. *Azeka Place Shopping Center, Box 1223, S. Kihei Rd., Kihei, HI 96753; tel. 808-875-4244. Open daily.*

◆ **Wings on the Wind.** Kites, wind socks, dual and quad-line stunt kites, repairs, and kite-flying lessons. *1280 S. Kihei Rd., Suite 120, Kihei, HI 96753; tel. 808-874-5050. Open daily. In Azeka Place Shopping Center.*

BEST FOOD SHOPS

SANDWICHES: ◆ **Stella Blues Cafe & Deli.** Huge sandwiches, veggie and otherwise. *1215 S. Kihei Rd., Kihei, HI 96753; tel. 808-874-3779. Open daily. In Long's Center near Kihei's northern end.*

SEAFOOD: ◆ **Fresh Island Fish Co.** You can buy fish here or eat lunch at the Maalaea Fish Market & Cafe, which this company operates on the same site. *RR 1, Box 373B, Wailuku, HI 96793; tel. 808-244-9633. Open daily. On Maalaea Rd. at Maalaea Harbor.*

FRESH PRODUCE: ◆ **Aloha Flea Market.** A collection of market stalls selling fresh produce and fruit. *S. Kihei Rd., Kihei, HI 96753. Open daily. On the ocean side of the road near the Azeka Place Shopping Center.*

BAKERY: ◆ **Cinnamon Roll Fair.** Terrific fresh, hot cinnamon rolls. *2463 S. Kihei Rd., Kihei, HI 96753; tel. 808-879-5177. Open daily. In Kamaole Shopping Center.*

ICE CREAM: ◆ **Tobi's Ice Cream and Shave Ice.** Try *azuki* beans and ice cream in a shave ice. *1913 S. Kihei Rd., Kihei, HI 96753; tel. 808-879-7294. Open daily.*

BEVERAGES: ◆ **Surfside Spirits & Deli.** *1993 S. Kihei Rd., Kihei, HI 96753; tel. 808-879-1385. Open Mon.-Sat.*

WINE: ◆ **Kihei Wine & Spirits.** *300 Ohukai Rd., Kihei, HI 96753; tel. 808-879-0555. Open Mon.-Sat. Off Piilani Hwy. in Kihei Commercial Center.*

SPORTS
FISHING

◆ **Ocean Activities Center.** Deep-sea fishing aboard *NoKaOi III*, a 37-foot Trollycraft. Also offers a wide variety of other ocean sports tours. *1847 S. Kihei Rd., Kihei, HI 96753; tel. 808-879-4485. Open daily.*

◆ **Rascal Charters.** Light or heavy tackle, share or private fishing charters aboard a 31-foot Bertram. *Box 1047, Kihei, HI 96753; tel. 808-874-8633. Open daily. Departs from Maalaea Harbor.*

BOATING

◆ **Kelii's Kayak Tours.** Kayak/snorkel adventure and other shoreline paddles to several areas otherwise inaccessible. Knowledgeable local guides. *Kihei, HI 96753; tel. 808-874-7652, 808-879-3957. Open daily. Departs from beach locations at Olowalu, Makena, and Kahana.*

◆ **Kihei Hawaiian Canoe Club Malama Ula.** For a donation to the canoe club, paddlers will take visitors on a genuine outrigger canoe ride in the afternoon. By reservation. Contact Kihei Destination Association for details (*see* Tourist Information). *Kalama Park, Kihei.*

◆ **Maui Classic Charters.** Pick your vintage vessel: a glass-bottom catamaran with water slide, a 1926 Biloxi Pilot Schooner, or a 1929 68-foot racing yacht. They cruise to Molokini for snorkeling, seek out whales in season, and fish a little on the way. Rents underwater videocameras and also conducts snuba dives (air hoses tethered to a surface tank). *1215 Kihei Rd., Kihei, HI 96753; tel. 808-879-8188. Departs daily. Office in Long's Center.*

◆ **Pacific Whale Foundation.** When humpback whales cruise into Hawaiian waters for the winter, the humans cruise out to get a glimpse of them. Greg Kaufman's foundation runs ten trips a day, with informed commentary by naturalists on board. If you don't see whales, you go again free. Snorkel cruises to Molokini also offered. Profits support efforts to save the whales. *101 N. Kihei Rd., Kihei, HI 96753; tel. 808-879-8811, 808-879-4253. Open daily. Departs from Maalaea and Lahaina harbors.*

◆ **South Pacific Kayaks & Outfitters.** Guided kayak tours along Maui's inner coastline, often with views of whales, dolphins, and endangered Hawaiian monk seals. A portion of tour proceeds is donated to Whales Alive International. *2439 S. Kihei Rd., Suite 101B, Kihei, HI 96753; tel. 808-875-4848, 800-776-2326. Open daily.*

SURFING

◆ **Local Motion.** Rents gear, togs, surfboards, and body boards. *1819 S. Kihei Rd., Kihei, HI 96753; tel. 808-879-7873. Open daily. In Kukui Mall Shopping Center.*

DIVING

◆ **Ed Robinson's Diving Adventures.** Morning dives daily. Wednesday dive trips to Lanai with buffet lunch. Thursday night dives at sunset with buffet. Robinson is an accomplished underwater photographer and diver who knows these waters. *Box 616, Kihei, HI 96753; tel. 808-879-3584, 800-635-1273; fax 808-874-1939. Open daily. Departs from Kihei Boat Ramp on S. Kihei Rd.*

BICYCLING

◆ **South Maui Bicycles.** Rentals, service, sales, and accessories. *1913 S. Kihei Rd., Kihei, HI 96753; tel. 808-874-0068. Open daily.*

GOLF

Kihei has the advantage of being just minutes away from half of Maui's 16 golf courses, including Kihei's own Silversword Golf Club. Not only are the five renowned Wailea and Makena resort golf courses nearby but Sandalwood and the private Waikapu Golf Club are just up the slope of the West Maui Mountains, between the airport and Kihei.

◆ **Silversword Golf Club.** This par-71 18-hole public course was created in 1987 by architect W. J. Noewis. Tee times required. Golf carts included in the fee. *1345 Piilani Hwy., Kihei, HI 96753; tel. 808-874-0777. Open daily. Admission. From town, go north on S. Kihei Rd. 2 mi. to Liposa St. Turn right and head mauka (to the mountains) on Liposa, across Piilani Hwy. Turn right at entry sign to the club.*

TENNIS

Tennis is popular in South Maui, where the weather's right for daily action. Public courts are located at Kalama Beach Park and Waipuilani Park. Many of Kihei's condominiums and hotels offer courts for guests' use. Some, listed below, share their courts with others. Tennis schools and resort courts are located nearby at Wailea and Makena (*see* Chapter 9, Wailea, and Chapter 11, Maluaka).

◆ **Luana Kai.** Four public courts, no charge. *940 S. Kihei Rd., Kihei, HI 96753; tel. 808-879-1268. Open daily.*

◆ **Maui Schooner Resort.** Four public courts, no charge. *980 S. Kihei Rd., Kihei, HI 96753; tel. 808-879-5247. Open daily.*

SAFETY TIPS

Reefs protect most of Maui's southwest beaches, making them the safest on the island for swimmers of all capabilities. Beware the winter sea, however, when dangerous waves and rip currents lash the shore. Most Kihei beaches are sandy coves embraced by sharp lava points that can slash a bare foot like a straight razor. Wear reef walkers or even tennis shoes if you plan to explore the lava points. Protect your feet on land, too, from the sharp spines of the kiawe tree, which are capable of piercing a car tire.

TOURIST INFORMATION

◆ **Kihei Destination Association.** No formal hours, but president Sam Garcia provides information by mail or phone. *2836 Panepoo St., Kihei, HI 96753; tel. 808-874-9400.*

◆ **Maui Visitors Bureau.** *1727 Wili Pa Loop, Wailuku, HI 96793; tel. 808-244-3530. Open Mon.-Fri. 8-4:30.*

CHAPTER 11

Maluaka

Raw and rugged, the wilderness coast of Maui begins on Makena Bay where golden sand gives way to sharp fingers of lava that ran to the sea in 1790, the last time Haleakala volcano exploded.

But first, the beaches get bigger and wider on this southwest coast—one is even named Big Beach—before they disappear under baseball-sized black lava rocks hurled from Haleakala's rift zone. Finally, the coast becomes one jagged black landscape so hellish even Dante would be delighted.

Beauty	A
Swimming	B
Sand	B+
Hotels/Inns/B&Bs	B
House rentals	C
Restaurants	A
Nightlife	C
Attractions	B
Shopping	NA
Sports	A
Nature	A

The beaches, when you find them, are often down red-dirt jeep trails to the coast through bramble forests of cactus and kiawe, the dominant flora of this deep southwestern shore. One secluded beach is popular with nudists.

After the densely packed resort zoning of Wailea, the undisturbed landscape of Makena, with its thorny kiawe forests and jagged black lava, is welcome visual relief. This is what Maui looked like 200 years ago, based on the journals and etchings of early European explorers.

Only one stark, man-made object, a three-story structure that looks like a county hospital, violates the natural order. This lone oasis is the Maui Prince Hotel, erected by Japanese railway heir Yoshiakai Tsutsumi, one of the world's richest men. It's a bit of Tokyo come to rest on this arid coast. This stark, white hostelry is elegant, expensive, and utterly alone on 2,500 undisturbed coastal acres.

Once you are here, in splendid isolation, the zen quality of the place takes hold and enhances the sound of whale splash, the scent of plumeria, and the night watch of the Milky Way. For those who seek solitude in civilized wilderness, this is the perfect beach retreat.

The Prince sits not on, but very near, the best beach in these parts, Maluaka, a golden crescent in the lee of Pu'u Olai, a 360-foot-high red cinder cone that dominates the raw frontier like a sentinel. Beyond are lava fields, empty beaches, ancient house sites and fishponds, and a chunky lava trail known as the King's Highway, which leads to Maui's deserted boulder and pebble beaches.

The kiawe tree, a fixture along the dry coast of Maui, from Kaanapali to Makena, dominates the landscape at the southwestern end. It also poses a threat to unsuspecting barefoot beachgoers, who may encounter its needle-sharp spines. The half-inch-long spines are capable of piercing car tires. Avoid

HOW TO GET THERE

◆ Maui is a 35-minute jet flight from Honolulu International Airport. Most arrivals on Maui, including many direct flights from the mainland, are at Kahului Airport. From Kahului Airport (55 minutes from Maluaka Beach), drive south on Mokulele Hwy. (Hwy. 35) to Pi'ilani Hwy. (Hwy. 31), and continue on that, bypassing the town of Kihei. Turn right onto Wailea Iki Dr. and proceed toward the coast. Turn left on Wailea Alanui, which becomes Makena Alanui as it heads south. Turn right on Makena Rd., a two-lane coastal road that leads to Maluaka Beach, in front of the Maui Prince Hotel. On Maui, rental cars and small four-wheel-drive vehicles are available at the airport and through the hotels.

seeking shade under kiawe trees, because they shed spine-filled twigs year-round.

Originally imported from Peru, the kiawe does have a couple of redeeming attributes: The blossoms make a tasty honey, available in most Hawaii markets, and the charcoal, a relative of mesquite, contributes a delicious smoke flavor to grilled meats, poultry, and fish.

MALUAKA BEACH PARK

Maluaka (*Ma-loo-AH-ka*) is one of Maui's most beautiful beaches because of its setting on this rugged coast and the view it commands. Molokini, the crescent islet that shelters marine life, is three miles offshore, and the uninhabited island of

Beauty	A
Swimming	A
Sand	B+
Amenities	A

Kahoolawe, formerly used by the U.S. Navy for target practice, is clearly visible. Beyond is the blue Pacific. On the land side, behind the beach, the tawny foothills of 10,023-foot-high Haleakala give no hint of its massive grandeur.

A small but wide palm-fringed crescent of gold sand, Maluaka is guarded by two black lava points and bounded by sand dunes. If it sounds like a postcard beach, it is.

On the south shore stands the landmark Pu'u Olai, a 360-foot-high red cinder cone, and on the north is the historic Keawala'i Congregational Church, constructed in 1831 of coral blocks cut from the reef. The church is named for the protected sea cove it sits on; *Keawala'i* is Hawaiian for "the calm bay."

Maluaka Beach is the most direct departure point for snorkel cruises to Molokini (*see* Boating). A catamaran launches from the beach, while others sail from Maalea Bay to the north. *Go south on Pi'ilani Hwy. (Hwy. 31) to Makena Alanui and continue south 5 mi. to the "Shoreline Access" sign near the Maui Prince Hotel.*
Swimming: This is the best swimming beach in Makena Bay, with friendly waves and a gentle shore break. But take care to avoid underwater boulders at the surf line.
Sand: Golden, grainy. Beware of kiawe thorns under trees bordering the beach.
Amenities: Rest room, showers, landscaped park. Lifeguard on duty.

Sports: Snorkeling, hiking to Pu'u Olai.
Parking: Roadside.

PU'U OLAI BEACH

On the seaward side of the landmark cinder cone is a secluded gold-sand beach known locally as Little Beach. This unusual natural beach, reached by a coastal trail around the foot of Pu'u Olai (*POO-oo OH-lye*), is a popular nude beach,

Beauty	A
Swimming	A
Sand	B+
Amenities	NA

despite an ordinance banning displays of flesh as "lewdness." This vestigial missionary rule is largely overlooked, although nudists are periodically cited for skinny-dipping. *Go south on Pi'ilani Hwy. (Hwy. 31) to Makena Alanui and continue south 5 mi. Stop at Pu'u Lai cinder cone, just past Maui Prince Hotel. The north coastal trail around the cinder cone is used to reach the beach. The trail to the summit is on the south side of the cinder cone.*
Swimming: Excellent, with a sandy bottom and gentle shore break.
Sand: Golden, grainy.
Amenities: None.
Sports: Snorkeling, bodysurfing, body boarding. No lifeguard.
Parking: Along the road.

ONELOA BEACH

Everyone calls it Big Beach, and it's easy to see why. Nearly a mile long and more than 100 feet wide, it is one of Maui's most popular undeveloped beaches. Ancient Hawaiians called it Oneloa (*Ow-nee-LO-ah*), which means "long sand." It seems

Beauty	B
Swimming	C
Sand	B+
Amenities	B

longer only when you're walking under the hot, tropical sun.

This beach on Ahihi Bay, which extends from Pu'u Olai to Cape Kina'u, is the last sand beach before the start of Maui's black lava coast. Size, not beauty, is the main attribute of Big Beach and most of the other pocket beaches nearby. True, the sheltering bluffs, sand dunes, and wide expanses of golden sand make for a beautiful setting. But it's also somewhat bland, lack-

ing the lush tropical foliage usually associated with Hawaii travel posters. *Drive about 3 mi. south of the Maui Prince Hotel and turn right on a dirt road that runs down to a parking lot at the beach.*
Swimming: Not the best for swimming because it has a strong shore break, a steep slope inshore, and a sharp offshore drop.
Sand: Golden, grainy.
Amenities: Rest rooms, showers. No lifeguard.
Sports: Snorkeling, bodysurfing, board surfing.
Parking: Ample free parking in dirt lot.

HOTELS/INNS/B&Bs

◆ **Maui Prince Hotel** (very expensive). Alone on a green hillside facing the sea, Makena Resort is an oasis set on Maui's most desolate coast. The refinements inside the Maui Prince, especially the vast atrium, help to offset the bland exterior. There are lush gardens, spare furnishings, outstanding cuisine, and a choice of magnificent beaches. Overall, it's exclusive without being intimidating. *5400 Makena Alanui, Kihei, HI 96753; tel. 808-874-1111, 800-321-6284; fax 808-879-8763. Almost at the end of the Alanui road that connects Makena and neighboring Wailea.*

HOUSE RENTALS

◆ **Makena Surf.** Ocean-front luxury condominium with large, fully equipped units overlooking the ocean. *96 Makena Alanui, Kihei, HI 96753; tel. 808-874-0616, 808-879-1595; fax 808-874-6455. On the way to Makena Resort from Wailea Resort.*

RESTAURANTS

Makena Resort's only restaurants are those in the Maui Prince Hotel. In addition to the three listed here, there is a golf course clubhouse restaurant (tel. 808-879-1154).
◆ **Hakone** (expensive). Here's an authentic Japanese restaurant and sushi bar that looks as if it fell out of the sky from Tokyo. It's only a few yards from the Prince Court restaurant but a world removed. When you dine here, you come away with a finer appreciation for

Japanese culture and cuisine. Best seats are in the sushi bar. *5400 Makena Alanui, Kihei, HI 96753; tel. 808-874-1111. Open Tue.-Sat. for dinner. In the Maui Prince Hotel.*

◆ **Prince Court** (expensive). This intimate restaurant is the showcase for chef Roger Dikon, a pioneer of Hawaii regional cuisine who directs all of the Maui Prince's food operations. The candlelit room on the hotel's second floor is a rarity for Hawaii: a beach restaurant with no ocean view. The focus is on the plate. Don't miss the Pacific salmon with potato string crust in balsamic vinegar and port wine sauce. And there's the exotic sugarcane-grilled swordfish with vine-ripened tomato-basil vinaigrette and grapefruit-avocado butter. *5400 Makena Alanui, Kihei, HI 96753; tel. 808-874-1111. Open daily for dinner, Sun. brunch. In the Maui Prince Hotel.*

◆ **Cafe Kiowai** (moderate). An open-air bistro tucked between a man-made waterfall and a Japanese koi carp pond in a tropical garden. The best seats are outside on the flagstone lanai, by the pond where the huge, brilliantly colored fish cruise up as if to peer at your plate. Try Oriental noodles with lobster and shrimp for lunch and smoked Pacific salmon on a toasted bagel for breakfast. *5400 Makena Alanui, Kihei, HI 96753; tel. 808-874-1111. Open daily for breakfast and lunch. In the Maui Prince Hotel.*

NIGHTLIFE

◆ **Molokini Lounge.** Live entertainment in this lounge by the Prince Court is Makena's only nightlife. *5400 Makena Alanui, Kihei, HI 96753; tel. 808-874-1111. Open every evening. In the Maui Prince Hotel.*

ATTRACTIONS

◆ **Keawalai Congregational Church.** Built of coral block cut from the reef, this little missionary church dates from 1831. It was restored in 1952. Sunday services are conducted in Hawaiian. The church is on a protected cove with a golden sand beach. *190 Makena Rd., Kihei, HI 96753; tel. 808-879-5557. Open daily. Beachside, just north of the Maui Prince Hotel.*

SHOPPING

◆ **Maui Prince Hotel.** Posh shops in the hotel lobby sell gifts and Hawaiiana, constituting the only shopping in the immediate area. *5400 Makena Alanui, Kihei, HI 96753; tel. 808-874-1111. Open daily.*

SPORTS

There's plenty to do at the Maui Prince Hotel, but there are no local sports shops. (For listings on nearby fishing, surfing, diving, and bicycling enterprises, *see* Chapter 9, Wailea, and Chapter 10, Kamaole III.)

BOATING

◆ **Makena Boat Partners.** The fastest (15 minutes) and most pleasant way to cruise out to Molokini crater for snorkeling and lunch is aboard the *Kai Kanani* catamaran. Snorkelers get a half hour or so of private time at the popular snorkel crater to meet the rainbow-colored fish before other boaters arrive. They then cruise to La Perouse Bay and head home along the south shore for more private snorkeling. Whales (in season) and dolphins are often seen on the way. Custom cruises for 12 or more people. *5400 Makena Alanui, Kihei, HI 96753; tel. 808-879-7218; fax 808-879-1850. Snorkel cruises Tue., Thu., Sat. Departs from the beach in front of the Maui Prince Hotel.*

GOLF

◆ **Makena Golf Course.** This par-72 18-hole course was designed by Robert Trent Jones, Jr. The course extends more than 203 coastal acres with 64 sand traps and ocean vistas from every fairway. *5415 Makena Alanui, Kihei, HI 96753; tel. 808-879-3344. Open daily. Admission. Next to the Maui Prince Hotel.*

TENNIS

◆ **Makena Tennis Clubs.** Six courts, two with lights, as well as ball machine and rentals. Peter Burwash International manages the club, offering private and group lessons and social events.

5400 Makena Alanui, Kihei, HI 96753; tel. 808-879-8777; fax 808-879-8763. Open daily. Admission. At the Maui Prince Hotel.

HORSEBACK RIDING

◆ **Makena Stables.** Guided rides on a 20,000-acre ranch, climbing up to the 4,000-foot level of Haleakala. Daily morning or sunset rides of three hours, or ride to the Tedeschi Winery, about five and a half hours away. *7299-A S. Makena Rd., Kihei, HI 96753; tel. 808-879-0244. Open Mon.-Sat.*

SHOOTING

◆ **Papaka Sporting Clays.** Try your skill at shooting clay targets in an old volcanic crater. The day includes use of a Beretta shotgun, 75 targets and shells, instruction, protective gear, and shuttle from Wailea or Makena. *1325 S. Kihei Rd., Suite 212, Kihei, HI 96753; tel. 808-879-5649. Open daily.*

HISTORY

Makena has an interesting background. The resort was part of the huge ranch above it on the slope of Haleakala, now known as Ulupalakua Ranch. In Victorian times, it was the Rose Ranch, owned by a former sea captain. Hawaiian royalty attended the parties held there. Makena Landing was the place where cattle were herded into the sea and forced to swim to ships bound for market. Haleakala's most recent eruption, in 1790, deposited the lava flow where the road ends south of Makena at La Perouse Bay.

NATURE

Take a hike up to the top of the Pu'u Olai cinder cone, 360 feet, to reach Maui's best land-based whale-watching perch. Even if you don't go in the whale season (December through April), you'll still have a grand view of neighboring Kahoolawe Island, Molokini crater, and, in the distance, Lanai. The hike is fine for the family and takes about half an hour from the southern side of the hill, reached from Ahihi Beach.

SAFETY TIPS

Protect your feet from the sharp spines of the kiawe tree, and don't seek shade beneath one at any time of year, because they're always shedding twigs, which are filled with the two-inch-long spines.

TOURIST INFORMATION

◆ **Maui Visitors Bureau.** *1727 Wili Pa Loop, Wailuku, HI 96793; tel. 808-244-3530. Open Mon.-Fri. 8-4:30.*

CHAPTER 12

Kaanapali

This is the beach that made Maui famous. When people think of Maui, they almost always have Kaanapali Beach on their mind, even if they can't pronounce the Hawaiian name of Maui's biggest, most popular beach (say *Kah-AH-NA-pah-lee*). In the 1970s, when Maui decided to embrace tourism, travel marketers realized that few except Polynesians could pronounce a word with four *A*s, but almost everybody could say Maui (rhymes with *wowie*). The rest is history.

Today, Maui attracts more than

Beauty	B
Swimming	B
Sand	B
Hotels/Inns/B&Bs	A
House rentals	B
Restaurants	A
Nightlife	B
Attractions	B
Shopping	A
Sports	A
Nature	A

two million visitors a year, second only to Oahu, and this four-mile-long golden-sand beach at the foot of a dozen hotels and condominiums is the reason. Popular with families and honeymooners, Kaanapali Beach is awash with surfers, snorkelers, scuba divers, and whale watchers. It's home port for sunset cruises, kayaks, pedal boats, and everything else aquatic.

Kaanapali didn't just happen. When conceived 30 years ago, it was not only the first major Hawaiian resort beyond Oahu but the first planned tourist destination anywhere on the islands. This playland on the former sugarcane coast of West Maui set a precedent for development in Hawaii and around the world. Its six hotels were set back from the ocean on extra-large lots, height restrictions were imposed, and public beach access was required. Another stipulation: plenty of free parking.

When a sunburn prevents another hour on the beach, nearby Lahaina provides relief from the rays. Lahaina was a rowdy whaler's playground in its 19th-century glory days, as well as home to missionaries and the first school west of the Rockies (Lahainaluna High School, which is still teaching). Historians have preserved the old structures and picturesque features of Lahaina, so you can walk from a Chinese temple to a mission-ary's home and dream of sailing on an old brig like the one moored in the harbor.

Inevitably, history must vie with schlock pop culture in Lahaina, which teems with bad whale art, airbrushed T-shirts with sappy slogans, and now a Planet Hollywood starring a nude, life size fiberglass replica of Sylvester Stallone next to a replica of Free Willie, the killer orca whale of Friday Harbor fame. Lahaina has a few outstanding restaurants, such as David Paul's Lahaina Grill and Mark Ellman's Avalon. And there's no

HOW TO GET THERE

◆ Maui is a 35-minute jet flight from Honolulu International Airport. Most arrivals on Maui, including many nonstop flights from the mainland, are at Kahului Airport. From Kahului Airport (40 minutes from Kaanapali Beach), drive southwest 8 1/4 mi. on Kuihelani Hwy. (Hwy. 38) to Honoapiilani Hwy. (Hwy. 30) and continue on this as it swings northwest up the coast. Pass through Lahaina and drive another mile or so to Kaanapali Resort. Turn right to enter the resort, and look for "Shoreline Access" signs.

◆ Kaanapali is also served by West Maui Airport, which han-dles interisland flights by Mahalo Airlines, IslandAir, and Hawaiian Air. From there, it's a 15-minute shuttle ride to resort hotels. Rental cars are available through the hotels and at both airports.

finer harbor-front perch in all of Maui than the open-air corner tavern at the Pioneer Inn.

KAANAPALI BEACH

Kaanapali combines the classic beauty of a tropical beach with all the comforts of home—and then some. The gorgeous four-mile stretch of golden sand jammed with beachgoers curves around Hanokoo Point and tucks inside the lee of 85-foot-

Beauty	A-
Swimming	B
Sand	B
Amenities	A

high Keka'a Point, often called Black Rock. A serpentine sidewalk hugs the coast as it runs along the shore from the Swan Court of the Hyatt Regency to Keka'a Point, the westernmost extremity of Maui. The beach promenade is crowded from sunrise to sunset.

The coco palm-fringed beach is the centerpiece of this 600-acre beach-front resort set between the West Maui Mountains and the deep blue Pacific. First-time visitors with videocameras spin in the sand, trying to capture on film the 360-degree tropical panorama of Kaanapali. Offshore, sailboats and motorboats dot the ocean. Across Au'au Channel, the pineapple island of Lanai shows like a lump of brown rock.

Oddly, for such a popular beach, no lifeguards are provided by either Maui County or the resorts. Since the water can often be dangerous, especially for first-time visitors, this apparent oversight requires everyone to be alert to changing sea conditions. A simple flag system warns swimmers of the daily changes in current, weather, and surf conditions. Red flags signal heavy tide, strong undertow, or other dangerous ocean conditions. Yellow flags warn of potential hazards. *After entering Kaanapali Resort, look for "Shoreline Access" signs.*

Swimming: One of Maui's best suntanning beaches, this isn't the best for swimming. A dangerous shore break and backwash often churn sand into the waves. The water is usually safe enough for swimming, however, and its temperature hovers in the mid-70s year-round.

Sand: Coarse golden sand mixed with black lava and some detritus from the high shore. The beach, which slopes gently to the water, is narrow in most places. Soft sandy bottom with scattered rocks.

Amenities: With a major resort in its backyard, every possible amenity is present except lifeguards.

Sports: Snorkeling, surfing, sailing, kayaking, volleyball.

Parking: Free parking in paved lots.

PU'U KEKA'A BEACH

In 1963 Sheraton Maui built a beach hotel on and around historic Keka'a Point, a black rock lava bluff that rises 85 feet above this wide, curving black and gold beach. Pu'u Keka'a (*POO-oo Kay-KAH-ah*) is the best at Kaanapali for swimming,

Beauty	A-
Swimming	B
Sand	B
Amenities	A-

snorkeling, and sunbathing, but it should be avoided until 1997 because the hotel is in the midst of a major reconstruction. If you don't mind noise, though, head for Keka'a Point. *At the north end of Kaanapali Beach.*

Swimming: Safe for swimming and snorkeling; the water is protected by the black lava point that juts into the sea.

Sand: Coarse golden sand mixed with black lava. Steep, sometimes deep slope to water. Submerged lava rocks and coral heads.

Amenities: Plenty of resort amenities. No lifeguard.

Sports: Snorkeling, surfing.

Parking: Free parking on paved lot.

HANAKA'O'O POINT

Lively water at this sandbar point makes this a hot spot for surfers, both beginner and expert. Usually gentle two- to three-foot waves wrap the point from the west. This high-energy point at Hanaka'o'o (*Hah-nah-KAH-oh-oh*) attracts surfers,

Beauty	B
Swimming	C
Sand	B
Amenities	A

who delight in the constant swells. It's a great place to watch the action, even if you aren't a surfer. *On the south side of Kaanapali Beach in front of the Hyatt Regency Maui.*

Swimming: Swimmers beware: This is a surfing beach.

Sand: Soft, golden, and clean.
Amenities: None. No lifeguard.
Sports: Surfing. Excellent for body surfers and body boarders, too.
Parking: Ample free parking in paved lot.

HANAKA'O'O BEACH PARK

Another good beach for swimming. The sand is a grainy black and tan, not the prettiest combo, but the warm, limpid water is the main attraction. This beach is a popular launch site for Maui canoe clubs because gentle waves enable easy access.

Beauty	B
Swimming	A-
Sand	B
Amenities	B

Some shade inshore provides relief on hot afternoons. This is a good spot to enjoy the view of Lanai across the channel. A red-dirt Japanese graveyard bounds the beach. *On the south end of Kaanapali Beach.*

Swimming: Gentle little waves, no strong currents.
Sand: Black and tan sand, often spiked with needle-sharp kiawe tree thorns. Watch your step.
Amenities: Rest rooms. Lifeguard on duty.
Sports: Snorkeling, kayaking.
Parking: Free parking in tree-shaded dirt lot.

KAHEKILI BEACH PARK

A royal little beach park named for Maui's King Kahekili (*Kah-hee-KEY-lee*), the "feather cloaked mighty thunderer" who reigned from 1766 to 1793 and built houses of skulls to intimidate his foes. The grassy park leads down to a palm-fringed

Beauty	B
Swimming	B
Sand	B
Amenities	A

beach with a dash of golden sand. It's ideal for beachgoers who don't like sand. Just grab a spot on the green under the coco palms and cool out at this jewel of a beach. If only King Kahekili could see Maui now! *Open daily 6 a.m to 6:30 p.m. From Kaanapali Beach Resort, drive north on Honoapi'ilani Hwy. 1 mi. past the condos. Look for a gated drive to the beach park on the left.*
Swimming: Gentle waves, sandy bottom.

115

Sand: Grainy and golden with black lava flecks.
Amenities: Rest rooms, outdoor showers, picnic tables, barbecue grills, benches, telephone. No lifeguard.
Sports: Bodysurfing.
Parking: Adequate free parking in a tree-shaded paved lot.

WAHIKULI STATE WAYSIDE PARK

This shoreline park with a panoramic view attracts weekend crowds (the name means "Noisy Place" in Hawaiian), but it's empty weekdays. One of Maui's many roadside, drive-up beaches, Wahikuli (*Wah-hee-KOO-lee*) is an ideal ocean-front

Beauty	B
Swimming	B
Sand	B
Amenities	B

picnic spot for families. It enjoys a good view of Lanai and Kahoolawe islands, plus whales in season. *From Kaanapali Beach Resort, drive south 1 1/2 mi. on Honoapi'ilani Hwy. Look for signs on the right.*
Swimming: Good swim and snorkel spot, safe for children, reef-protected beach.
Sand: Grainy, firm sand flecked with black lava. Boulder-lined shore.
Amenities: Rest rooms, outside showers, open-air shade pavilions, picnic tables, barbecue grills. No lifeguard.
Sports: Snorkeling.
Parking: Free parking in dirt lot.

HOTELS/INNS/B&Bs

Kaanapali spans four miles of beach and is a self-contained playground, with six hotels, six vacation condominium complexes, restaurants, shopping, and entertainment. It also offers golf, tennis, water sports, and its own shuttle trolleys. Neighboring Lahaina, three miles away, is a better bet for moderately priced accommodations: They may not be on the beach, but they'll be near the waterfront and affordable.

◆ **Hyatt Regency Maui** (very expensive). Kaanapali's southernmost and largest beach-front hotel, down a shady lane full of tropical trees and flowers, features lush gardens and a pool complex with waterfall, grotto, hanging bridge. The lobby itself is a tropical garden with winding paths, exotic birds, and plenty of artwork, hallmarks of a state-of-the-art Hawaiian resort. *200 Nohea Kai Dr., Lahaina, HI 96761; tel. 808-661-1234, 800-233-1234; fax 808-667-4498.*

◆ **Westin Maui** (very expensive). To enter this lobby is to arrive in a tropical Shangri-la where everyone is happy. The sounds pull you in: rushing waterfalls, squawking cockatoos, kids playing on the waterslide and swimming in the huge pool complex that dominates the center of the hotel. The pools, with rock islands and bridges to link them, are edged with other pools that are alive with fish and swans. Secluded walks, decorated with a variety of sculpture and art, lead to the beach. *2365 Kaanapali Pkwy., Lahaina, HI 96761; tel. 808-667-2525, 800-228-3000; fax 808-661-5764.*

◆ **Kaanapali Beach Hotel** (expensive). Hawaiian atmosphere is carefully nurtured here, despite a preponderance of glitz in the neighborhood. This hotel wins awards for its efforts to be culturally correct. The result for the guest is a friendly experience and a chance to learn something about Hawaiian people and their hospitality. Low-rise, beach-front garden setting. *2525 Kaanapali Pkwy., Lahaina, HI 96761; tel. 808-661-0011, 800-233-1014; fax 808-667-5978.*

◆ **Lahaina Shores Beach Resort** (moderate). The beach isn't Kaanapali, but it's right in front of this reasonably priced, attractive hotel, which features full kitchens in 151 studio, one-bedroom, and penthouse units. Room/car package available. Walking distance from downtown Lahaina. *475 Front St., Lahaina, HI 96761; tel. 808-667-1666, 800-642-6284; fax 808-661-1025. South of central Lahaina, next to the shopping and restaurant complex at 505 Front St.*

◆ **Pioneer Inn** (moderate). A funky, two-story wood-frame hotel on the waterfront, this turn-of-the-century gem has 48 guest rooms and is a prime choice of those who collect old hotels with "character." Guests feel at home here. It offers a way to enjoy a Maui beach vacation at a reasonable rate and also be near restaurants and shops. *658 Wharf St., Lahaina, HI 96761; tel. 808-661-3636, 800-457-5457.*

117

HOUSE RENTALS

Resort condominiums share the same wonderful beach and amenities as neighboring hotels at Kaanapali. For a family, two couples traveling together, golfing buddies, or others who want more space and a kitchen and a relaxed atmosphere, condos are a popular choice. Some individual residences within the resort are available for rental through the listing agent, but they tend toward the palatial and are priced accordingly.

◆ **Elite Properties.** Very expensive vacation rental homes with two to seven bedrooms, as plush as the purse will bear, including chefs, massages, limos, and concierge on call. *Box 5273, Lahaina, HI 96761; tel. 808-665-0561; fax 808-669-2417. Open Mon.-Fri.*

◆ **Kaanapali Alii.** Beachfront luxury complex of 264 spacious one- and two-bedroom units surrounded by gardens, lawns, and pools steps away from the beach. Tennis courts, daily maid service, hotel restaurants on either side. *50 Nohea Kai Dr., Lahaina, HI 96761; tel. 808-667-1400, 800-642-6284. Open daily.*

RESTAURANTS

Maui's menu of restaurants has improved considerably in recent years, and Kaanapali Beach Resort and neighboring Lahaina offer some of the best.

◆ **Sound of the Falls** (very expensive). An open-air restaurant faces the sea and the sunset, not to mention eight islets in a koi carp lagoon, each bearing a royal palm and assorted flamingos. And, of course, roaring waterfalls. Pacific Rim cuisine lives up to the promise of this fantasy setting. Try the New Zealand abalone in ginger-mango sauce or the grilled Lanai venison with mixed island greens. *2365 Kaanapali Pkwy., Lahaina, HI 96761; tel. 808-667-2525. Open Mon.-Wed., Fri., and Sat. for dinner. At the Westin Maui.*

◆ **Swan Court** (very expensive). This continental restaurant has a romantic setting that's perfect for a special occasion, especially with its sunset ocean view, reflecting pool, and cruising swans. Island cuisine is well represented here by such dishes as grilled fresh papio and sea scallops and ono with Maui onion-and-tomato sauce. Reservations requested. *200 Nohea Kai Dr., Lahaina, HI 96761; tel. 808-661-1234. Open daily for brunch and dinner. Reservations requested. At the Hyatt Regency Maui.*

◆ **Avalon Restaurant & Bar** (expensive). Owner Mark Ellman is one of the most innovative chefs creating Hawaii regional cuisine. He combines Southeast Asian and Western cookery with fresh Maui produce and seafood. Worth searching for (it's in a small shopping-complex courtyard with indoor/outdoor tables). Don't leave without a Caramel Miranda dessert (fresh fruit heaped under ice cream and caramel sauce). *844 Front St., Lahaina, HI 96761; tel. 808-667-5559. Open daily for lunch and dinner.*

◆ **Roy's Kahana Bar & Grill and Roy's Nicolina** (expensive). Chef Roy Yamaguchi's two side-by-side restaurants bring his style of Hawaii regional cuisine to Maui, offering the same excellent East/West concoctions for which Roy's is known on Oahu and other islands. *4405 Honoapiilani Hwy., Kahana, HI 96761; tel. for Bar & Grill 808-669-6999; Nicolina 808-669-5000. Open daily for dinner. From Kaanapali Beach Resort, turn left on Honoapiilani Hwy. and drive 6 mi. to Kahana Gateway Shopping Center. Kahana Bar & Grill and Nicolina are on the second floor.*

◆ **Hula Grill and Barefoot Bar** (moderate). Best bet in the Kaanapali Beach Resort area for people interested in good food that's creatively prepared, served on the beach front, and priced well. Chef Peter Merriman is one of Hawaii's best and brightest. His new restaurant recalls a 1930s plantation house—friendly and informal, with some outdoor tables on a patio and some planted in the sand. *2435 Kaanapali Pkwy., Lahaina, HI 96761; tel. 808-667-6636. Open daily for lunch and dinner.*

◆ **Tiki Terrace Restaurant** (moderate). Indoor/outdoor restaurant surrounded by ocean-front garden. Pleasant and affordable. Try the Hawaiian-style breakfast: eggs, Portuguese sausage, and rice. Dinner menus include local specialties, such as *lumpia* (a Filipino spring roll) of chicken and fresh vegetables, baked Maui onion soup, and fish baked with taro leaves, grilled bananas, steamed sweet potato, and homemade poi. *2525 Kaanapali Pkwy., Lahaina, HI 96761; tel. 808-661-0011. Open* *daily for breakfast and dinner. In the Kaanapali Beach Hotel.*

◆ **Cheeseburger in Paradise** (inexpensive). Cheeseburgers, mai tais, and rock and roll with great views of the harbor and sunsets over the sea. Fare includes salads and some of Hawaii's best burgers. Bring the kids. *811 Front St., Lahaina, HI 96761; tel. 808-661-4855. Open daily for lunch and dinner.*

◆ **Rusty Harpoon** (inexpensive). Here's a good way to start the day: Watch for whales while you eat pineapple sausage and waffles heaped with toppings from the waffle bar. The view is excellent at this reasonably priced, family-oriented, indoor/outdoor eatery right on the beach. *2435 Kaanapali Pkwy., Lahaina, HI 96761; tel. 808-661-3123. Open daily for breakfast, lunch, and dinner. In Whalers Village.*

NIGHTLIFE

Evening entertainment has quieted from the disco dreams of the 1980s, but if there's going to be bright lights and boogying on Maui, Lahaina is the place to find it. Resort luaus are lively, with several to choose from in the area.

◆ **Blue Tropix.** Dinner and dancing five nights a week. Different themes, with DJs and recorded music or live bands; $5 cover after 9 p.m. *900 Front St., Lahaina, HI 96761; tel. 808-667-5309. Open Thu.-Mon. In Lahaina Center shopping area.*

◆ **Old Lahaina Luau.** Begins on the beach with some performers arriving by outrigger canoe and continues with island-style feast and Hawaiian music and dance. *505 Front St., Lahaina, HI 96761; tel. 808-667-1998. Open Mon.-Sat. Admission.*

◆ **World Cafe.** Come here for drinks and a relaxing game of pool. *900 Front St., Lahaina, HI 96761; tel. 808-661-1515. Open daily. In Lahaina Center shopping area.*

ATTRACTIONS

◆ **Hawaii Experience Domed Theater.** A gigantic screen brings to life the Hawaiian Islands' most dramatic scenery in the 40-minute film *Hawaii, Islands of the Gods. 824 Front St., Lahaina, HI 96761; tel. 808-661-8314. Open daily 10-10. Admission.*

◆ **Lahaina, Kaanapali & Pacific Railroad.** The perky little Sugar Cane Train tootles along a 12-mile round-trip through the canefields upslope from Lahaina and Kaanapali. Board at three stations for a different look at the West Maui Coast and the history of the trains that once carried cane from plantation to shipping wharf. Call for station details. *Honoapiilani Hwy., Lahaina, HI 96761; tel. 808-661-0089. Open daily 8:55-4:40. Admission.*

◆ **Whale Center of the Pacific Museum.** Whaling memorabilia from West Maui's early days. A massive skeleton of a sperm whale hangs by the entrance. He's real except for his rubber teeth, inserted after tourists swiped the real ones. *Whalers Village, 2435 Kaanapali Pkwy., Lahaina, HI 96761; tel. 808-661-5992. Open daily 9:30 a.m.-10 p.m.*

SHOPPING

Whalers Village shopping complex augments the substantial shopping areas of the hotels at Kaanapali, and Lahaina adds still another dimension. Art galleries heavy on marine art are very popular and busy, as are the resort-wear shops and the jewelers featuring good coral and Hawaiian Niihau shell necklaces. Plenty of European boutiques court an increasing number of Asian visitors here.

◆ **Collections by Liberty House.** Collections, located in the lobbies of both the Westin Maui and the nearby Hyatt Regency Maui, is a resort-wear branch of Hawaii's Liberty House stores. Good selection of bathing suits and other clothing appropriate to the setting. *2365 Kaanapali Pkwy., Lahaina, HI 96761; tel. for Westin Maui 808-661-5083; Hyatt Regency Maui 808-667-7785. Open daily.*

◆ **Lahaina Galleries.** Whimsical works by Guy Buffet and marine fantasies by Robert Lyn Nelson, plus other contemporary paintings, sculpture, and prints stressing local artists and subjects. Scene of the annual Ocean Arts Festival, held January through April. *Two locations in West Maui: 728 Front St., Lahaina, HI 96761; tel. 808-667-2152; Kapalua Bay Hotel, 808-669-0202.*

◆ **Lahaina Printsellers.** One of three Maui outlets (another, larger shop is located in Lahaina Cannery Mall). Interesting collection of old maps and reproductions of the fine pen-and-ink sketches of Hawaiian people and scenery drawn by Captain Cook's crew. *2435 Kaanapali Pkwy., Lahaina, HI 96761; tel. 808-667-7617. Open daily. In Whalers Village.*

◆ **Lei Spa Maui.** Maui-made spa products: cosmetics, oils, creams, shampoos, scrubs, aromatherapy perfumes, and gift baskets. Available by mail-order as well as in the store. *505 Front St. No. 105, Lahaina, HI 96761; tel. 808-661-1178; fax 808-667-7727. Open daily.*

◆ **Maui Monkey.** Original designs and prints of "tropical rain forest" patterns inspired by scenery on Maui's Hana Highway. Andrina Cochrane's creations are made of lightweight cotton. Also plush toys at this factory-outlet store. Goods available by mail-order. *78 Front St., Lahaina, HI 96761; tel. 808-661-7979, 800-939-5678. Open daily. In Lahaina Shopping Center.*

◆ **Maui To Go.** Pleasant corner shop in re-created seaside whalers' village features Maui Gourmet products such as Hawaiian coffees, tropical fruit jellies and syrups (all of which can be mail-ordered), as well as tropically scented soaps and cosmetics. An adjoining gallery and clothing shop has an excellent selection of men's silk aloha shirts and women's airy sundresses. *505 Front St., Suite 128, Lahaina, HI 96761; tel. 808-667-0727, 800-717-6284. Open daily.*

◆ **Sandal Tree.** Great spot to find informal or dressy sandals and other beach-oriented footwear. *In lobby shops at the Hyatt Regency Maui (tel. 808-661-3495) and the Westin Maui (tel. 808-667-5330). Open daily.*

◆ **Totally Hawaiian.** Hawaiian gifts, including bowls and boxes of native koa wood, Niihau shell lei and necklaces, and heirloom quilts. *1221 Honoapiilani Hwy., Lahaina, HI 96761; tel. 808-667-2558. Open daily. In Lahaina Cannery Mall.*

BEST FOOD SHOPS

SANDWICHES: ◆ **Mr. Sub.** *129 Lahainaluna Rd., Lahaina, HI 96761; tel. 808-667-5683. Open daily.*

SEAFOOD: ◆ **Nagasako Super Market.** *Lahaina Shopping Center, Lahaina, HI 96761; tel. 808-661-0575. Open daily.*

BAKERY: ◆ **Pikake Bakery.** *300 Ohukai Rd., Suite 305, Lahaina, HI 96761; tel. 808-879-7295. Open Mon.-Sat.*
ICE CREAM: ◆ **Lappert's Ice Cream.** *693 Front St., Lahaina, HI 96761; tel. 808-661-3310. Open daily.*
WINE: ◆ **Maui Bottle Shop, Whalers Village.** *2435 Kaanapali Pkwy., Lahaina, HI 96761; tel. 808-661-3708. Open daily.*

SPORTS

Most sports here are wet and wild, since the sea is so accessible. But golf runs a close second to water activities, and tennis is an important third in this healthy atmosphere.

FISHING

◆ **Absolute Sportsfishing.** Captain Marty Sands pursues Hawaii's delicious and trophy-candidate deep-sea fish on half-day or full-day charters, private or shared, aboard the *Absolute*, a tournament-equipped 31-foot Bertram with a cruising speed of 25 knots. *Box 10511, Lahaina, HI 96761; tel. 808-669-1449. Sails daily from Kaanapali Beach.*

BOATING

Lahaina is one of Maui's busiest harbors, with tour boats, charter boats, snorkel/sails, sunset cruises, and whale-watching cruises in winter. All this plus a one-hour passenger ferry to Lanai, as well as charter fishing and private yachts.
◆ **Gemini Charters.** Half-day picnic snorkel/sails and whale watching (December to April), as well as private charters aboard the 64-foot catamaran *Gemini*. Free valet parking at the Westin Maui, closest hotel to mooring. *Box 10846, Lahaina, HI 96761; tel. 808-661-2591. Operates daily.*
◆ **Hawaii Ocean Rafting.** Whale-watching December through April and snorkel adventures to Lanai and Molokini in the most exciting transport: a high-tech ocean-going hard-hulled raft that takes up to 14 passengers. *Box 381, Lahaina, HI 96761; tel. 808-667-2191. Operates daily.*
◆ *Navatek II.* Specially designed to minimize ocean motion and seasickness, the Navatek crosses the channel each morning to

snorkel off Lanai Island. Snorkeling gear, breakfast, and lunch included. *162 Lahainaluna, Lahaina, HI 96761; tel. 808-661-8787. Operates daily.*

◆ **Trilogy Excursions.** Family operation famous for sailing expertise offers snorkel/sails to Lanai with access to the Hulopoe Bay marine preserve and private park and to Molokini Crater. Overnight Lanai tours available, as well as packages combining sailing adventures with helicopter rides, golf, and other sports. Custom charters and seasonal whale watching (December to April). *Box 1119, Lahaina, HI 96761; tel. 808-661-4743, 800-874-2666. Daily departures from Lahaina Harbor.*

SURFING

◆ **Nancy Emerson School of Surfing.** Certified instructors teach using a special method. Group or private lessons by the hour or day. *Box 463, Lahaina, HI 96761; tel. 808-244-7873. Open daily.*

DIVING

◆ **Dive Maui.** Diverse diving trips to Molokini Crater, Lanai, and Maui sites. Tours for every budget depart from a number of locations. Equipment sales and rentals. *900 Front St., Lahaina, HI 96761; tel. 808-667-2080. Open daily.*

◆ **Lahaina Divers.** Two dive boats offer introductory dives, refresher dives, two-tank dives, three-day scuba trips, and night diving. *143 Dickenson St., Lahaina, HI 96761; tel. 808-667-7496. Operates daily.*

GOLF

Golf is so much a part of the appeal that Maui resorts banded together to create the Maui Golf Coast. Kaanapali Beach Resort's courses wind throughout the resort, coating hillsides and rolling terrain with a carpet of green.

◆ **Royal Kaanapali Golf Courses.** Two par-71 18-hole championship courses, the scene of annual televised tournaments. North Course designed by Robert Trent Jones, Sr., South Course by Arthur Jack Snyder. Greens fees are high. Club rentals, pro shop. Priority starting times (and slightly cheaper fees) for Kaanapali resort guests, with two-day advance registration. *Kaanapali Pkwy., Lahaina, HI 96761; tel. 808-661-3691; fax 808-661-0203. Open daily. Admission.*

TENNIS

Most of Kaanapali's hotels and condos have tennis facilities, ranging from a court or two to a full-on tennis tournament complex. If you prefer an ocean breeze while you play, the Maui Marriott's five-court facilities are beach front.

◆ **Maui Marriott Resort.** Tennis with an ocean view. Beach front, beside the hotel, are five courts, three of them lighted. Rentals, ball machine, instruction, pro shop. *100 Nohea Dr., Lahaina, HI 96761; tel. 808-667-1200. Open daily. Admission.*

◆ **Royal Lahaina Tennis Ranch.** Complex includes 11 courts, 7 of them with lights. Stadium court, ball machine, pro shop, rentals, daily activities. Play is free for guests of Royal Lahaina. *2780 Kekaa Dr., Lahaina, HI 96761; tel. 808-661-1753; fax 808-661-3538. Open daily. Admission.*

HORSEBACK RIDING

◆ **Ironwood Ranch.** Guided rides through pineapple plantation. Sunset, picnic, and private rides also available. Pickups and deliveries in Kaanapali. *5095 Napilihau Rd., Lahaina, HI 96761; tel. 808-669-4991.*

◆ **Mendes Ranch and Trail Rides.** Breathtaking four-hour morning ride with barbecue lunch on private coastal West Maui Mountains ranch. Beach, waterfalls. Also, package with helicopter tour. Kaanapali pickups and deliveries. *RR 1, Box 150, Wailuku, HI 96793; tel. 808-871-5222; fax 808-249-0466.*

HISTORY

◆ **Baldwin House Museum.** Former home of the Rev. Dwight Baldwin and his medical mission, restored and furnished to reflect the mid-1800s. *668 Front St., Lahaina, HI 96761; tel. 808-661-3262. Open daily 10-4:30.*

◆ *Brig Carthaginian II.* Replica of a 19th-century square-rigged ship is a floating museum with video, whalers songs, and other lore. *Lahaina Harbor Wharf, Lahaina, HI 967561; tel. 808-661-*

8527. Open daily 10-4.

◆ **Wo Hing Chinese Cultural Museum.** Look for a fine example of Chinese Victorian architecture and you'll readily find the Wo Hing temple, built in 1912 as a residence for Chinese immigrant men (they had to leave their families behind). Artifacts and photographs tell their story. *858 Front St., Lahaina, HI 96761; tel. 808-661-5553. Open daily 10-4.*

SAFETY TIPS

Swimming can be perilous, even for the strongest swimmer, in winter along Kaanapali Beach. Don't swim at that time of year. Even at other times, study the ocean before you enter. If in doubt, stay out.

Sharp coral and slippery rocks are a hazard at some places along the beach. Falling lava rocks pose a danger at Keka'a Point. Also, sharp kiawe (mesquite) thorns fall in the sand and puncture passing feet at the south end of Kaanapali.

TOURIST INFORMATION

◆ **Kaanapali Beach Resort Association.** *45 Kai Ali Dr., Suite 118A, Lahaina, HI 96761; tel. 808-661-3271. Open Mon.-Fri. 8-5.*
◆ **Maui Visitors Bureau.** *1727 Wili Pa Loop, Wailuku, HI 96793; tel. 808-244-3530. Open Mon.-Fri. 8-4:30.*

CHAPTER 13

Hanalei Bay

For natural beauty, there is no finer beach in Kauai, maybe in all of Hawaii, than Hanalei. Coconut trees line the golden sand. Sheer volcanic ridges laced with waterfalls rise to 4,000 feet inland. Gentle waves roll across the face of Hanalei Bay, running up the wide, half-moon beach. Hanalei, which means "heavenly garland," is truly divine.

Beauty	A
Swimming	A
Sand	B+
Hotels/Inns/B&Bs	B
House rentals	B
Restaurants	B
Nightlife	D
Attractions	B
Shopping	B
Sports	A
Nature	A

Hanalei (*Ha-na-LAY*) stands for more than a beach, however. It embraces a bay, a wetland refuge for endangered waterbirds, a laid-back, old plantation town, and, arguably, a state of mind. It also happens to be Kauai's best beach-vacation bargain, offering an assortment of water sports, unparalleled scenery, and a variety of accommodations.

Its relative isolation and two major hurricanes in ten years have held back "progress," but what really keeps Hanalei from becoming just another stop on the tourist trail is a rickety one-lane bridge over the Hanalei River that is too small for a tour bus to cross. If it ever goes, it will probably be rebuilt bigger and wider, with at least two lanes, spelling doom for a beach town that, so far, has evaded developers' schemes for marinas, hotels, and grandiose resorts.

For now, the town is a rustic charmer of plantation-style houses, shops, and restaurants, including the famous Tahiti Nui, a funky roadside nightspot that hosts Hawaiian music concerts and luaus and serves the island's best mai tai. With streets named for Hawaiian fish and dogs snoozing in the middle of them, Hanalei seems to have just the right energy level for a languid beach holiday. The toughest choice each morning is deciding which beach to enjoy. Some are perfect for snorkeling, others for just sitting and staring at the spectacular beauty. Still others are excellent for swimming, bodysurfing, or beachcombing. What's your pleasure?

HANALEI BAY BEACH

One of the most famous beaches in Hawaii, Hanalei is celebrated in song and hula and is featured on travel posters, postcards, and in movies.

Beauty	A
Swimming	A
Sand	B
Amenities	B

It owes its natural beauty to its age of maybe 70 million years or more. Kauai is the oldest, most geologically complex Hawaiian island, and Hanalei Bay is an ancient sunken valley with "post-erosional" cliffs (that's how geologists explain the aesthetics).

Surfers benefit greatly from this geology. Not only is the bay two miles wide, but it extends inland a full mile and has coral reefs on both east and west sides, with a patch of coral in the

HOW TO GET THERE

◆ From Honolulu International Airport, it's a 20-minute flight by jet to Kauai's Lihue Airport, which is a 45-minute drive from Hanalei. From Lihue, drive north 31 mi. on Kuhio Hwy. (Hwy. 56). Hanalei is the only major town on the North Shore. Cross the one-lane bridge over the Hanalei River, and you're there. Mahalo Airlines, IslandAir, and Hawaiian Air fly prop planes between Honolulu International and Princeville Airport, which serves Kauai's North Shore. On Kauai, rental cars and small four-wheel-drive vehicles are available through the hotels and at Lihue and Princeville airports.

middle. The reefs ripple the waves and make the long ride to shore a delight.

Actually, the bay is so big it has several beaches, from Black Pot on the eastern shore to Waikoko on the west. Each is different in its own way. Hanalei Bay Beach, almost in the middle at the beach park off Weke Drive, is the most popular for sunbathing, body boarding, and general splashing about in the water. Swimming is excellent year-round, especially in summer when Hanalei Bay becomes what lifeguard Norman Hunter calls "one big lake."

Hunter, who is based at Hanalei Bay Beach, is the only lifeguard for miles around. His nearest colleague is at Ke'e Beach at the end of Highway 56. They stay in touch via short-wave radio but still have too many beaches to watch. *After crossing the bridge into town, turn right at Aku Rd. Drive 1 block, turn right at Weke Rd., then left at beach park.*

Swimming: Excellent, but a strong undertow.

Sand: Reddish gold and grainy mixed with small amounts of black soil from runoff.

Amenities: Rest rooms, showers, picnic tables. Lifeguard on duty.

Sports: Swimming, surfing, body boarding, fishing, kayaking, sailing.

Parking: Ample and free.

HANALEI PAVILION COUNTY PARK

A popular launch spot for surfers, beachgoers with picnics, and sunset observers, this beach park has the most public facilities of any on the east side of Hanalei Bay. Picturesque Hanalei Pier, a popular spot for anglers and photographers, juts into the

Beauty	A
Swimming	A
Sand	B
Amenities	B

bay. *From Kuhio Hwy., turn right on Aku Rd. and drive to Weke Rd. Turn right and go almost to the end of the road. The beach is on the left.*

Swimming: Good to excellent except in winter, when strong undertow and big waves pose a risk.

Sand: Grainy reddish golden with some sediment from the Hanalei River.

Amenities: Rest rooms, outdoor showers, picnic tables, barbecue

grills. No lifeguard.
Sports: Surfing, bodysurfing, fishing.
Parking: Ample free parking.

BLACK POT BEACH

A small, busy beach at the mouth of the Hanalei River, it takes its name from the missionary's cook pot that simmered for years here. This 1 1/4-acre beach park on the east side of the bay affords spectacular views of the mountains and bay, framed by

Beauty	A
Swimming	A
Sand	B
Amenities	B

ironwood trees. The river mouth is the launch site for kayak and rafting expeditions up the Na Pali Coast. *Turn right off Kuhio Hwy. onto Aku Rd. Turn right on Weke Rd. and drive to the east end of the road. There's a dirt parking lot in the ironwood grove.*
Swimming: Safe in shallows near the river mouth.
Sand: Golden and grainy mixed with black dirt from river runoff.
Amenities: Rest rooms, showers, picnic tables. No lifeguard.
Sports: Kayaking.
Parking: Free parking in the dirt lot.

WAIOLI BEACH PARK

Almost in the middle of the Hanalei Bay shoreline, Waioli (*Why-OH-lee*) is a small, grassy overlook at the surf break known locally as Pinetrees because of the iron-woods on the shore. A great place to swim or, if you're surfing, pick up a gentle ride.

Beauty	A
Swimming	A
Sand	B
Amenities	B

Turn right off Kuhio Hwy. onto Aku Rd. Turn left at Weke Rd. and drive 1/2 mi. until dirt road leads to parking lot in an ironwood grove.
Swimming: Excellent swimming in summer. Sandy bottom, easy waves.
Sand: Hard-packed and reddish golden with some dirt from Waioli Stream runoff.
Amenities: Rest rooms, outside showers, picnic tables. Lifeguard on duty.
Sports: Surfing, body boarding, sailing.
Parking: Ample lot.

WAIKOKO BEACH

Under ironwood trees, this natural roadside beach is perfect for a picnic or a
plunge. The calm water, protected by
Waikoko (*Why-CO-CO*) Reef, is safe for
swimming and good for beginner snorkelers. However, the pale green Princeville

Beauty	B
Swimming	A
Sand	A
Amenities	NA

Hotel on the eastern bluffs of Hanalei Bay is visible in the dis-
tance from here, intruding on the natural beauty of the beach
and bay. *Take Kuhio Hwy. beyond Hanalei town to west side of
Hanalei Bay. No signs mark the beach—only a wide turnoff on hard-
packed sand under ironwood trees.*
Swimming: Safest swimming on Hanalei Bay—reef-protected
and sheltered from onshore waves.
Sand: Reddish golden sand often mixed with stream runoff.
Amenities: None. No lifeguard.
Sports: Snorkeling.

LUMAHAI BEACH

One of Hawaii's most photographed
beaches, Lumahai (*Loo-MA-high*) is beautiful but deadly. The same waves that create dramatic Hollywood-style splashes
when they break on the islets a few yards
offshore can also dash you against the

Beauty	A
Swimming	C
Sand	A
Amenities	NA

cliffs. So be content just to take a picture and drink in the
scenery. Don't be surprised if it looks familiar. Framed by lush
foliage at the foot of a sheer black lava cliff, Lumahai starred in
the 1957 film classic *South Pacific* and has appeared in nearly
every visitor's home video since. *Take Kuhio Hwy. beyond Hanalei
town to west side of Hanalei Bay. Pass the turnoff for Waikoko Beach
and drive a short way to a scenic overlook. Take a picture from here,
but do not try to reach the beach by descending the sheer cliffs. Drive
on to Wainiha Beach Park and hike back.*
Swimming: For experts and even then only in a summer calm.
No one should attempt to swim here in winter, when huge
waves smash the coast and run up on the cliffs.
Sand: Coarse reddish golden.

Amenities: None. No lifeguard.
Sports: None.
Parking: At Wainiha Beach Park.

HOTELS/INNS/B&Bs

Other than the Princeville Resort, Hanalei area accommodations are strictly vacation rental houses, cottages, and bed-and-breakfasts. The village serves as gateway and support system for campers, hikers, and boat passengers bound for the Na Pali wilderness and for visitors setting up housekeeping on the North Shore. Princeville offers luxury hotels and a full array of condominiums, along with golf, tennis, and other resort amenities, including a small airport.

◆ **Princeville Hotel** (very expensive). Sheer luxury, with Hawaiian warmth and as spectacular a setting as mountains and sea can create. The glitzy 252-room hotel steps down the cliffs overlooking Hanalei Bay. Full of Italian marble and glass, the Princeville looks like Versailles-by-the-Sea. Its enormous lobby takes in the splendid panorama of Kauai's North Shore scenery. *5520 Kahaku Rd., Princeville, HI 96722; tel. 808-826-9644; fax 808-826-1166.*

◆ **Hanalei Bay Resort** (expensive). Hotel rooms and one- and two-bedroom luxury condominium suites with kitchens in a breathtaking setting overlooking Hanalei Bay. Amenities include tennis, pool with waterfall and sandy beach area for kids, as well as a real beach with snorkeling reefs near shore. *Box 220, Hanalei, HI 96714; tel. 808-826-6522, 800-367-5005; fax 808-826-6680. At Princeville Resort.*

HOUSE RENTALS

◆ **Aloha Rental Management.** Beach-front vacation cottages, homes, and condos on the North Shore. *Box 1109, Hanalei, HI 96714; tel. 808-826-7288, 800-487-9833. Open daily.*

◆ **Bed & Breakfast Hawaii.** This is a reservation service for houses, cottages, and condominium units on Kauai and other Hawaiian islands. *Box 449, Kapaa, HI 96746; tel. 808-822-7771,*

800-733-6132; fax 808-822-2723. Open daily.

◆ **Blue Water Vacation Rentals.** *Princeville Center, Hanalei, HI 96714; tel. 808-826-9229. Open daily.*

◆ **Kauai Paradise Vacations, Inc.** Condo rentals for several Princeville complexes, including ocean-front units. *Box 1080, Hanalei, HI 96714; tel. 808-826-7444, 800-826-7782; fax 808-826-7673. Open daily.*

◆ **Kauai Vacation Rentals.** Houses, condos, and cottages for vacation rentals throughout the North Shore. *3-3311 Kuhio Hwy., Lihue, HI 96766; tel. 808-245-8841; fax 808-246-1161. Open daily.*

RESTAURANTS

◆ **Hanalei Dolphin Restaurant** (moderate). Fresh fish and steaks, vegetarian dishes, and rich desserts. Open-air casual bistro in the garden. *Hanalei, HI 96714; tel. 808-826-6113. Open daily for dinner. Beside the river, at the entrance to Hanalei town.*

◆ **Tahiti Nui** (moderate). With a bow to Quinn's Bar in Tahiti, this tropical bar and restaurant has a friendly, colorful atmosphere that smacks of island adventure. Owner is fabled Tahitian *tutu* ("grandmother" or "auntie") Louise Marston. She serves local fish and other uncomplicated entrées. Terrific down-home luau Wednesday and Friday nights. Tables indoors, or out on the lanai. *Hanalei, HI 96714; tel. 808-826-6277, 808-826-7320. Open daily for breakfast, lunch, and dinner. In the heart of Hanalei town.*

◆ **Cafe Luna** (moderate). Italian fare with a wood-burning oven for pizzas served either in a pleasant, plantation-style room or outdoors on the large, covered lanai. Full bar. *Hanalei Center, Hanalei, HI 96714; tel. 808-826-1222. Open daily for lunch and dinner.*

◆ **Bubba Burgers** (inexpensive). Burgers made from local beef, as well as chicken, fish, Italian sausage, and hot dogs. Try the Slopper, a chiliburger, or, if you dare, the Hubba Bubba: rice, hamburger, hot dog smothered in chili and onions. *Hanalei, HI 96714; tel. 808-826-7839. Open daily 10:30-6. Walk-up stand in Hanalei Center.*

◆ **Hale O'Java** (inexpensive). Italian sandwiches, Italian and Hawaiian coffees, Calabrese pizza, baked goods, desserts, fresh tropical juices, Italian sodas. Outdoor seating. *Princeville Center, Princeville, HI 96722; tel. 808-826-7255. Open daily for breakfast, lunch, and dinner. In Princeville Center.*

◆ **Hanalei Gourmet** (inexpensive). Hearty California-style food, baked goods, salads, and sandwiches in an old, high-ceilinged plantation schoolroom with a view of taro patches and waterfalls on the distant mountains. Picnic lunches, bar, gourmet shop. *Old School, Hanalei Center, Hanalei, HI 96714; tel. 808-826-2524; fax 808-826-6007. Open daily for breakfast, lunch, and dinner.*

NIGHTLIFE

The Princeville Hotel, the Hanalei Bay Resort, and several restaurants feature music at night, particularly on weekends, but the North Shore is primarily a quiet place devoted to the next day's fun.

◆ **Tahiti Nui.** Local-style luaus on Wednesday and Friday nights, plus live entertainment in the bar on weekends. Patrons are encouraged to sit in with musicians and to dance when the spirit moves them. *Hanalei, HI 96714; tel. 808-826-6277, 808-826-7320. Open daily. In the heart of Hanalei town.*

SHOPPING

The North Shore, especially Hanalei, has Kauai's most interesting shops to poke around in and find a treasure or two. Hanalei's "commercial district"—all one block of it—is divided into several small, off-the-road complexes of shops, one in an old schoolhouse. In Princeville Center, there are more shops and restaurants as well as a market, so shoppers can stay busy on a misty morning or a hot, après-beach afternoon.

◆ **Bamboo Silks.** Womenswear of hand-painted silk, including local creations. *Hanalei, HI 96714; tel. 808-826-1811. Open daily. In Hanalei Center.*

◆ **On the Road to Hanalei.** Pareus to tie around a bathing suit, gifts, clothing with flair. *Box 787, Hanalei, HI 96714; tel. 808-826-7360. Open daily. In the center of Hanalei town.*

◆ **Rainbow Ducks.** Children's clothing and playthings. *Hanalei*

Center, Hanalei, HI 96714; tel. 808-826-4741. Open daily.

◆ **Yellowfish Trading Co.** Hawaiiana, island kitsch, collectibles, antique and contemporary furniture, and such books as *Lust* and *Over My Dead Body*. Also, soft boudoir boxes made of Japanese patterned material. *Box 1049, Hanalei, HI 96714; tel. 808-826-1227. Open daily. In Hanalei Center.*

BEST FOOD SHOPS

SANDWICHES: ◆ **Big Save.** Hanalei's supermarket. *Hanalei, HI 96714; tel. 808-826-6652. Open daily. In Ching Young Village Shopping Center in central Hanalei.*

SEAFOOD: ◆ **Hanalei Dolphin Fish Market.** Fresh catch, calamari, fresh bread. *Hanalei, HI 96714; tel. 808-826-6113. Open daily. At the entrance to Hanalei town behind Dolphin restaurant.*

FRESH PRODUCE: ◆ **Hanalei Natural Foods.** Sweet, local sunrise papaya, avocados, salad greens, fresh herbs, sandwiches, fresh-baked breads, plus the usual natural food store wares. *Hanalei, HI 96714; tel. 808-826-6990. Open daily. In Ching Young Village Shopping Center in central Hanalei.*

BAKERY: ◆ **Kauai Ohana Bakery.** Fresh baked goods, specialty breads (including sundried tomato and basil), and taro rolls. *Princeville Center, Princeville, HI 96722; tel. 808-826-7711. Open Mon.-Sat.*

ICE CREAM: ◆ **Hanalei Shave Ice.** Nothing cools on a very hot day like a Hawaiian shave ice (a fine snow cone). Try such tropical flavors as *lilikoi* and guava. Or how about a Hanalei Rainbow: strawberry, orange, banana, vanilla, and grape, and get a scoop of ice cream underneath for good measure. Also served here: saimin, Hawaii's noodle soup, and plate lunches. *Hanalei Center, Hanalei, HI 96714. Open Tue.-Sun. A stand at Hanalei Center.*

◆ **Lapperts of Princeville.** *Princeville Center, Princeville, HI 96722; tel. 808-826-7393. Open daily.*

BEVERAGES: ◆ **Foodland Super Market.** *Princeville Center, Princeville, HI 96722; tel. 808-826-9880. Open daily.*

WINE: ◆ **Big Save.** *Hanalei, HI 96714; tel. 808-826-6652. Open daily. In Ching Young Village Shopping Center in central Hanalei.*

SPORTS
BOATING

Hanalei and the North Shore take water sports seriously. Hanalei River is a great stream for kayaking. Guided tours go out into the bay. A boat trip not to be missed (weather permitting): the Capt. Zodiac ride along the wilds and cliffs of the Na Pali Coast. Clancy Greff, who started the Zodiac tour, has accumulated competitors, but he's still the best option.

◆ **Bluewater Sailing.** Half-day sail, including snorkeling and lunch, and two-hour sunset sails with Captain Rick Marvin aboard the *Lady Leanne II*. Also private charters. *P.O. Box 1318, Hanalei, HI 96714; tel. 808-828-1142. Open Mon.-Sat. in summer. In Hanalei town, turn right on Aku Rd., right again on Weke. Park by the pier for departure from the Hanalei River mouth.*

◆ **Capt. Zodiac Rafting Expeditions.** Fabled raft ride up the Na Pali Coast: sea caves, snorkeling, lunch on a remote beach with an ancient village site and burial caves nearby. Campers bound for Kalalau State Park can get a ride one-way or round-trip. *Box 456, Hanalei, HI 96714; tel. 808-826-9371, 808-826-7197; fax 808-826-7704. Open daily. Office in the center of Hanalei town.*

◆ **Kayak Kauai Outfitters.** Kayak rentals and guided tours on the placid Hanalei River and out into the bay to snorkel and perhaps ride a wave back to shore. Also whale watching, sea kayaking, snorkel tours. *Box 508, Hanalei, HI 96714; tel. 808-826-9844, 800-437-3507; fax 808-822-0577. Open daily. At start of Hanalei town, near the river.*

◆ **Pedal n' Paddle.** Guided kayak trips along the Na Pali Coast from mid-May to mid-September, with all gear provided. Rentals of kayaks, body boards, and snorkeling equipment, including masks with corrective lenses. Also rents camping gear. *Hanalei, HI 96714; tel. 808-826-9069. Open daily. In Ching Young Village.*

SURFING

◆ **Hanalei Surf Company.** Rents snorkeling equipment, body boards, surfboards, and other gear. Windsurfing lessons. *Box 790, Hanalei, HI 96714; tel. 808-826-9000, 808-828-2056; fax 808-826-7295. Open daily. In Hanalei Center.*

◆ **Windsurf Kauai.** Surfing lessons on Hanalei Bay. Call for appointment. *Box 323, Hanalei, HI 96714; tel. 808-828-6838. Open Mon.-Sat..*

BICYCLING

◆ **Kayak Kayai Outfitters.** Mountain bike rentals and tours. *Hanalei, HI 96714; tel. 808-826-9844, 800-437-3507; fax 808-822-0577. Open daily. Near the river, at the edge of Hanalei town.*

◆ **Pedal 'n Paddle.** Rentals of mountain bikes and mopeds. *Hanalei, HI 96714; tel. 808-826-9069. Open daily. In Ching Young Village.*

GOLF

Princeville's two golf courses are highly ranked for both scenic beauty and challenging layout.

◆ **Princeville Golf Club, Makai Course.** *Box 3040, Princeville, HI 96722; tel. 808-826-3580; fax 808-826-9738. Open daily. Admission. Off the main road in Princeville development.*

◆ **Princeville Golf Club, Prince Course.** Designed by renowned Robert Trent Jones, Jr., this is a par-72 championship layout. Besides a handsome clubhouse, there's also a restaurant and a health spa on site. *Box 3040, Princeville, HI 96722; tel. 808-826-5000; fax 808-826-4653. Open daily. Admission. Just south of Princeville on Kuhio Hwy.*

TENNIS

◆ **Princeville Tennis Center.** Six courts, pro shop, rentals, private lessons, and daily clinics. *Box 3040, Princeville, HI 96722; tel. 808-826-9823. Open daily. Admission. In Princeville development, near the clubhouse for Princeville Golf Club.*

HORSEBACK RIDING

◆ **Pooku Stables.** Guides lead up to six riders on a morning waterfall picnic ride through the beautiful uplands of the North Shore. Other private rides available. Call for reservations. *Box 888, Hanalei, HI 96714; tel. 808-826-6777. Open Mon.-Sat. Near the Princeville Airport; the turnoff on the mountain side of the road is marked by a sign.*

HISTORY

◆ **Waioli Mission House Museum.** Docents greet guests as though it were the mid-1800s, when Lucy and Abner Wilcox lived in this charming, white house. Excellent example of heathens converting the missionaries: broad lanais, separate cookhouse, lava-rock chimney. From the house, the view of steepled mountains ribboned with waterfalls inspires reverential awe. Reservations accepted three months in advance. *Hanalei, HI 96714; tel. 808-245-3202. Tours Mon., Wed., Thu. at 10 and 1. Admission. Back toward the mountains on a lane behind the green Waioli Huiia Church in Hanalei.*

TOURIST INFORMATION

◆ **Hawaii Visitors Bureau, Kauai Chapter.** *3016 Umi St., Suite 207, Lihue, HI 96766; tel. 808-245-3971. Open Mon.-Fri. 8-4:30.*

CHAPTER 14

Kalapaki

Beauty	A-
Swimming	B
Sand	B
Hotels/Inns/B&Bs	A
House rentals	B
Restaurants	B
Nightlife	B
Attractions	B
Shopping	A
Sports	A
Nature	A

Kalapaki is a gold-sand beach in a brown-shoe town. It dazzles wondrously at the lip of Lihue, a gritty, sun-baked plantation town of 4,000 founded by sugar barons more than 100 years ago. Serious beachgoers pass as quickly as possible through Lihue's traffic to the big, wide, U-shaped beach.

Tucked in the lee of Ninini Point, Kalapaki (*Ka-la-POCK-ee*) looks out at a spectacular view. Steepled, 2,200-foot-high peaks of the majestic Ha'upu Ridge shield Nawiliwili Bay and set a ragged course inland toward 5,148-foot Mount Waialeale. Reputed to be the wettest spot on earth, where 450 inches of rain is the annual average, it's only 12 miles inland. Don't worry, it almost never rains on Kalapaki.

The beach is "Action Central" by day, crowded with surfers, sunbathers, swimmers, and divers. Kayakers paddle up the Huleia River (you saw it in *Raiders of the Lost Ark*), which flows into this natural harbor often visited by luxury cruise ships from distant lands. Commanding the shore, the Marriott Resort & Beach Club glistens amid acres of sparkling fountains, enormous pools, and tropical gardens.

At night, honeymooners walk hand in hand under palm trees along the serpentine promenade as moonbeams dance on the blue velvet water. Romance, adventure, and fantasy are all here at Kalapaki Beach. Somebody should write a song.

KALAPAKI BEACH

Only ten minutes from Lihue, this great beach is naturally protected by steep cliffs on one side and the harbor jetty on the other. A quarter mile long and about 50 yards wide, it's nestled in a natural bowl blanketed with tropical flowers. Kalapaki

Beauty	A-
Swimming	B
Sand	B
Amenities	B

is the postcard beach on Kauai's south shore and certainly the finest swimming beach in Lihue.

A high-energy beach, Kalapaki is busy day and night with a multitude of activities and sometimes seems as crowded as Waikiki. This is especially true on weekends, when interisland cruise ships dock here.

The noise of nearby Nawiliwili Harbor, the island's main port of call, may break the laid-back vacation mood, but despite the din, Kalapaki is a top choice for any vacation beachgoer. *From the Marriott Resort, turn right at "Shoreline Access" sign.*
Swimming: Excellent, with gently sloping sandy bottom. Protected by a jetty that dampens the waves to swimmers' delight.
Sand: Fine reddish golden sand on a wide crescent beach with a black lava rock in the middle of the strand.
Amenities: Rest rooms, showers. Food and drinks are available

H O W   T O   G E T   T H E R E

◆ Kauai's Lihue Airport is a 20-minute flight by jet from Honolulu International Airport via Mahalo Airlines, Aloha Airlines, or Hawaiian Airlines. From Lihue Airport (5 minutes from Kalapaki Beach), go south on Kapule Hwy. (Hwy. 51) to Rice St. Turn left and drive to the entrance of the Marriott Resort on the left. Look for sign. Enter the resort, and, if you're staying there, drive under the hotel's porte cochere. To reach the beach, go past it and turn right at the "Shoreline Access" sign.

at the Marriott Resort & Beach Club. Lifeguard on duty.
Sports: Snorkeling, sailing. Waves break perfectly for beginner surfers.
Parking: Ample and free.

KIPU KAI BEACH

Kipu Kai (*KEE-poo KIGH*) is one of four beaches on the two-mile-long coast at the foot of the Ha'upu ("Hoary Head") Ridge that can be reached only by water. One of the longest beaches on Kauai, Kipu Kai is a privately owned coastal ranch held in trust as a nature preserve. There is no public access by land.

Beauty	A
Swimming	B
Sand	A
Amenities	NA

Since all beaches in Hawaii are public, day-trippers come by kayak, sailboat, and motor launch to picnic, sunbathe, and swim in the sheltered cove in the lee of Molehu Point. They also enjoy beachcombing for bottles (look for a note), glass balls, fishing floats, and the assorted flotsam that washes up on the southwestern shore of the beach. *Charter a boat at Nawiliwili Small Boat Harbor on the south side of Nawiliwili Harbor. From the Marriott Resort, go past Nawiliwili Harbor on Wilcox Rd. Turn left on dirt road at sign for Small Boat Harbor.*
Swimming: Excellent swimming in protected cove on northeast side of beach.
Sand: Grainy reddish golden sand.
Amenities: None. No lifeguard.
Sports: Snorkeling.

NAWILIWILI BEACH PARK

More a park than a beach, Nawiliwili (*NAH-willy-willy*) is in the backyard of a mini shopping mall. An open-air bar with ocean-front lanai makes it a popular spot among tourists and locals. Some call the beach the Pine Tree Inn, a reference to

Beauty	B+
Swimming	C
Sand	C
Amenities	A

the native *wilwili* trees, from which ancient Hawaiians made the canoes that once plied the waters above the harbor.

The beach is a thin strip of sand with a lot of grass and shade trees bordering the concrete seawall that juts into the harbor. It's a popular afternoon perch for all who like to hang out at the beach, talk, fish off the concrete jetty, kick back under the coconut trees, or just watch the boats go by.

On the other side of the port area is the Small Boat Harbor, the starting point for charter fishing, diving, and Na Pali Coast tours. *On the west side of Kalapaki Beach. From the Marriott Resort, turn left on Kapule Hwy. (Hwy. 51), which becomes Wilcox Rd. Turn left into Anchor Cove minimall.*

Swimming: Okay for a dip, but Kalapaki is right there and so much better.

Sand: Reddish golden coral sand mixed with red dirt.

Amenities: Rest rooms, showers, picnic tables. Minimall with T-shirt shops, art gallery, waterfront restaurant, and bar. No lifeguard.

Sports: Surfing, fishing.

Parking: Ample and free.

HOTELS/INNS/B&Bs

Accommodations at Kalapaki Bay are varied but limited. More lodgings are located north of Lihue in the Wailua River area.

◆ **Kauai Marriott Resort & Beach Club** (very expensive). Kauai's largest resort and only high-rise (ten stories), it was converted from a fantasy resort into a 355-room hotel with 232 time-share units. To Hawaiianize public areas, Marriott ditched millions of dollars worth of plaster statues and fake Asian art and replaced a two-acre Las Vegas-style reflecting pond with a rock fountain, lawns, and tropical gardens. Now it's a nice luxury hotel with Hawaii's largest (26,000 square feet) swimming pool. *Kauai Lagoons Resort, 3610 Rice St., Lihue, HI 96766; tel. 808-245-5050, 800-228-9290; fax 808-246-5920. At Kauai Lagoons Resort, overlooking Nawiliwili Harbor, just south of Lihue town.*

◆ **Outrigger Kauai Beach Hotel** (expensive). A 346-room beachfront hotel with pools, restaurants, lounges, shops, and entertainment. *4331 Kauai Beach Dr., Lihue, HI 96766; tel. 808-245-1955, 800-462-6262; fax 808-246-9085. On Kuhio Hwy., 4 mi. north of Lihue Airport. Look for entrance sign on right.*

◆ **Aston Kauai Beach Villas** (moderate). Studio and one- and two-bedroom condominium units, some fronting on the beach. Neighboring Outrigger Kauai Beach Hotel provides restaurants, lounges, entertainment, and shops within walking distance. *4330 Kauai Beach Dr., Lihue, HI 96766; tel. 808-245-7711, 800-922-7866; fax 808-245-5550.*

◆ **Garden Island Inn** (inexpensive). Small, clean rooms with comfy touches, in-room coffeemakers, and some kitchen facilities. Partial ocean views. *3445 Wilcox Rd., Kalapaki Beach, HI 96766; tel. 808-245-7227, 800-648-0154; fax 808-245-7603. At Nawiliwili Harbor, across from Kauai Lagoons Resort.*

HOUSE RENTALS

◆ **Pali Kai Cottages.** Six cottages are available through Kauai Vacation Rentals & Real Estate. *3-3311 Kuhio Hwy., Lihue, HI 96766; tel. 808-245-8841, 800-367-5025; fax 808-246-1161. Open Mon.-Fri. Ocean front, on cliff overlooking Kalapaki Beach and harbor.*

RESTAURANTS

◆ **A Pacific Cafe** (expensive). Kauai's best restaurant features chef Jean-Marie Josselin's version of Hawaii regional cuisine. Fresh seafood, local produce. Dishes are part Hawaii, part Asia, part Provence, and totally memorable. Served on unusual china created and painted by Josselin's wife. *Kauai Village Shopping Center, Kapaa, HI 96746; tel. 808-822-0013. Open daily for dinner. Off Kuhio Hwy., 20 minutes north of Lihue.*

◆ **Cafe Portofino** (moderate). Tasty Italian fare: fresh pasta, veal, seafood, baked goods, espresso, gelato. *3501 Rice St., Lihue, HI 96766; tel. 808-245-2121. Open daily for dinner; Mon.-Fri. for lunch. Across from the entrance to Kauai Lagoons Resort.*

◆ **Gaylord's at Kilohana** (moderate). An outdoor, covered courtyard facing lawns and flowers makes eating here feel like being a guest in someone's gracious home. Fresh fish, ribs, steaks, prime rib, salads, fruit, and desserts are all good. *3-2087 Kaumualii Hwy., Lihue, HI 96766; tel. 808-245-9593. Open daily* *for lunch and dinner; Mon.-Sat. for lunch; Sunday for brunch. 1 mi. west of Lihue on Kaumualii Hwy. (Hwy. 50), in the restored plantation manor called Kilohana.*

◆ **JJ's Broiler** (moderate). Bar and casual open-air restaurant overlooking the beach. Menu is basic surf and turf: mahimahi, steak, chicken. Bar is equipped with binoculars for checking out surfers and beach sights. *3416 Rice St., Lihue, HI 96766; tel. 808-246-4422. Open daily for lunch and dinner. At south end of Kalapaki Beach.*

◆ **Hamura Saimin Stand** (inexpensive). Saimin, Hawaii's noodle soup, prepared by local experts who cook the broth in steaming kettles and add fresh noodles to order. Flavored with pink and white pinwheels of fish cake, Chinese *char siu* barbecued pork or shrimp tempura. You'll not find better. *2956 Kress St., Lihue, HI 96766; tel. 808-245-3271. Open daily for lunch and dinner. 1 1/2 blocks off Rice St.*

NIGHTLIFE

◆ **Hap's Hideaway Satellite Sports Bar.** Darts, drinks, jukebox, and ball games live via satellite, which can be important when you are on vacation but your favorite team is not. *4347 Rice St., Lihue, HI 96766; tel. 808-245-3473. Open daily.*

◆ **Kauai Coconut Beach Resort Luau.** Traditional feast modified for tourists. Hawaiian entertainment presented in a pavilion among tall coco palms. Pig cooked in underground oven. Evening launched with torch-lighting ceremony. *Box 830, Kapaa, HI 96746; tel. 808-822-3455. Open Sat.-Thu. Admission. In Kapaa, about 20 minutes north of Lihue in the Coconut Beach Hotel behind Coconut Marketplace.*

ATTRACTIONS

Kauai Lagoons Resort is in and of itself an attraction, complete with a visitors center. Besides golf and tennis, there are carriage rides in which you are drawn by giant Clydesdale horses, more than a mile of man-made lagoons and waterways plied by mahogany motor launches and outrigger canoes, six islands filled with exotic wildlife, and several restaurants and lounges. Looking is free, but rides and sports are not.

◆ **Grove Farm Homestead Museum.** Life held sweet promise in 1864 when George Wilcox created one of Hawaii's early sugar plantations here. Careful preservation of the buildings, furnishings, and gardens on this estate allows modern visitors a look at what it must have been like. Two-hour tours by reservation. *Nawiliwili Rd., Lihue, HI 96766; tel. 808-245-3202. Admission. Atop a hill on the road between Kukui Grove Center and Nawiliwili Harbor. Look for a sign pointing to the turn.*

◆ **Kauai Museum.** Kauai's history, in a small museum with photos, artifacts, shells, old Hawaiian quilts, and feather leis. *4428 Rice St., Lihue, HI 96766; tel. 808-245-6931. Open Mon.-Fri. 9-4:30, Sat. 9-1. Admission. Next door to Kauai's county government building.*

◆ **Kilohana Plantation.** Restored 1930s sugar plantation manor with boutiques, restaurants, carriage rides around the estate, polo grounds. A taste of life in the sweet era when sugar was king. *Box 3121, Lihue, HI 96766; tel. 808-245-5608; fax 808-245-7818. Open daily 9 a.m.-9:30 p.m. 1 mi. west of Lihue on Kaumualii Hwy. (Hwy. 50).*

SHOPPING

Kauai's largest shopping center is the Kukui Grove Center, about two miles from Kalapaki Beach on Nawiliwili Road. Besides the traditional Liberty House and Sears department stores, there's a K-Mart that carries some Hawaii products, a rash of boutiques, a huge Borders bookstore, fast-food outlets, movies, and other suburban comforts. Kauai products, notably foods, scents, clothes, arts and crafts, and wood bowls, are sold here and at many other places on the island.

◆ **Hilo Hattie Fashion Center.** There's free transport from most resorts to this aloha-wear mecca. It's not the best or most original, but there's lots to choose from in the way of shirts, muumuus, dresses, T-shirts, rubber slippers, and jewelry. *3252 Kuhio Hwy., Lihue, HI 96766; tel. 808-245-4724. Open daily. In central Lihue. Free transportation from Kauai Marriott, as well as Wailua and Poipu area hotels.*

◆ **Kapaia Stitchery.** Original needlepoint design, handmade originals, Hawaiian quilting, and Hawaiian fabrics. *Box 1327, Lihue, HI 96766; tel. 808-245-2281. Open Mon.-Sat. On Kuhio Hwy. 1/2 mi. north of Lihue.*

◆ **Kilohana Galleries.** Sells shell leis from the island of Niihau plus jewelry, scrimshaw, and Hawaiiana. *3-2087 Kaumualii Hwy., Lihue, HI 96766; tel. 808-245-9452. Open daily. In Kilohana Plantation.*

BEST FOOD SHOPS

SANDWICHES: ◆ **Deli & Bread Connection.** Fresh bread and baked goods, classic sandwiches, soups and salads, gourmet kitchenware, gifts, and goody baskets. *Kukuki Grove Center, Lihue, HI 96766; tel. 808-245-7115. Open daily.*

SEAFOOD: ◆ **The Fish Express.** Fresh local catch, smoked fish, poke (Hawaiian marinated fish), and other seafood. *3343 Kuhio Hwy., Lihue, HI 96766; tel. 808-245-9918; fax 808-246-9188. Open daily.*

FRESH PRODUCE: ◆ **Star Market.** *Kukui Grove Center, Lihue, HI 96766; tel. 808-245-7777. Open daily.*

BEVERAGES: ◆ **ABC Stores.** Sundries, snacks, drinks, Hawaii gifts. *Anchor Cove Shopping Center, Lihue, HI 96766; tel. 808-245-7071. Open daily. At the south end of the beach.*

WINE: ◆ **City Liquor.** *4347B Rice St., Lihue, HI 96766; tel. 808-245-3733. Open daily.*

SPORTS
FISHING

◆ **Gent-Lee Sportsfishing Charters.** Shared or private half- to full-day fishing charters on a 36-foot powerboat with handmade lures by owner Bo Jordan. Boat keeps a share of the catch and cuts fish for everyone. Call for reservations. *Box 1691, Lihue, HI 96766; tel. 808-245-7504; fax 808-245-1853. Open daily. Departures from Nawiliwili Harbor.*

◆ **Sea Lure Fishing Charters.** Half- to full-day fishing trips in the rich waters of Kauai's south and east coasts in a 28-foot powerboat with Captain Bill Lawrence. Call for reservations. *Box 413,*

Kapaa, HI 96746; tel. 808-822-5963. Open daily. Departures from Nawiliwili Harbor.

◆ **True Blue Charters.** Shared or private fishing charters aboard the 30-foot *Pamelita* for half- to full-day trips, accommodating up to six passengers. Call for reservations. *Box 1722, Lihue, HI 96766; tel. 808-246-6333. Open daily. On Kalapaki Beach next to Duke's Restaurant.*

BOATING

◆ **Kauai River Adventures.** Kayak tours up the gentle Huleia River into the heart of the Huleia National Wildlife Refuge. Paddling lessons and life jackets included. *Box 3370, Lihue, HI 96766; tel. 808-245-9662. Open daily. Office near Small Boat Harbor at Nawiliwili.*

◆ **Paradise River Rentals.** Kayak and powerboat rentals, with jeeps for towing plus picnic tarp, cooler, and topographical maps. *Box 388, Eleele, HI 96705; tel. 808-245-9580. Open daily. At Kilohana Plantation, 1 mi. west of Lihue.*

SURFING

◆ **Kauai Water Ski & Surf Co.** Surfing rentals (boards, gear), snorkeling equipment, kayaks, body boards, and water ski gear for skiing the Wailua River, one of the few places in Hawaii to enjoy this sport. *4-356 Kuhio Hwy., Kapaa, HI 96746; tel. 808-822-3574. Open daily. In Kinipopo Shopping Center at Wailua, about 10 minutes north of Lihue.*

DIVING

◆ **Nitrox Tropical Divers.** Scooter dives from shore for certified divers to fishy reefs off the South Shore and such sites as Ammo Drop, where cargo was jettisoned off Lihue from a German ship in World War II. *Box 1255, Kapaa, HI 96746; tel. 808-822-7333, 800-695-3483. Open daily. At Kalapaki Beach Center.*

GOLF

◆ **Kauai Lagoons Golf Club.** Two highly ranked, challenging par-72 golf courses: the 7,070-yard Kiele Course and the links-style 6,942-yard Lagoons Course. Jack Nicklaus designed them both.

Kalapaki Beach, Lihue, HI 96766; tel. 808-241-6000, 800-634-6400. Open daily. Admission.

◆ **Wailua Municipal Golf Course.** One of the nation's top-rated municipal courses. Its fees are a fraction of those at the famous resort courses. Club rentals available, along with pro shop, restaurant, and driving range. *3-5351 Kuhio Hwy., Lihue, HI 96766; tel. 808-245-8092. Open daily. Admission. 5 mi. north of Lihue.*

TENNIS

◆ **Kauai Lagoons Golf & Racquet Club.** Eight courts, one a stadium with 600 seats. Call a day in advance for reservations. *Kalapaki Beach, Lihue, HI 96766; tel. 808-241-6000, 800-634-6400; fax 808-241-6025. Open daily. Admission.*

HORSEBACK RIDING

◆ **South Sea Tours at Kauai Lagoons.** Three daily trail rides through Kauai Lagoons Resort's tropical landscape, with views of ocean, mountains, and lagoons. *3901 Mokulele Loop, Box 32, Lihue, HI 96766; tel. 808-245-2222; fax 808-246-9586. Open daily.*

HISTORY

◆ **Menehune Fishpond.** Legend has it that Kauai's ancient inhabitants, an industrious race of elfin engineers known today as *menehune*, constructed the fishpond in a single night. Its rock-wall enclosure is built without mortar, just stone. Best seen by kayak. *On the Huleia River behind Nawiliwili Harbor.*

◆ **Wailua River.** North of Lihue, the Wailua River runs to the sea, the only truly navigable river in Hawaii. Its shores are full of historic sites. Go by kayak. *Drive north on Kuhio Hwy., which crosses the Wailua River at the southern edge of Wailua town.*

NATURE

◆ **Kauai Mountain Tours.** Four-wheel-drive van tours into Kauai's scenic backcountry, high forests, and Waimea Canyon, nicknamed the Grand Canyon of the Pacific. Call for reservations. *Box 3069, Lihue, HI 96766; tel. 808-245-7224. Admission.*

Transportation provided from your door.

◆ **Ohana Helicopter Tours.** Flight-seeing tours over Kauai's fabled landscape, including waterfalls and inaccessible wilderness coast. *Anchor Cove Center, Lihue, HI 96766; tel. 808-245-3996. Open daily.*

◆ **Opaekaa Falls.** A splendid waterfall along the Wailua River that can be seen easily from an overlook on the road. *Drive north on Kuhio Hwy. and, just after crossing the bridge at Wailua, turn left onto Rte. 580. From there, it's 3 mi. to the overlook.*

◆ **Wailua Falls.** A spectacular falls, it will look familiar to fans of TV's *Fantasy Island. Drive north 1 mi. on Kuhio Hwy. to Kapaia and, where the highway veers right toward Hanamaulu, turn left onto Maalo Rd. (Rte. 583). Drive 3 mi. through the cane fields to the falls.*

TOURIST INFORMATION

◆ **Hawaii Visitors Bureau, Kauai Chapter.** *Lihue Plaza Bldg., Suite 207, 3016 Umi St., Lihue, HI 96766; tel. 808-245-3971. Open Mon.-Fri. 8-4:30. Beside the Kauai County buildings.*

CHAPTER 15

Poipu

One of Kauai's favorite beach resorts, Poipu (*Poy-POO*) took a direct hit in September 1992 when Iniki, the biggest hurricane in Pacific history, smashed into the island with sustained 185-mile-an-hour winds. Along with most of the other beaches on the South Shore, Poipu Beach, namesake for this coastal strip of condos and resort hotels, got blown away. It's open again, however, thanks to many tons of sand trucked in from the dunes of Polihale on the western part of the island, where there's plenty of sand.

Beauty	A
Swimming	B-
Sand	B
Hotels/Inns/B&Bs	A
House rentals	B
Restaurants	B
Nightlife	NA
Attractions	B
Shopping	B
Sports	B
Nature	A

Hotels and condos are still being rebuilt in this once-prime vacation spot that continues to look like a disaster recovery area three years later because of lawsuits, insurance wrangles, and corporate indecision. Condemned hotels such as the Sheraton and Waiohai stand like contemporary ruins along the shore, an atypical image in this otherwise idyllic setting.

First of the big resorts to reopen was the Hyatt Regency Poipu, which received light damage. The popular Kiahuna Plantation resort, which was demolished, recently reopened. Others may never return, but the buzz and rap of saw and hammer is expected to continue for at least another year as hard-hat crews reassemble this great beach resort.

Not really a town, Poipu Beach Resort is an ancient Hawaiian district now officially zoned as a resort area. It sits on a sloping sugarcane plain between the Ha'upu ("Hoary Head") Ridge and the Pacific Ocean on the sun-washed southernmost extremity of Kauai. Two more hotels, a residential neighborhood, and commercial development in the sugarcane fields are planned on the west side, near Kukuiula Harbor. Three miles inland, the sugar plantation town of Koloa has been recycled into shops and restaurants.

Though diminished, Poipu shows signs of recovery—in addition to the two resorts that have reopened. There's a seafood restaurant, a surf shop, a souvenir stand, a neighborhood of new rental condos by the sea—and a great beach.

Incidentally, the Hawaiian word *poipu* can mean either "overcast" or "crashing." The latter probably applies here, since the sun always shines at Poipu and waves crash endlessly ashore.

POIPU BEACH

There are other beaches on this coast, but none is more popular than Poipu. It's crowded every day of the year with sunbathers, swimmers, and surfers. The reason is simple: It's handy, safe, and beautiful. It's a big, wide south-shore beach with

Beauty	A
Swimming	A
Sand	B
Amenities	A

HOW TO GET THERE

◆ From Honolulu International Airport, it's a 20-minute flight by jet to Kauai's Lihue Airport, which is a 35-minute drive from Poipu Beach. After leaving Lihue Airport, turn left on Kaumuali'i Hwy. (Hwy. 50) and drive 7 mi. through sugarcane fields that stretch to the 3,000-foot-high Kahili Mountains. Turn left onto Maluhia Rd. (Hwy. 520) and drive along the tree-lined stretch known locally as the Eucalyptus Tree Tunnel, then 3 1/4 mi. to Koloa. One block south of town, turn left onto Poipu Rd. and drive 1 1/2 mi. down to Poipu.

a grassy park, a green lagoon embraced in black lava rock, and lively cobalt-blue water beyond.

An unusual beach, Poipu is divided in two by a sandbar. On the left, a sandy-bottom pool is guarded by the lava rock jetty. On the right, the bay is swept by waves. The pool on the left is ideal for small children to splash in, while the open bay attracts confident swimmers. Heavy surf poses a danger to swimmers. *After turning onto Poipu Rd., go 1 mi. to Ho'owili Rd. Turn right.*
Swimming: Excellent except in winter or high-surf conditions.
Sand: Grainy, reddish golden.
Amenities: Rest rooms, showers, picnic tables. Restaurant, grocery, and beach-gear rental shop nearby. Lifeguard on duty.
Sports: Snorkeling, surfing, windsurfing.
Parking: Ample free parking in dirt lot across the street.

BRENNECKE'S BEACH

This popular surfing beach virtually disappeared when Hurricane Iniki hit, and it hasn't revived yet, although it's scheduled for resanding. That means tons of sand will be dumped on the exposed rock to recreate the beach. Meanwhile, Brennecke's

Beauty	A
Swimming	C
Sand	B
Amenities	A

still attracts bodysurfers to endless summer waves created by an offshore submerged sandbar. *To reach Brennecke's Beach, walk east from Poipu Beach a few hundred yards.*
Swimming: Not advised because of heavy surfing traffic.
Sand: Golden and grainy (when it returns).
Amenities: Rest rooms, showers, picnic tables. No lifeguard.
Sports: Surfing, bodysurfing, body boarding.
Parking: Roadside.

KEONELOA BEACH

This big, beautiful beach in front of the Hyatt Regency Poipu is framed by rocky headlands and coves frequented by sea turtles and endangered Hawaiian monk seals. Hawaiians named this nearly two-mile-long beach *Keoneloa (Kay-OH-nee-lo-*

Beauty	A
Swimming	C
Sand	B
Amenities	A

ah), which means "long sands," and it's also called Shipwreck Beach after a wooden boat that wrecked here years ago. Makawehi Point, the imposing landmark on the east side of the beach, is used by surf casters and by young men who dive off the headlands into the waves. On the western shore are sand dunes with ancient Hawaiian burial grounds. *From Poipu Beach, return to Poipu Rd. Turn right and go east 2 mi. to Hyatt Regency Poipu. Turn into the resort and drive to the east side of the hotel. Turn right at "Shoreline Access" sign and park.*

Swimming: Dangerous because of pounding shore break and strong rip currents. High surf warning flags and "Danger" signs are posted in front of the Hyatt.

Sand: Reddish golden and gravelly.

Amenities: Rest rooms, showers, walkway along the dunes. No lifeguard.

Sports: Locals launch Windsurfers against incoming waves here to go airborne and gain "hang-time." Pole fishermen cast their bait to the wind from Makawehi Point.

Parking: Ample free parking in paved lot.

BEACH HOUSE BEACH

Beauty	C
Swimming	A
Sand	B
Amenities	B

Not much to write home about, Beach House Beach is a small, roadside beach that disappears at high tide and makes it possible for the Beach House restaurant to offer ocean-front dining. The beach is named for the restaurant, which was destroyed in 1982 by Hurricane Iwa, rebuilt, and flattened again in 1992 by Iniki. The restaurant is back, and so's the beach at low tide. *From Poipu Beach, return to Poipu Rd. Turn left and drive 2 mi. to Lawai Rd. Turn left and head down to the coast. The beach is across from the Lawai Beach Resort on Lawai Rd.*

Swimming: Good for a dip, but better for snorkeling and surfing.

Sand: Reddish golden pebbly sand.

Amenities: Rest rooms, showers, beach-front restaurant. No lifeguard.

Sports: Excellent snorkeling offshore on reef. Three great surfing breaks.

Parking: Paved lot.

MAHAULEPU BEACH

A natural beach of outstanding beauty, Mahaulepu (*Ma-hah-OO-LEE-poo*) may be the best-looking south coast beach. This two-mile-long strand is backed by big sand dunes and framed by a windbreak of ironwood trees. The wide, flat beach

Beauty	A
Swimming	B
Sand	B
Amenities	NA

seems endless. There's scarcely a person in sight, and no sign of development. A great beach for a romantic liaison or total isolation. *From the Hyatt Regency Poipu, drive east 3 mi. on a red dirt road, passing the golf course and stables. Turn right at T-intersection and stop at security guardhouse. Register there and drive 1 mi. to a big sand dune. Turn left and drive a half mile to offroad parking under trees.*

Swimming: Risky except in reef-protected shallows 200 yards west of the parking lot.

Sand: Reddish golden and grainy. Big sand dunes forested by ironwood trees.

Amenities: None. No lifeguard.

Sports: Surf casting, net throwing, snorkeling.

Parking: Unpaved lot.

POLIHALE BEACH

If you want to explore a great, empty beach, head for Polihale (*PO-LEE-hah-lay*). One of the longest continuous sand beaches in Hawaii, it's an awesome 17-mile stretch of desert on Kauai's north-western shore. The beach, wide as three

Beauty	A
Swimming	D
Sand	A
Amenities	C

football fields, starts at the former plantation town of Kekaha and seems to go forever. It runs around Mana Point, the western extremity of Kauai, skirts Waimea Canyon State Park's rippled ridgebacks, and ends in the 140-acre Polihale State Park, on the western border of the Na Pali Coast.

The beach includes ancient Hawaiian heiau and burial sites, a seabird sanctuary, and the famed Barking Sands Beach, where the friction of a footfall makes a sound like a dog. Also within its boundaries are Nohili Dune, which stretches nearly three miles and ranges from 50 to 100 feet high, and the Pacific Missile Range Facility, a U.S. surveillance center that snooped on Russian submarines during the Cold War. *From Poipu, return to intersection of Maluhia Rd. (Hwy. 520) and Kaumuali'i Hwy. (Hwy. 50) and drive 22 mi. west through Hanapepe and Waimea to Kekaha, where the beach begins. Entrance to Polihale State Park is another 11 mi.*

Swimming: Don't go in the water. It's treacherous year-round, with powerful rip currents that run out to sea and dangerous surf that often covers the entire beach. Safe swimming is possible only at Queen's Pond, a sandy-bottom reef-protected pool in Polihale State Park. Even here, stay on guard for rogue waves.

Sand: There's more sand here than you can imagine: long stretches of deep, golden, grainy sand.

Amenities: Rest rooms, showers, picnic pavilions, camping facilities. No lifeguard.

Sports: Sunbathing, beachcombing, surf casting.

Parking: Ample and free.

HOTELS/INNS/B&Bs

Three years after a devastating storm, Poipu's only operative hotel is thriving, but the others (Sheraton's Kauai Beach Resort and Stouffer's Poipu Beach and Waiohai hotels) have yet to be repaired. However, Poipu's attractive condominium complexes offer plenty of moderate-to-expensive choices, especially for vacationing families.

◆ **Hyatt Regency Kauai** (very expensive). One of Hawaii's most appealing luxury resorts, it spreads down a hill to the beach. Aquatic complex with pool, water slide, and falls surrounded by lush tropical gardens. Stunning plantation-style architecture: 600 rooms under green-tile roofs, open-air Art Deco lobby. Tennis, golf, spa. Guided nature walks through neighboring dunes, lectures by local historians. *1571 Poipu Rd., Koloa, HI 96756; tel. 808-742-1234, 800-233-1234; fax 808-742-6229. At the eastern end of Poipu Beach Resort.*

◆ **Gloria's Spouting Horn Bed & Breakfast** (expensive). Charming ocean-front five-room inn features rooms practically overhanging the surf, with panoramic views from seaside balconies. Sunken tubs, wet bar with fridge and microwave. Tropical continental breakfast, three-night minimum. There is a sandy beach and an outdoor lava rock shower under mango tree. *4464 Lawai Beach Rd., Koloa, HI 96756; tel. 808-742-6995. On the road to Spouting Horn.*

HOUSE RENTALS

◆ **Kauai Vacation Rentals.** *3-3311 Kuhio Hwy., Lihue, HI 96766; tel. 808-245-8841, 800-367-5025; fax 808-246-1161.*

◆ **Poipu Bed & Breakfast Inn & Vacation Rentals.** Cottages, homes, B&B, and suites at budget levels in Poipu and nearby Kalaheo. *2720 Hoonani Rd., Poipu, HI 96756; tel. 808-742-1146, 800-22POIPU, 800-552-0095; fax 808-742-6843.*

◆ **Kiahuna Plantation.** Kiahuna's 333 newly renovated one- and two-bedroom condos in two-story plantation-roofed buildings are spread along a hillside and down to the beach, with shady old trees, abundant flowers, and rolling green lawns. It was the site of a historic plantation home that was famous for its gardens. Golf, tennis, shopping, and dining close by. Hawaiian-oriented activities for kids. Cost becomes moderate with four to six persons per unit. *2253 Poipu Rd., Koloa, HI 96756; tel. 808-742-6411, 800-367-7052; fax 808-742-7233. On ocean side of Poipu Rd.*

◆ **Poipu Kapili.** This ocean-front complex has 60 one- and two-bedroom upscale condos, with amenities inside and out. Tennis, pool. The surf will lull you to sleep. The nearest swimming beach is a short walk away from the complex. *2221 Kapili Rd., Koloa, HI 96756; tel. 808-742-6449, 800-443-7714; fax 808-742-9162. From Poipu Rd., turn right onto Kapili Rd. just after the road to Spouting Horn.*

◆ **Koloa Landing Cottages.** There are five cottages ranging from studios to two-bedroom units. *2704B Hoonani Rd., Koloa, HI 96756; tel. 808-742-1470; fax 808-332-9584. Off Poipu Rd. on the ocean side.*

◆ **Suite Paradise.** Condo rentals at several complexes in the

Poipu resort area. Car/condo packages available. *2827 Poipu Rd., Koloa, HI 96756; tel. 808-742-7400, 800-367-8020; fax 808-742-9121.*

RESTAURANTS

Kauai's abundance of fresh fish is the highlight of most restaurant menus in the Poipu area. The restaurants range from moderate to expensive, plain to inspired, but the fish is usually great regardless of price.

◆ **Beach House at Poipu Beach** (expensive). Hugging a promontory just above the waves (most of the time), this restaurant should get a perseverance award since it continues to rebound after each devastating storm. It's known for such seafood dishes as opakapaka with ginger and lemon butter and bouillabaisse with lobster and clams. Great location for sunset cocktails. *5022 Lawai Rd., Koloa, HI 96756; tel. 808-742-1424. Open daily for breakfast, lunch, and dinner. West of Poipu Beach Resort on Lawai Rd., by the water.*

◆ **Roy's Poipu Bar & Grill** (expensive). Roy Yamaguchi, perhaps Hawaii's most acclaimed chef, specializes in a sort of Eurasian fusion cuisine, reflected in the standing menu that ranges from pizza to pot roast to pot stickers and the daily specials, which are determined when the local fish catch comes in. *2360 Kiahuna Plantation Dr., Koloa, HI 96756; tel. 808-742-5000; fax 808-742-5050. Open daily for dinner. In Poipu Shopping Village.*

◆ **Brennecke's Beach Broiler** (moderate). Friendly, casual fish house on the second floor, with stunning sunset and sea views, a competent chef, and fresh fish. Proud of its mai tais and its salad bar. Also known for barbecued ribs, prime rib, and steaks. Early-bird specials served from 4 to 6 p.m. Gift shop and beach rentals in Brennecke Beach Center downstairs. *2100 Hoone Rd., Koloa, HI 96756; tel. 808-742-7588. Open daily for lunch and dinner. Across the street from Poipu Beach Park.*

◆ **Kimo's Paradise** (moderate). Casual atmosphere with a stream running through the tropical interior. Seafood and taco bar for light fare. Dinner features several preparations of island fish, ribs, chicken, and steaks. Vegetarian offerings. Children's menu.

2360 Kiahuna Plantation Dr., Koloa, HI 96756; tel. 808-742-7534. Open daily for dinner. In Poipu Shopping Village.
◆ **Tomkats Grill** (inexpensive). Burgers, salads, sandwiches, and light fare. Children's menu. *Old Koloa Town, Koloa, HI 96756; tel. 808-742-8887. Open daily.*

NIGHTLIFE

Nightlife in Poipu consists largely of sunset cocktails, alfresco dinners by the sea, after-dinner beach walks, a moonlit dip under manmade waterfalls at the Hyatt, or perhaps a romantic comedy on the hotel movie channel. Is it any wonder Poipu is a honeymoon haven? Some hotels and condos maintain libraries for guests, but bring your own CDs if you want to listen to anything other than Hawaiian music, which is in the air everywhere.

ATTRACTIONS

◆ **Spouting Horn.** A blowhole in a coastal cliff where crashing waves pop through like geysers and render a mournful sound. The sight draws so many tourists that local vendors have turned the parking lot into an open-air shopping mall. Booths sell everything from inexpensive trinkets to exquisite Niihau shell leis. Tip: Check prices of expensive Hawaiian handicrafts like these before you come to Poipu. The Spouting Horn vendors have a fine selection, and their prices are considered fair. *At the end of Lawai Rd.*
◆ **National Tropical Botanical Gardens.** A double treat for plant-lovers: the nation's only Congressionally chartered tropical research gardens, plus scenic formal gardens of the Allerton Estate (if it looks familiar, that's because part of *Fantasy Island* was shot here). Sampan tours give visitors a look at the rare tropical trees, medicinal plants, and other botanical splendors. After that, you can walk through the Allerton Estate gardens and among the sculptures. Call for reservations. *Box 340, Lawai, HI 96765; tel. 808-332-7361. Open daily. Admission. Sampans leave from Spouting Horn.*

◆ **Olu Pua Gardens.** Tropical flowers and trees on a wonderful historic plantation, plus a visit to the home designed by Hawaii's influential architect, C. W. Dickey. *Kalaheo, HI 96741; tel. 808-332-8182, 808-332-8334. Open daily 9-4. Admission. From Koloa, drive west on Koloa Rd. to Kaumuali'i Hwy. (Hwy. 50). Continue west on Kaumuali'i Hwy. A sign points out the turn 1 mi. past the town of Kalaheo.*

SHOPPING

Kauai's best shopping finds aren't always discovered in posh stores. Outdoor stalls (*see* Attractions), arts-and-crafts fairs, and stores in such funky old plantation towns as Hanapepe and Koloa present wares that are often straight from the artist. Some Kauai products to look for: soaps and lotions with tropical scents, hand-painted silks and other clothing, one-of-a-kind necklaces and other jewelry made from tiny shells by the women of Niihau, the "Forbidden Island," just west of Kauai.

◆ **Cane Field Clothing.** Nice selection of casual and evening tropical-weight clothing for women. *3878 Hanapepe Rd., Hanapepe, HI 96716; tel. 808-335-3191. Open Mon.-Sat. In Hanapepe, a ramshackle sugar plantation town 10 mi. west of Koloa, now becoming a shopping district.*

◆ **Crazy Shirts.** High-quality T-shirts and tropical sportswear. *2360 Kiahuna Plantation Dr., Koloa, HI 96756; tel. 808-742-9000. Open daily. In Poipu Shopping Village and other Kauai locations.*

◆ **Old Hawaiian Trading Post.** Niihau shell jewelry, gifts. *Box 430, Lawai, HI 96756; tel. 808-332-7404. Open daily. At the intersection of Kaumuali'i Hwy. (Hwy. 50) and Koloa Rd. in Lawai, a small community west of Koloa.*

◆ **Overboard/Onboard.** Tropical clothes with style for women (Overboard) and men (Onboard). Bathing suits, casual wear. *2360 Kiahuna Plantation Dr., Koloa, HI 96756; tel. 808-742-1299; fax 808-742-8402. Open daily. In Poipu Shopping Village.*

◆ **Paradise Sportswear/Tropical Shirts.** Kauai's nearly indelible brick-red soil is going to get your white shorts and Ts anyway, so why not buy them stained that color? So goes the theory behind Kauai's Red Dirt Shirts, a clever and attractive line of sports gear with humorous messages that Kauai visitors will enjoy. *Box 1027, Kalaheo, HI 96741; tel. 808-335-5670. Open daily. Factory outlet store next to fire station. Tropical Shirts store in Poipu Shopping Village.*

BEST FOOD SHOPS

SANDWICHES: ◆ **La Griglia.** Italian sandwiches, coffee, pasta, soda, burgers, and pizza. *2360 Kiahuna Plantation Dr., Koloa, HI 96756; tel. 808-742-2147. Open daily. In Poipu Shopping Village.*

SEAFOOD: ◆ **Koloa Fish Market.** *5482 Koloa Rd., Koloa, HI 96756; tel. 808-742-6199. Open Mon.-Sat. Across from Koloa post office.*

FRESH PRODUCE: ◆ **Kukuiula Store.** *Koloa, HI 96756; tel. 808-742-1601. Open daily. In a cluster of stores on the right of the road into Poipu Beach Resort from Koloa.*

BAKERY: ◆ **Omoide Bakery & Delicatessen.** Famous for custard-filled "Long Johns" and other pastries. *Kaumuali'i Hwy., Hanapepe, HI 96716; tel. 808-335-5291. Open daily. A 10-minute drive west of the Poipu Beach Resort.*

◆ **Roy's Logo Shop.** Fresh-baked bread, muffins, and cookies from Roy's Poipu Bar & Grill. *2360 Kiahuna Plantation Dr., Koloa, HI 96756; tel. 808-742-5000. Open daily. Across walkway from Roy's Poipu Bar & Grill.*

ICE CREAM: ◆ **Lapperts Aloha Ice Cream & Gourmet Coffee.** Lapperts' rich, tropical-flavored ice cream, made at the factory in Hanapepe, is sold in many parts of Hawaii. *Koloa Rd., Koloa, HI 96756; tel. 808-742-1272. Open daily.*

BEVERAGES: ◆ **Whalers General Store.** Drinks, snacks, sundries. *2360 Kiahuna Plantation Dr., Koloa, HI 96756; tel. 808-742-9431. Open daily. In Poipu Shopping Village.*

WINE: ◆ **Big Save Market.** *Koloa Rd., Koloa, HI 96756; tel. 808-742-1614. Open daily.*

SPORTS
FISHING

◆ **JJ's Big Bass Tours.** Believe it or not, freshwater big-mouth and peacock bass cruise the waters of Kauai's inland reservoirs.

Pursue them in a 17-foot boat for up to three passengers, full or half day. Call for reservations. *Box 248, Kalaheo, HI 96741; tel. 808-332-9219, 808-654-4153.*

◆ **Sport Fishing Kauai.** Captain Julian Chapa pilots the *Vida Del Mar* in search of Hawaii's delectable denizens of the deep: marlin, shark, snapper, jack, mahimahi, ahi (tuna), ono (wahoo), and others. Four-, six-, and eight-hour charters, private or shared. Call for reservations. *Box 1195, Koloa, HI 96756; tel. 808-742-7013. Open daily. Departs from Kukuiula Harbor on the road to Spouting Horn.*

BOATING

◆ **Capt. Andy's Sailing Adventures.** Four-hour morning snorkel sails with lunch, two-hour daytime sails, sunset sails. Six-hour Na Pali Coast cruise from Port Allen in summer, whale-watching in winter. *Box 1291, Koloa, HI 96756; tel. 808-822-7833; fax 808-332-9379. Open daily. Departures from Kukuiula Harbor on the road to Spouting Horn or from Port Allen Small Boat Harbor on Hwy. 541 at Hanapepe.*

◆ **Outfitters Kauai.** One- and two-person kayaks for rent, along with car racks, straps, life jackets, and maps to peaceful nearby rivers with waterfalls. Also, guided ocean paddles along the south shore to Spouting Horn and along the Na Pali Coast wilderness. Basic paddling lesson included. *2827-A Poipu Rd., Koloa, HI 96756; tel. 808-742-9667. Open Mon-Sat. In Poipu Plaza at the beginning of Poipu Beach Resort.*

SURFING

◆ **Margo Oberg's Surfing School.** A seven-time world-champion surfer and her staff teach on land and sea and guarantee that students will ride a wave before school is out. Call for reservations. *2253 Poipu Rd., Koloa, HI 96756; tel. 808-742-6411. Open daily. Based at Kiahuna Plantation resort.*

DIVING

◆ **Mana Divers.** Introductory or advanced dives for up to six persons aboard the 33-foot *Mana Kai*, in waters off Poipu and the island of Niihau. Call for reservations. *Kukuiula Harbor, Koloa,*

HI 96756; tel. 808-742-9849. Open daily. Look for the Mana Kai *at Poipu's small-boat dock on the road to Spouting Horn.*

◆ **Sea Sports Divers.** Daily snorkel and scuba classes, introductory dives, and certification courses. Day or night dives for experienced divers, refresher dives, and instructor courses. Special charter to the waters off Niihau. Also rents snorkel gear, body boards, surfboards, beach equipment, and scuba gear. Trips by advance reservation. *Box 638, 2827 Poipu Rd., Koloa, HI 96756; tel. 808-742-9303, 800-685-5889. Open daily. Look for the yellow submarine next to the Spouting Horn turnoff.*

◆ **Snuba Tours of Kauai.** Diving with an air source tethered to a floating raft on surface during guided tours lets you go deeper than snorkeling. Tours depart hourly. *5795 Lauloa Pl., Kapaa, HI 96746; tel. 808-823-8912. Open Mon.-Sat. Tours depart from Lawai Beach in Poipu.*

BICYCLING

Mountain biking is popular on the jeep trails of scenic Waimea Canyon, a baby Grand Canyon in West Kauai. Coastal roads tend to be level or slightly rolling.

◆ **Bicycle John.** Call 24 hours ahead and mountain bike rentals are delivered free of charge and picked up when you're finished. *3142 Kuhio Hwy., Lihue, HI 96766; tel. 808-245-7579, 808-639-4750; fax 808-245-6690. Open daily.*

◆ **Outfitters Kauai.** Mountain bike rentals, extensive local trail information, and tours into the Waimea Canyon's high forests. *2827-A Poipu Rd., Koloa, HI 96756; tel. 808-742-9667. Open Mon.-Sat. In Poipu Plaza at the beginning of Poipu Beach Resort.*

GOLF

◆ **Kiahuna Golf Club.** Designed by Robert Trent Jones, Jr., this scenic par-70 course winds around ancient rock walls and other historic features, including a heiau, or temple site, in the middle of the links-style layout. Driving range and restaurant. *2545 Kiahuna Plantation Dr., Koloa, HI 96756; tel. 808-742-9595; fax 808-742-7445. Open daily. Admission. Beyond Poipu Shopping Village, in the middle of Poipu Beach Resort.*

◆ **Poipu Beach Resort Golf Course.** Championship 18-hole,

links-style course designed by Robert Trent Jones, Jr., and site of the annual PGA Grand Slam of Golf professional competition. Four major water hazards and distractingly stunning views. *2250 Ainako St., Koloa, HI 96756; tel. 808-742-8711. Open daily. Admission. Adjoining the Hyatt Regency Kauai at Poipu Beach.*

TENNIS

Several Poipu properties have their own courts, including Poipu Kapili condos and the Hyatt Regency Kauai. The Kiahuna Tennis Club is a full-service complex.

◆ **Kiahuna Tennis Club.** Ten courts, rentals, pro shop, ball machine, lessons, restaurant, and pool. *Box 334, Koloa, HI 96756; tel. 808-742-9533; fax 808-742-1296. Open daily. Admission. On the uphill side of Poipu Rd. Look for the sign by the turn.*

HORSEBACK RIDING

◆ **CJM Country Stables.** Horseback trail rides to a "secret" beach three times a day: early morning (with breakfast), mid-morning, and early afternoon. *1731 Kelaukia St., Koloa, HI 96756; tel. 808-742-6096; fax 808-742-6015. Open Mon.-Sat. At the end of Poipu Rd.*

NATURE

The wild eastern end of the Poipu area features a long stretch of unusual wild and historic dunes. Ancient Hawaiians used these sand dunes as a burial ground. The Hyatt offers guided dune walks with a naturalist, but anyone can walk the dune trail near the hotel.

TOURIST INFORMATION

◆ **Hawaii Visitors Bureau, Kauai Chapter.** *3016 Umi St., Suite 207, Lihue, HI 96766; tel. 808-245-3971. Open Mon.-Fri. 8-4:30.*

CHAPTER 16

Anini

Too often overlooked in the pell-mell rush to see Hanalei and explore the wild Na Pali Coast, Anini Beach isn't usually mentioned in tourist brochures. Folks around here, such as celebrity neighbors Bette Midler, Sylvester Stallone, and Kareem Abdul-Jabbar, prefer it that way.

Beauty	A-
Swimming	B+
Sand	A
Hotels/Inns/B&Bs	C
House rentals	C
Restaurants	C
Nightlife	NA
Attractions	B
Shopping	B
Sports	A
Nature	A

But the word's getting out. For spectacular beauty, it's hard to match this three-mile-long golden beach on an ancient blue lagoon at the foot of emerald cliffs. What's more, it also happens to be Kauai's safest beach for swimming, windsurfing, and camping. It's protected from the open ocean by a great, fringing reef that makes Anini *(Ah-NEE-nee)* the very best snorkeling spot on Kauai, even for beginners.

Anini is the main beach in Kilauea, an ex-plantation town of about 1,685 people. The area, which is gradually being gentrified into country estates for horsey gentlepersons, is worth a visit on a number of counts besides its gorgeous beach. It's the site of historic Kilauea Point Lighthouse, which oversees a national seabird preserve renowned as a rookery for red-footed boobies. There's also a great local bakery and the Kong Lung Store, which displays an eclectic taste in art, crafts, and style.

While accommodations on Anini Beach are limited to either rustic camping or private homes, those lucky enough to find lodging in this idyllic place return year after year. Anini is the perfect beach vacation spot for families or anyone who seeks to get off the tourist trail without spending a fortune.

For those who prefer the lap of luxury, of course, the marbled, pampering palace of Princeville Resort, where suites come with butlers, is only a few miles up the coastal highway.

ANINI BEACH COUNTY PARK

Anini Beach looks like something out of a South Seas painting, with its big lagoon, coconut trees, lush greenery, and tropical flowers. It has a spacious beach-side park, a polo field, a beach-park campground, and several vacation rentals but, thankfully, no hotels.

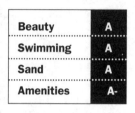

Beauty	A
Swimming	A
Sand	A
Amenities	A-

Anini is a popular choice among tent campers, picnickers, and day-trippers, especially families. The swimming is prob-

HOW TO GET THERE

◆ From Honolulu International Airport, it's a 20-minute flight by jet to Kauai's Lihue Airport, which is a 45-minute drive from Anini Beach. After leaving Lihue Airport, turn right on Kuhio Hwy. (Hwy. 56) and follow it to the town of Kilauea. Pass the first exit for Kalihiwai Rd. west of Kilauea and turn off at the second. (The road used to loop through Kalihiwai Bay, but the bridge is washed out.) Drive 1/2 mi. toward the ocean and turn left at Anini Beach Rd.

◆ Mahalo Airlines, IslandAir, and Hawaiian Air fly prop planes between Honolulu International and Princeville Airport, which is a 20-minute drive from Anini Beach. ◆ On Kauai, rental cars and small four-wheel-drive vehicles are available through the hotels or at Lihue and Princeville airports.

lem-free, and the beach is made for combing. Cowries and sometimes even rare Niihau shells can be found here. It's as rewarding underwater as it is above. A channel runs through the reef on the west and drops to 60 feet, which makes it an ideal spot for scuba diving. *On Anini Beach Rd.*

Swimming: Safest swimming on Kauai's North Shore, Anini is on a reef-protected lagoon. Water and waves are safe enough year-round for small children. Shallow water, about four feet deep, extends 1,000 to 1,500 yards out to the reef, which runs 2 1/2 miles along the coast.

Sand: Reddish gold, fine-grain sand.

Amenities: Rest rooms, showers, picnic tables, cook grills. Big, safe, well-equipped beach campground. No lifeguard.

Sports: Excellent snorkeling and scuba diving. Windsurfing conditions are ideal, since the prevailing wind is onshore, saving neophytes from being blown out to sea.

Parking: Ample and free.

KALIHIWAI BEACH

On this coast of good-looking beaches, Kalihiwai (*Kah-LEE-hee-why*) is no ugly step-sister. A pocket of golden sand, it sits at the head of half-mile-wide Kalihiwai Bay, under sheltering ironwood trees in a lush tropical set-

Beauty	A
Swimming	B
Sand	A
Amenities	B

ting. A stream runs through the middle of this wide beach, creating a small, sand-bottom pool on the west side that is ideal for children. A tire swing dangles over the water from a tree limb. To the east, Kapukamoi Point, a 150-foot-high cinder cone, stands guard. *West of Kilauea, turn off Kuhio Hwy. at first intersection with Kalihiwai Rd., which leads to beach.*

Swimming: Safe for all, especially children.

Sand: Reddish golden sand mixed with stream runoff.

Amenities: Rest rooms, showers, and picnic tables. No lifeguard.

Sports: Good surfing.

Parking: Ample and free.

KAUAPEA BEACH

A little hard to find, wide, sandy Kauapea (*Kow-ah-PEE-ah*) Beach is one of Hawaii's most popular nude beaches. Often called Secret Beach, it's a dirt-trail hike down sea cliffs to this beach just west of Kilauea Point. The beach is 100 feet wide and

Beauty	A
Swimming	B
Sand	A
Amenities	NA

nearly a mile long. *About 1/2 mi. west of Kilauea on Kuhio Hwy., turn right onto an unmarked dirt road and go 1 mi. Look for "Beach Trail" sign. From there, it's a 15-minute hike to the beach.*
Swimming: Generally safe in summer, but a pounding shore break can make swimming risky, especially in winter.
Sand: Grainy, reddish golden sand.
Amenities: None. No lifeguard.
Sports: Snorkeling, surfing.
Parking: Roadside at the trailhead.

HOTELS/INNS/B&Bs

Anini Beach lacks resort or commercial development, which is part of the charm for its many devotees. The nearest hotels and condominiums are at Princeville Resort to the north (*see* Chapter 13, Hanalei). However, a limited number of vacation-home rentals and bed-and-breakfast rooms in homes or cottages are available in the area.

◆ **Glo Manor** (inexpensive). This family estate includes two comfortable studios and an 1,800-square-foot two-bedroom apartment, all with kitchen facilities. A secluded getaway by the sea. *Box 221, Kilauea, HI 96754; tel. 808-828-0328. E-mail address: dinky@aloha.net. At the end of Anini Beach Rd.*

◆ **Hale Ho'o Maha** (inexpensive). Four rooms in a home on five acres with a pond. Ten-minute walk from Kalihiwai Beach. *Box 422, Kilauea, HI 96754; tel. 808-828-1341, 800-851-0291. Almost 1 mi. north of Kilauea on Kuhio Hwy., turn right on the first of two turnoffs for Kalihiwai Rd. Go 1/4 mi. and turn left on the gravel road at the sign for Hale Ho'o Maha. Proceed up the hill to the split-level home overlooking a pond and stream.*

◆ **Makai Farms Orchids** (inexpensive). Bed-and-breakfast cottage that sleeps four. Kitchen facilities. *Box 93, Kilauea, HI 96754; tel. 808-828-1874; fax 808-828-1874. Just outside Kilauea.*

HOUSE RENTALS

◆ **Anini Beach Vacation Rentals.** Vacation homes on Anini Beach and throughout the North Shore. *Box 1220, Hanalei, HI 96714; tel. 808-826-4000, 800-448-6333. Internet address: http://www.anini.com.*

RESTAURANTS

One just closed, reducing the number of full-service restaurants in town to zero. Your best bet is to drive north to Princeville and Hanalei.

◆ **Kilauea Bakery and Pau Hana Pizza** (moderate). Pizza, whole or by the slice, served with fresh salad. *Imaginative* is the word for the pizza menu. Try the Billie Holiday: smoked ono fish, swiss chard, roasted onion, gorgonzola, rosemary sauce, and cheese. *Box 630, Kilauea, HI 96754; tel. 808-828-2020. Open Mon.-Sat. for breakfast, lunch, and dinner. At Kong Lung Center on Lighthouse Rd.*

NIGHTLIFE

If you came to Anini for nightclubs, discos, or even bowling alleys, you came to the wrong place. Anini nightlife consists of sunsets and moonrises, night rainbows, and singing frogs. If you require more, seek the bright lights of Tahiti Nui, the major roadside attraction, a few miles down Kuhio Highway in the town of Hanalei (*see* Chapter 13, Hanalei).

ATTRACTIONS

◆ **Makai Farms Orchids.** An orchid nursery and greenhouse with unusual species from around the world. Organic fruit orchard. *Box 93, Kilauea, HI 96754; tel. 808-828-1874; fax 808-828-1874. Open Sun.-Tue. or by appointment. Just outside Kilauea.*

SHOPPING

◆ **Kong Lung Co.** A classy collection of gifts, artifacts, clothing, and art in an old, high-ceilinged store that earned the sobriquet "Gumps in the cane field." It's not Gumps, but it's a pleasant, air-conditioned stop with enticing wares. *Box 36, Lighthouse Rd., Kilauea, HI 96754; tel. 808-828-1822; fax 808-828-1227. Open daily. On the right-hand side of the road to the Kilauea Lighthouse.*

BEST FOOD SHOPS

SANDWICHES: ◆ **Farmers Market.** Deli sandwiches, drinks, groceries. *Box 400, Kilauea, HI 96754; tel. 808-828-1512. Open daily. Next to Kong Lung Center.*

SEAFOOD: Nearest is at Princeville Foodland, about eight miles north of Anini Beach.

FRESH PRODUCE: ◆ **Banana Joe's.** Tropical fruit farm and stand that sells smoothies, dried fruit, salads, fresh fruit. *5-2719 Kuhio Hwy., Kilauea, HI 96754; tel. 808-828-1092. Open daily. On the mountain side of Kuhio Hwy., just north of Kilauea.*

BAKERY: ◆ **Kilauea Bakery and Pau Hana Pizza.** Hearty fresh breads, pastries, and pizza. *Box 630, Kilauea, HI 96754; tel. 808-828-2020. Open Mon.-Sat. At Kong Lung Center on Lighthouse Rd.*

BEVERAGES: ◆ **Menehune Food Mart.** *2521 Kolo Rd., Kilauea, HI 96754; tel. 808-828-1771. Open daily. At the corner of Kuhio Hwy. and Kolo Rd.*

WINE: ◆ **Farmers Market.** Wines, champagnes, and liquors in a little country store. *Kilauea, HI 96754; tel. 808-828-1512. Open daily. Next to Kong Lung Center.*

SPORTS

Anini Beach is an ideal place to learn windsurfing: safe, uncrowded, no witnesses. The lagoonlike water is shallow and protected by a reef. Winds tend to blow onshore.

◆ **Anini Beach Windsurfing.** Windsurfing lessons; equipment sales and rentals. Travel packages available. *Box 1602, Hanalei, HI 96714; tel. 808-826-9463. Open daily.*

FISHING

◆ **Anini Fishing Charters.** Experienced local guides for sport- and bottom fishing aboard the six-passenger *Sea Breeze IV.* Call for reservations. *Box 594, Kilauea, HI 96754; tel. 808-828-1285.*

◆ **Robert McReynolds.** Private or shared charters, from half- to full-day, for up to six passengers aboard 30-foot sportfishing boat *Hoomaikai.* Call for reservations. *Box 767, Kilauea, HI 96754; tel. 808-828-1379.*

DIVING

No shops in the area rent equipment. Snorkeling is excellent along Anini's accessible reef: very shallow on one side, an abyss on the other.

BICYCLING

No shops or rentals in this area (*see* Chapter 13, Hanalei).

GOLF

Although the Prince Golf Course of the Princeville Resort is practically alongside Anini Beach, it's an eight-mile drive to get there. Worth the effort, though, and it's the only course on the North Shore.

TENNIS

No courts in the area (*see* Chapter 13, Hanalei, and Chapter 14, Kalapaki).

HISTORY

◆ **Kilauea Point Lighthouse.** Built in 1913, the 52-foot lighthouse is a National Historical Landmark. Said to have the largest clamshell lens in the world, it flashes its beam 90 miles out to sea. The public is not allowed inside, but the setting alone is worth a visit. *Kilauea, HI 96754. From Kuhio Hwy., turn onto Kilauea Rd. and look for sign to the lighthouse. Go 1 mi. north on paved road to the parking lot by the lighthouse.*

NATURE

◆ **Kilauea Point National Wildlife Refuge.** Black lava boulder beaches on either side of Kilauea Point, the northernmost extremity of Kauai, are inaccessible to humans but provide perfect habitat for red-footed boobies, wedge-tailed shearwaters, and other seabirds. And the 165-foot-high point is an ideal perch from which humans can observe the birds in mating and nesting rituals on the cliffs and on Mokuaeae Island, a hulking rock 200 yards offshore. Bring binoculars. *Box 87, Kilauea, HI 96754; tel. 808-828-1413; fax 808-828-6634. Open Mon.-Fri. 10-4, except federal holidays. From Kuhio Hwy., turn onto Kilauea Rd. and look for sign to Kilauea Point Lighthouse. Go 1 mi. north on paved road to the parking lot by the lighthouse.*

SAFETY TIPS

Anini Stream cut a channel through the reef on the western end of Anini Beach that can cause strong currents in the immediate area, so avoid it. Swimmers exploring the offshore reef in other areas will want to wear reef walkers.

TOURIST INFORMATION

◆ **Hawaii Visitors Bureau, Kauai Chapter.** *3016 Umi St., Suite 207, Lihue, HI 96766; tel. 808-245-3971. Open Mon.-Fri. 8-4:30.*

CHAPTER 17

Tunnels

Some of Hawaii's best beaches begin at Ha'ena, a wide spot on a wiggly road on Kauai's North Shore that's filled with extraordinary beauty. Cross over waterfall streams on one-lane wooden bridges to discover this little piece of paradise.

Beauty	A
Swimming	B
Sand	B+
Hotels/Inns/B&Bs	NA
House rentals	B
Restaurants	B
Nightlife	NA
Attractions	B
Shopping	D
Sports	A
Nature	A

Here, at the foot of volcanic peaks and next to turquoise lagoons, beaches like no others on earth lead down to the blue sea. There are little coves under steepled mountains, curving strands lapped by gentle waves, and remote wilderness beaches accessible only by boat or on foot.

Haena (*Ha-AY-nah*) is a 230-acre beach park between two natural wonders. On the east is Wainiha Bay, where some of the torrential rain that falls on 5,148-foot Mount Waialeale runs to the sea in a river so wide it requires two bridges to span it. To the west is Ke'e Beach, with a dandy reef that's made for snorkeling.

Along this idyllic four-mile coast, ancient Hawaiians built houses, agricultural terraces, and sacred heiau, the ruins of which have yet to be uncovered by archaeologists. The Hawaiians called the coast Haena, which means "Red Hot," probably because it's such a great place to catch a sizzling Pacific sunset.

Today, the rich and famous inhabit the Haena Coast in million-dollar beach houses occupied intermittently by the likes of the Beach Boys, Jeff Bridges, Billie Jean King, and entertainer Charo, who lends her name to the neighborhood's sole beach-front bar and grill.

Ha'ena is the gateway to the Na Pali Coast, Hawaii's premier wilderness escape, with deep narrow valleys, waterfalls, and beaches. Other than exceptional natural beauty, often empty beaches, and the occasional puka shell that washes up on the golden sand, there's not much going on in Ha'ena, which is the best recommendation for a great Hawaiian beach vacation. P.S.: Bring your own book (no libraries out this way).

TUNNELS BEACH

Even if you've never been to Hawaii, you've probably seen this beach. It appears regularly in almost any photo illustrating the beauty of Hawaii's beaches. If only every beach looked so good. Spiky volcanic peaks stand as the backdrop for this

Beauty	A
Swimming	A
Sand	A
Amenities	B

HOW TO GET THERE

◆ From Honolulu International Airport, it's a 20-minute flight by jet to Kauai's Lihue Airport, which is a one-hour drive from Tunnels Beach. From Lihue, drive north 31 mi. on Kuhio Hwy. (Hwy. 56) to Hanalei, and buy beach supplies there (*see* Chapter 13, Hanalei). Continue on Kuhio Hwy. for 5 mi. as it winds in and out of the coast across one-lane bridges, passing Charo's, the best-known landmark, into the town of Haena. Proceed for 1 mi. and turn right down a dirt road into a grove of ironwood trees to get to the beach.

◆ Mahalo Airlines, IslandAir, and Hawaiian Air fly prop planes between Honolulu International and Princeville Airport, which serves Kauai's North Shore. On Kauai, rental cars and small four-wheel-drive vehicles are available through the hotels or at Lihue and Princeville airports.

meandering golden strand and its sparkling blue-green lagoon. Offshore, a coral reef keeps guard, and beyond that, the deep blue Pacific falls away over the horizon to Japan. In early times, this beach was called Makua ("Cave" in Hawaiian), but today everyone calls it Tunnels because of the reef's submarine lava tubes. Some of these are occupied by tiger sharks, so you probably won't want to go out of your way to explore them.

But the big, wide, deep lagoon at Tunnels is great to explore with snorkel, mask, and fins. The long, curvy beach is sheltered on the inner shore by a coastal forest of ironwood trees that provide welcome shade in the tropical heat. No facilities exist at Tunnels, but Haena Beach Park, with its full facilities, is a half-mile hike to the west.

Tunnels is the home of the puka shell, the tiny, pearly white seashell almost everyone wore in the 1970s. Waves that wrap around Haena Point carry seashells across the reef to shore, along with precious flotsam such as green glass balls lost from Japanese fishing nets. According to local lore, the puka-shell necklace craze began when Ha'ena resident Howard Taylor gave one to his sister Liz (yes, *that* Liz Taylor). She wore it in public, and you know the rest. *From Haena, drive west 1 mi. on Kuhio Hwy. and turn right down a dirt road into a grove of ironwood trees to access the beach. If the parking lot is full, return to the highway, drive west 1/2 mi. to Haena Beach Park, and hike back.*
Swimming: Excellent nearly all year.
Sand: Coarse, grainy, and golden.
Amenities: None, but some can be found at Haena Beach Park. No lifeguard.
Sports: Snorkeling, windsurfing, surfing, fishing.
Parking: Small unpaved lot.

HAENA BEACH PARK

This spot on Maniniholo Bay is a great place to picnic or camp in summer, but it's dangerous for swimming in winter. A wide, grassy plain sits along Kuhio Highway, across from two lava-tube sea caves scoured out by wave action over the

Beauty	A
Swimming	C
Sand	B
Amenities	B

millennia. Dunes lead to the wide, sandy beach on the bay, which has no protection from the open ocean. Reefs on either side of the bay channel the waves into monsters during winter's high surf. *Driving west on Kuhio Hwy., look for "Haena Beach Park" sign on right across from two sea caves. Turn right into the lot.* *Swimming:* Safest in June, July, and August, when the ocean is calm. Winter surf is high, with dangerous waves, rip currents, and strong undertow.
Sand: Grainy and golden.
Amenities: Rest rooms, showers, picnic tables, food wagons, camping facilities. No lifeguard.
Sports: Snorkeling.
Parking: Ample and free.

WAINIHA BEACH PARK

Here's a half-mile-long broad sandy beach that's great for beachcombing and sunbathing but risky for swimming at any time of year. The bay is an open bight with no protection from the ocean. Many people get washed out to sea by huge, rogue

Beauty	A
Swimming	F
Sand	B
Amenities	C

waves at Wainiha (*Why-NEE-hah*), which is why local rescue teams jocularly call it Tourist Beach. *From Hanalei, drive west on Kuhio Hwy. for 5 mi. After crossing the Wainiha River, (the one with two bridges), look for parking lot in a grove of ironwood trees.*
Swimming: Don't. It's too dangerous.
Sand: Grainy, golden sand, often blown by wind.
Amenities: None. No lifeguard.
Sports: Fishing from shore.
Parking: Ample off-road lot that is free.

KE'E BEACH

The road ends here at a beach on a reef-protected cove flanked by fluted volcanic cliffs. The setting is picture-perfect, which undoubtedly is why Ke'e Beach appeared as a backdrop in *The Thornbirds.* At the entrance to Na Pali Coast State

Beauty	A
Swimming	A
Sand	A
Amenities	B

Park, Ke'e (*KAY-ay*) is the North Shore's last public beach accessible by vehicle. Big winter waves tear away the beach, exposing shoreline tree roots and uncovering rock, but when the sand comes back in the summer, there's no finer beach. *From Hanalei, drive west on Kuhio Hwy. 7 mi. to the end of the road.*
Swimming: Safe inside the reef, dangerous outside for those unfamiliar with Hawaiian waters.
Sand: Gravelly reddish golden sand.
Amenities: Rest rooms, showers. Lifeguard on duty.
Sports: Snorkeling, reef walking.
Parking: Roadside or in small sand lot.

NA PALI COAST STATE PARK

The trail to Na Pali Coast State Park and the wilderness beaches of Hanakapiai and Kalalau begins where the road ends at Ke'e Beach. Said to be in use for the past 1,000 years, this ancient path winds in and out of narrow valleys for 11 miles along

Beauty	A
Swimming	C
Sand	B
Amenities	NA

the otherwise impenetrable accordion coast known as Na Pali ("The Cliffs" in Hawaiian).

The beaches are remote and often empty, although some worry that the wilderness experience is being sorely tested by the *thwock* of flight-seeing helicopters, zooming tour boats, and abusive campers. As was the case with Hawaii's native birds, this coast's natural appeal may be its doom.

Still, a sense of isolation makes most people whisper and smile in the natural cathedral of the 4,000-foot-tall steepled cliffs, where descendants of Captain Cook's goats traverse thin trails and long-tailed tropic birds soar high on thermals. Whales leap out of the sea, rainbows arch across the sky, and towering waves pound the golden sand. Anyone who's been down the Na Pali (*NA-PAH-lee*) Coast yearns to return someday. It's that kind of place. *Trail begins at Ke'e Beach parking lot at the end of Kuhio Hwy. Park there, or have a taxi from Princeville Airport drop you off.*
Swimming: Dangerous currents at Hanakapiai. Both beaches are open to the ocean, and waves thunder ashore in winter, making it impossible to swim. Experienced swimmers can give it a try in

summer, but even then rogue waves may rise up and carry you out to sea.

Sand: Grainy, golden coral sand. At Kalalau, it's mixed with red-dirt runoff near the waterfalls on the west end.

Amenities: Kalalau has trash cans and portable toilets, but that's all. No lifeguard, no park ranger at either beach.

Sports: Exploring, hiking.

Parking: In Ke'e Beach parking lot.

Hanakapiai Beach

Easily reached with a 90-minute day hike, Hanakapiai (*Hah-naw-COP-ee-eye*) Beach is the first of two beaches in Na Pali Coast State Park that are accessible on foot or by boat. It's only two miles down the trail to this bouldered pocket beach. For those willing to do some more hiking for a freshwater plunge, a rough trail leads two miles inland through lush jungle to Hanakapiai Falls. Swimsuits optional.

Kalalau Beach

Kalalau (*Kah-LAW-lau*) Beach is best described by what's not there: roads, resorts, electricity, running water, stores or supplies (except what you pack in), shelters (beyond sea caves or tents), restaurants, gift shops, telephones, TV sets, and, usually, swimsuits. There's something about this beach that compels people to shed their togs and get close to nature.

Once the refuge of kings, scoundrels, hermits, and hippies, this golden coral-sand beach is now the primary goal of adventure travelers, who hike the precipitous trail across corrugated sea cliffs or race down the Na Pali Coast in inflatable rubber rafts. Permits are required for overnight camping (*see* Hotels/Inns/B&Bs).

Kalalau is a wilderness zone: no lifeguard, no park rangers, so prepare accordingly. Good hiking boots are a must on the steep, rocky trail. In heavy rain, streams rise dramatically, and flash floods occur. A waterproof tent will ensure a good night's sleep, since torrential ocean squalls often pelt the North Coast at night. A poncho is handy for daytime rain protection. All water should be boiled or purified before drinking. A backpacker's stove is essential. Firewood is scarce, and tree-cutting is prohibited. A light sleeping bag is all that's needed in summer. Bring first aid kit, sunscreen, flashlight. *From the trailhead at Ke'e Beach parking lot, allow at least 8 hours to hike into Kalalau Beach.*

HOUSE RENTALS

Kauai's North Shore is blessedly free of commercial development, but that limits the places to stay. There are no hotels. However, house rentals in the area provide an appealing alternative.

◆ **Anchorage Point/Kilauea Travel Group** (expensive). A two-bedroom, two-bath elevated (to escape storm tides) vacation house on the beach in a celebrity hideaway neighborhood. A wonderful retreat. Air/car vacation packages available. *Box 713, Kilauea, HI 96754; tel. 808-826-7090, 800-214-1314; fax 808-828-6661. Beach front in Haena, next door to Charo's.*

◆ **Hanalei Colony Resort** (moderate). Small complex of unpretentious, comfortable, well-tended two-bedroom condominium units, each with full kitchen and private lanai. Some beach-front units let you step off your lanai into sand. The setting is a dramatic vista of mountains and sea. One of Hawaii's little jewels. Condo/car vacation packages available. *Box 206, Hanalei, HI 96714; tel. 808-826-6235, 800-628-3004; fax 808-826-9893. Just past the last one-lane bridge, sharing the parking lot with Charo's.*

◆ **Ivy's Place/Kilauea Travel Group** (moderate). Two-bedroom restored plantation house perched on a shoulder of Wainiha Valley with views of ocean, waterfall, and rain forest. Five-minute drive downhill to beautiful beaches. *Box 713, Kilauea, HI 96754; tel. 808-826-7090, 800-214-1314. From Kuhio Hwy., just past Wainiha Store, turn left onto Wainiha Powerhouse Rd. and drive 1 1/4 mi. to the house. Watch out for sleeping dogs.*

◆ **Ainalani Tropical Farms** (inexpensive). Vacation rental studio with private lanai, kitchenette, and inspiring view of the mountains in secluded tropical-flower and fruit-farm setting. Short drive to the beaches. Three-day minimum. Obliging hosts allow guests who want to hike the Kalalau Trail to leave their cars on the property and get a ride to the trailhead. E-mail address: zim-cap@aloha.net. *Box 835, Hanalei, HI 96714; tel. 808-826-9400; fax 808-826-4154. 3/4 mi. inland from Kuhio Hwy. at Wainiha.*

◆ **Na Pali Coast State Park** (inexpensive). Camping permits must be obtained in advance from the address below. Bring your own tent (and everything else) if you plan to camp at Kalalau Beach. Other than sea caves, there is no shelter there. *Division of State Parks, 3060 Eiwa St., Room 306, Lihue, HI 96766; tel. 808-241-3444. Open Mon.-Fri. 8-4.*

RESTAURANTS

◆ **Charo's** (moderate). Mexican and fish dishes in a beach-front restaurant/cantina owned by the famed exotic dancer, who has forsaken Las Vegas for the simple life in Hawaii. She spends most of her time on stage elsewhere, but if she's on Kauai, you might meet her here. *Box 1007, Haena, HI 96714; tel. 808-826-6422. Open daily for lunch and dinner. Adjoining Hanalei Colony Resort.*

NIGHTLIFE

This remote stretch of the North Shore inspires visitors to get close to nature in general and the beach in particular. There are no pubs and thus there's no pub crawling.

ATTRACTIONS

◆ **Limahuli Garden.** This pleasant garden is part of the National Tropical Botanical Garden headquartered on the other side of Kauai at Lawai. *Hanalei, HI 96714; tel. 808-826-1053; fax 808-826-4759. Open Sun. and Tue.-Thu. Tours, at 10 a.m. and 1 p.m., are by reservation only. Admission. On uphill side of Kuhio Hwy. near its end.*

SHOPPING

There are no stores on the North Shore past the Wainiha General Store, so stock up on everything before you head this way.

BEST FOOD SHOPS

People planning to set up vacation housekeeping on the North Shore should buy groceries, including fresh produce and seafood, on the way to Haena. The largest markets are the Big Save in Hanalei and the Foodland at Princeville (*see* Chapter 13, Hanalei.). The little Wainiha General Store is stocked more for beach snacks and drinks.

SANDWICHES: ◆ Mr. Sandwich. The place for freshly made sandwiches, vegetarian or with deli meats. *Box 1553, Hanalei, HI 96714; tel. 808-826-4579. Open daily. Next door to Wainiha General Store.*

ICE CREAM: ◆ Wainiha General Store. *Hanalei, HI 96714; tel. 808-826-6251. Open daily. Located just past the one-lane bridges on Kuhio Hwy.*

BEVERAGES: ◆ Wainiha General Store. Cold drinks, snacks. *Hanalei, HI 96714; tel. 808-826-6251. Open daily. Just past the one-lane bridges on Kuhio Hwy.*

SPORTS

Windsurfing, surfing, beachcombing for shells, snorkeling in calm weather, and hiking the Na Pali Coast are the prime sports of the Haena area.

FISHING

The waters are full of fish, but there are no commercial charters or party boats in the area.

BOATING

Commercial boating in this area is based in Hanalei or on the south end of the Na Pali Wilderness in Port Allen, where captains specialize in offering tours of the wilderness coast.

SURFING

◆ **Last Chance.** Stop in to rent a surfboard. *Box 1553, Hanalei, HI 96714; tel. 808-826-7503. Closed Sun. Next to Wainiha General Store.*

DIVING

◆ **Last Chance.** Beach equipment rentals, snorkel rentals and sales, camping gear/tent rentals. *Box 1553, Hanalei, HI 96714; tel. 808-826-7503. Closed Sun. Next to Wainiha General Store.*

GOLF

Nearest golf is at Princeville Resort, 15 miles south of Haena (*see* Chapter 13, Hanalei).

TENNIS

Courts at Hanalei Colony Resort are reserved for guests.

NATURE

Near the end of the Kuhio Highway, across from Haena Beach Park, are some lava tube caves to explore. The yawning mouths of Waikapalae Wet Cave and Waikanaloa Wet Cave are right beside the road. Inside is frigid water and rock walls. The Maniniholo Dry Cave is about 150 yards uphill from a marker by the road.

◆ **Kalalau Falls.** This waterfall is on a stream coming from the heights of Mount Waialeale. Take a refreshing shower, but keep an eye on the color of the water. If it turns red, get out: Rain from a cloudburst is eroding the sea cliffs, and there's a risk of flash floods. *At the west end of Kalalau Beach.*

SAFETY TIPS

This is an untamed coast with strong currents, huge waves, undertows, and few lifeguards. Inshore reefs and coral heads make for excellent snorkeling but increase the risk of cuts. Hikers bound for Hanakapiai and Kalalau should be prepared for slippery mud and narrow cliff ledges.

TOURIST INFORMATION

◆ **Hawaii Visitors Bureau, Kauai Chapter.** *3016 Umi St., Suite 207, Lihue, HI 96766; tel. 808-245-3971. Open Mon.-Fri. 8-4:30.*

CHAPTER 18

Hapuna

Hawaii's greatest collection of luxury resorts rises like a mirage, shimmering in the heat waves from the black lava desert of the Kohala Coast. From the highway, it looks like the last place on earth any mortal would choose for a beach vacation.

Yet for 30 years, entertainers, high-powered executives, and other rich folks have spent small fortunes at Kohala resorts to be secluded from worldly pressures by a barren buffer zone of black lava. They keep coming back, and so do their children and grandchildren.

Beauty	A
Swimming	A-
Sand	B+
Hotels/Inns/B&Bs	A
House rentals	D
Restaurants	B
Nightlife	B
Attractions	C
Shopping	C
Sports	A
Nature	A

True, the accommodations are luxurious and the dining sumptuous, but the root cause of this infatuation is the area's extraordinary beaches. They are few in number, but each is magnificent in its own way. Hapuna is broad with a lava outcropping that divides it in half, Kaunaoa a nearly perfect crescent of golden sand in a big, blue bay framed by rocks and swaying palms. Anaehoomalu is a favorite of water-sports enthusiasts, and Kalahuipuaa is renowned for its views.

No wonder beach-front resorts have flowered beside the coastal desert. Mauna Kea was the first, then came Mauna Lani, Waikoloa, and the latest, Hapuna. They're carefully sited on the shore to take advantage of the beaches, the ocean and mountain views, and the wind, which blows in from the sea or down the slopes of those volcanic neighbors, Mauna Kea and Mauna Loa.

The resorts are new kids in an old neighborhood that includes ancient petroglyphs and shelter caves, village ruins, and, farther north, the birthplace of 18th-century King Kamehameha, who united the kingdom by conquering most of it. The nearest town is Waimea, also known as Kamuela for mailing purposes. Up the slope from Waikoloa, there's a shopping area, restaurant, golf, tennis, stables, and a gas station at Waikoloa Highlands, the nearest retail outpost.

The Kohala District, historic and harsh, regal and religious, is a sun-baked, arid land averaging less than ten inches of rain a year, but it has always been desirable. Yesterday's royal ruins and today's room rates are proof of that.

HAPUNA BEACH STATE RECREATION AREA

Hapuna is the largest beach on an island too young to have many beaches. This one is a winner: golden and flat, more than half a mile long. It's over 200 feet wide in spots, but the winter surf whittles it back to reveal a lava point that, like the

Beauty	A
Swimming	B+
Sand	A
Amenities	B+

bow of a ship, divides the strand in two. The public park is landscaped and sports a fringe of palms. The beach slopes gently into the water.

HOW TO GET THERE

◆ The Big Island of Hawaii is a 35-minute jet flight from Honolulu International Airport. From Keahole Airport in Kailua-Kona (30 minutes from the Kohala Coast resort area), turn left on Queen Kaahumanu Hwy. (Hwy. 19) and drive 26 mi. to the resorts. To reach any of the beaches, turn left off the highway and drive west 2 mi. across black lava fields to the coast.

◆ Rental cars are available through the hotels and at the airport, but be aware that there are few gas stations in West Hawaii. The resorts are served by limousine and shuttle.

On the north side of Hapuna (*Ha-POO-nah*) the black lava forms coves and tide pools, which are good for exploring, snorkeling, or private sunbathing. A bit farther along the beach front, the Hapuna Prince hotel's grassy lawns slope down to the beach and a public coastal path.

Because it's on the Big Island's arid side, Hapuna Beach is practically guaranteed to be hot, dry, and sunny, even in the depths of winter. When frozen snowbirds need a winter beach fix, Hapuna's the one. *From Queen Kaahumanu Hwy. (Hwy. 19), follow the "Shoreline Access" signs 1 mi. on a bumpy, two-lane paved road to the beach park.*

Swimming: Great when conditions are calm, dangerous in high winter surf.

Sand: Abundant, golden.

Amenities: Rest rooms, showers, picnic pavilions, paved walkways. Good access road from the highway. Four-person cabins for camping. Lifeguard on duty.

Sports: Bodysurfing. Good snorkel spots around the reefs at the ends of the beach. Fishing by pole or throw-net.

Parking: Paved lot.

ANAEHOOMALU BEACH PARK

This is a natural, movie-set beach, strikingly at odds with the barbecue pit of black lava that separates it from the highway. The long crescent of golden sand, with lots of rustling palms for shade, is a beach peninsula formed by the ancient

Beauty	A
Swimming	A
Sand	B
Amenities	A

fishpond complex behind it. The fishpond stocks were for kings' consumption only. Anaehoomalu (*A-NIGH-ee-ho-o-ma-loo*) means "Restricted Mullet." The royals enjoyed their fish and apparently liked to linger at the beach as well.

The sands slope gently into picturesque Anaehoomalu Bay, a fine site for swimming and all kinds of water sports. The paved public accessway leads into a coconut grove park area at the southern end of the beach, adjoining a fine party site for the nearby Royal Waikoloan Hotel and other Waikoloa resort properties. *From Queen Kaahumanu Hwy. (Hwy. 19), turn into*

Mauna Lanai Resort. Drive across lava fields to the Royal Waikoloan Resort. Turn left and follow the "Shoreline Access" signs to the beach.
Swimming: Safe except for storms.
Sand: Golden, flecked with black lava, and somewhat coarse.
Amenities: Rest rooms, showers, picnic tables, food available at the hotel. Paved walks, interpretive history signage around the fishponds. No lifeguard.
Sports: Canoeing, kayaking, snorkeling, scuba diving, windsurfing, fishing, and occasional surfing.
Parking: Paved inland public lot near the access.

KAUNAOA BEACH

In Kaunaoa's clear, buoyant waters, you may end up swimming with a turtle. Green sea turtles like to visit this spot, where there's good swimming for all creatures. Manta rays hang out by the rocky points, and at night, the Mauna Kea Hotel leaves floodlights on to attract the evening meal for them.

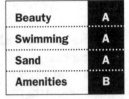

Beauty	A
Swimming	A
Sand	A
Amenities	B

The white-gold sands of the long, curved strand submerge gently into a sand-bottomed bay. Kaunaoa (*KOW-nah-o-ah*) is perfect for swimming or floating effortlessly on the salty waves. Snorkeling the sides of Kaunaoa Bay is rewarding and easier than at many sites, because the waters are relatively protected.

Although the beach seems to have been created just for the adjacent hotel, it is publicly accessible, like all Hawaiian beaches. Kaunaoa's access via coastal trail was won in a court fight. The resort's influence is pervasive, naturally. Everyone calls it Mauna Kea Beach, but it's real name is Kaunaoa, meaning "Native Dodder," either a mollusk or a lacy, yellow-orange vine.

From Queen Kaahumanu Hwy. (Hwy. 19), enter Mauna Kea Resort and drive 2 mi. across black lava fields to the coast. Turn left before the resort and look for "Shoreline Access" signs.
Swimming: Excellent in calm conditions. Good for families with children.
Sand: Golden, soft, and fine.
Amenities: Rest rooms, showers. No lifeguard, but hotel employees have made many rescues.

Sports: Snorkeling.
Parking: Free and ample.

KALAHUIPUAA BEACH

Mauna Lani means "Mountain Reaching Heaven," and a five-volcano view may have inspired the name of the resort built beside this shoreline scalloped with pocket beaches. Kalahuipuaa (*Kah-la-hooey-POOAH-ah*) Beach, the largest of the lot,

Beauty	A
Swimming	B
Sand	B
Amenities	A

fronts the Mauna Lani Bay Hotel & Bungalows. It offers the most protected swimming, in a cove enclosed by a fringe of reef. The reef beyond it is good for snorkeling and diving when the sea is calm.

A coastal trail links sections of the resort, winding along by the beaches and the kiawe forests between them. It's a great walk along a wild stretch of coast.

To the north, the trail leads to another delightful beach with protected swimming right beside the Ritz-Carlton. Public access to the trail and the Puako Petroglyph field is found at the north end of the hotel. The trail stops at a public beach park by the residential area of Puako. *From Queen Kaahumanu Hwy. (Hwy. 19), enter the Mauna Lani Resort and drive 2 mi. across black lava fields to the coast. Just before reaching Mauna Lani Bay Hotel & Bungalows, follow "Shoreline Access" sign to the beach.*
Swimming: Excellent in a wide, shallow, sandy-bottomed cove.
Sand: Golden in some places. In others, an unusual mix of white and black sand with plenty of white coral rocks thrown in.
Amenities: Minimal. This is a resort with public access rather than a public beach. No lifeguard.
Sports: Snorkeling, scuba diving.
Parking: Paved, marked lots.

HOTELS/INNS/B&Bs

◆ **Mauna Kea Beach Resort** (very expensive). Completely renovated during 1995. Its gracious charm, large art collection, superlative beach, and famous golf course assure continued top billing. *One Mauna Kea Dr., Kamuela, HI 96743; tel. 808-882-7222, 800-882-6060. Beach front at Mauna Kea Resort.*

◆ **Mauna Lani Bay Hotel & Bungalows** (very expensive). Gentle Hawaiian ways and first-rate hospitality make it special. Plan far ahead if you hope to stay in one of the five exclusive, butlered bungalows, usually booked year-round by the rich and famous. *68-1400 Mauna Lani Dr., Kohala Coast, HI 96743; tel. 808-885-6622, 800-356-6652; fax 808-885-4556. Beach front in Mauna Lani Resort.*

◆ **Ritz-Carlton, Mauna Lani** (very expensive). Ritz-Carlton's first Hawaii hotel is opulently furnished and landscaped, enjoying a scenic perch on a slope leading down to Pauoa Bay. *One N. Kaniku Dr., Kohala Coast, HI 96743; tel. 808-885-2000, 800-241-3333; fax 808-885-1064. Beach front in Mauna Lani Resort.*

◆ **Hilton Waikoloa Village** (expensive). Could rank as the most popular attraction on this coast, with its grand architectural features and theme-park amenities, which draw plenty of day-trip visitors. A light-rail tram and boats on tracks take people between buildings. There's a pool where guests can swim with dolphins and walkway galleries filled with Asian and Pacific art reproductions. No natural beach here, but it's fun. *425 Waikoloa Beach Dr., Kamuela, HI 96743; tel. 808-885-1234, 800-445-8667. In Waikoloa Beach Resort.*

◆ **Royal Waikoloan** (expensive). Best buy in the area: less luxury but more nature and an all-inclusive rate option that even takes care of the drinks. Overlooks an ancient fishpond and picturesque beach once enjoyed by royalty. *69-275 Waikoloa Beach Dr., Kamuela, HI 96743; tel. 808-885-6789, 800-822-4282. In Waikoloa Beach Resort.*

◆ **Elima Lani** (moderate). Well-equipped and well-priced two-bedroom condos with spas, pools, golf, and tennis. *68-3883 Lua Kula St., Waikoloa, HI 96738; tel. 808-883-8288, 800-367-5004. Hillside in Waikoloa Village.*

HOUSE RENTALS

◆ **South Kohala Management.** This company rents condos and other luxury vacation homes in all three Kohala Coast resort areas. *Box 3301, Waikoloa, HI 96743; tel. 808-883-8500, 800-822-4252. Open daily.*

RESTAURANTS

Kohala Coast hotels pride themselves on their cuisine and offer both fine dining and casual places to eat and drink. It's all open to the public.

◆ **CanoeHouse** (very expensive). Pacific Rim cuisine in an airy, indoor/outdoor, beach-front setting. Try the fresh coriander-crusted ahi (tuna) with curried eggplant, sticky rice, roasted Maui onion vinaigrette, and shiitake *namasu. 68-1400 Mauna Lani Dr., Kohala Coast, HI 96743; tel. 808-885-6622. Open daily for dinner. At Mauna Lani Bay hotel.*

◆ **Merriman's** (expensive). This fine restaurant features Contemporary Hawaii regional cuisine by one of its top chefs, Peter Merriman. He became famous for creating a seemingly endless variety of dishes using local lamb and for a wonderful concoction called wok-charred ahi, a cross between sashimi and fried fish. *Opelo Plaza, Waimea, HI 96743; tel. 808-885-6822. Open daily for dinner, Mon.-Fri for lunch. In Waimea, about half an hour's drive inland.*

◆ **Beach Bar at Hapuna Prince** (moderate). Excellent lunch fare and desserts in a casual outdoor atmosphere. *62-100 Kaunaoa Dr., Kamuela, HI 96743; tel. 808-880-1111. Open daily for lunch, snacks, sunset cocktails. By the Hapuna Prince pool in Mauna Kea Resort.*

◆ **Cafe Pesto** (moderate). *Kawaihae Shopping Center, Kawaihae, HI 96743; tel. 808-882-1071. Open daily for lunch and dinner. Across from the Kawaihae Harbor, a few minutes north of Mauna Kea Resort.*

NIGHTLIFE

Nightlife on the Kohala Coast doesn't take the form of bois-terous nightclubs and discos. It consists of oppulent luaus, live entertainment, Hawaiian music, and frequent hula per-formances at the hotels.

ATTRACTIONS

◆ **Parker Ranch Visitor Center and Historic Homes.** Parker Ranch's 225,000-acre cattle spread is the largest solely owned ranch in the United States. A small museum in Waimea details ranch history. On the property, a Victorian house and a historic home contain artifacts and notable collections of paintings and other artworks. *Box 458, Kamuela, HI 96743; tel. 808-885-7655. Open daily 9-5. Admission. Visitor Center at Parker Ranch Shopping Center in Waimea.*

SHOPPING

◆ **Cook's Discoveries.** Hawaiian handicrafts, wood carvings, and artworks in a historic setting. *1 Waimea Center, Kamuela, HI 96743; tel. 808-885-0550. Open daily. In the old Spencer House in Waimea.*

◆ **Kings' Shops.** Attractive cluster of shops and restaurants beside a lake with wonderful ancient-history exhibits scattered throughout. *Waikoloa Beach Dr., Kamuela, HI 96743; tel. 808-885-8811. Open daily. In Waikoloa Beach Resort.*

BEST FOOD SHOPS

SANDWICHES: ◆ **Waikoloa Beach Golf Clubhouse.** *Waikoloa Beach Resort, Kamuela, HI 96743; tel. 808-885-6131. Open daily for lunch. Up a hilly drive off Waikoloa Beach Dr.*

SEAFOOD: ◆ **Laau Fishing.** *Kawaihae Harbor, Kamuela, HI 96743; tel. 808-882-1052. Open Mon.-Sat.*

FRESH PRODUCE: ◆ **KTA Super Store.** *Waimea Center, Kamuela, HI 96743; tel. 808-885-8866. Open daily. A 30-minute drive up to Waimea.*

BAKERY: ◆ **Waikoloa Village Market.** Fresh pastries, breads, pies, doughnuts. *Waikoloa Highlands Center, Kamuela, HI 96743; tel. 808-883-1088. Open daily. 10 minutes uphill from Waikoloa.*

ICE CREAM: ◆ **Snackarama.** Makes its own ice cream and chili and also serves kosher hotdogs. *Kawaihae Shopping Center, Kamuela, HI 96743; tel. 808-882-1109. Open daily. Across from Kawaihae Harbor, north of Mauna Kea Resort.*

BEVERAGES: ◆ **Waikoloa Village Market.** *Waikoloa Highlands*

Center, Kamuela, HI 96743; tel. 808-883-1088. Open daily. 10 minutes uphill from Waikoloa.

WINE: ◆ **KTA Super Store.** *Waimea Center, Kamuela, HI 96743; tel. 808-885-8866. Open daily. A 30-minute drive up to Waimea.*

SPORTS

FISHING

The charter fishing fleet is based at Honokohau Harbor in Kailua-Kona. Sports activities centers or concierges at any of the Kohala Coast hotels can arrange a fishing trip.

BOATING

Snorkel/dive and whale-watching cruises, sunset sails, kayak trips, and other boating excursions can be arranged through hotel concierges or sports activities centers.

◆ **Maile.** Sailing trips ranging from sunset jaunts to ten-day interisland voyages aboard a 50-foot charter yacht. Four-passenger minimum. *Box 44335, Kamuela, HI 96743; tel. 808-326-5174, 800-726-7245. By reservation. Sails from Kawaihae Harbor.*

◆ **Red Sail Sports.** Snorkel/dive cruises, whale watching, kayak trips, sunset sails. Rents body boards, paddleboats, and bikes. *69-425 Waikoloa Beach Dr., Kamuela, HI 96743; tel. 808-885-2876. Open daily. At Waikoloa Beach Resort, Mauna Kea Resort, Ritz-Carlton, and Mauna Lani Resort.*

DIVING

Diving activities can be arranged through hotel concierges or sports activities centers.

◆ **Ocean Sports Waikoloa.** Reservations for snorkel and diving cruises and boat tours. Sailing, windsurfing, body boards, kayaks. *69-275 Waikoloa Beach Dr., Kohala Coast, HI 96743; tel. 808-885-5555. Open daily. At Waikoloa Beach Resort.*

BICYCLING

◆ **Red Sail Sports.** Rents bikes and water-sports equipment. *69-425 Waikoloa Beach Dr., Kamuela, HI 96743; tel. 808-885-2876.*

Open daily. At Waikoloa Beach Resort, Mauna Kea Resort, Ritz-Carlton, and Mauna Lani Resort.

GOLF

The challenging layouts of Kohala Coast golf courses draw devotees from around the world. Picture blankets of green winding around outcroppings of chunky black lava by the sea. Here a rough means really rough.

◆ **Hapuna Golf Course.** Rolling terrain of older volcanic rock with wild grasses and native wildflowers. This course by Arnold Palmer and Ed Seay runs from the 700-foot level to the shore and gets accolades for environmental sensitivity. *62-100 Kaunaoa Dr., Kamuela, HI 96743; tel. 808-880-3000; fax 808-880-3010. Open daily. Admission. At Mauna Kea Resort.*

◆ **Mauna Kea Golf Course.** The senior course on the coast is still the most popular. Judged "Hawaii's finest" by *Golf Digest*, it's a major item in anyone's book of favorites. *62-100 Kaunaoa Dr., Kohala Coast, HI 96743; tel. 808-880-3480; fax 808-882-7552. Open daily. Admission. At Mauna Kea Resort.*

◆ **Mauna Lani Francis H. I'i Brown Golf Courses.** Breathtaking seaside championship layouts over lava flows. Home of the annual PGA Senior Skins competition. *68-150 Ho'ohana, Kohala Coast, HI 96743; tel. 808-885-6655; fax 808-885-9612. Open daily. Admission. At Mauna Lani Resort.*

◆ **Waikoloa Beach and Kings' Golf Courses.** Daunting resort courses etched over lava by the sea. Beach Course by Robert Trent Jones, Jr.; Kings' Course by Weiskopf/Morrish. *600 Waikoloa Beach Dr., Kamuela, HI 96743; tel. 808-885-4647. Open daily. Admission. At Waikoloa Beach Resort.*

TENNIS

◆ **Hilton Waikoloa Village Tennis.** Eight courts, including two clay courts, one stadium, and a lesson court. Pro shop, rentals, instruction, clinics. *425 Waikoloa Beach Dr., Kamuela, HI 96743. Open daily. Admission.*

◆ **Mauna Kea Beach Resort Tennis.** Thirteen courts, 11 oceanside, plus video training, rentals, instruction, pro shop. *62-100*

Mauna Kea Beach Dr., Kamuela, HI 96743; tel. 808-882-7222, 800-882-6060. Open daily. Admission.

◆ **Mauna Lani Bay Hotel Tennis.** Ten courts, player-matching service, rentals, lessons, clinics, ball machine. *68-1400 Mauna Lani Dr., Kohala Coast, HI 96743; tel. 808-885-1485, 800-356-6652. Open daily. Admission.*

◆ **Mauna Lani Racquet Club.** Eight courts, including two grass. Weight room, lap pool, pro shop, instruction, steam rooms. *Box 4959, Kohala Coast, HI 96743; tel. 808-885-7765. Open daily. Admission.*

◆ **Royal Waikoloan Tennis.** Six courts, aerobics, rentals, lessons, clinics, pro shop. *69-725 Waikoloa Beach Dr., Kamuela, HI 96743; tel. 808-885-6789. Open daily. Admission.*

HORSEBACK RIDING

Trailriding is a natural way to get around Big Island ranch country, just uphill from the beach resorts. To ride Parker lands, contact Mauna Kea Beach Hotel Stables (tel. 808-885-4288).

HISTORY

You can ponder the meaning of petroglyphs, ancient pictographs carved into lava, at two nearby sites. It's a 1 1/2-mile walk to Puako Petroglyph Park, reached by the public access through Mauna Lani Resort. Waikoloa Petroglyph Field is easily accessible at the front of Waikoloa Resort, where there are trail signs and parking. Both resorts have ancient fishpond complexes—early aquaculture, where small fry came in on the tide, were trapped, and were raised to eating size.

◆ **Lapakahi State Historic Park.** A mile-long trail leads visitors through an ancient fishing village site. *North Kohala, Mahukona, HI 96719. Open daily 8-4. On the coast, 10 mi. north of Kawaihae Harbor.*

◆ **Mookini Heiau.** Tahitian priests performed sacrifices centuries ago at this spirit-laden, windswept fortress of stone. Adjacent is a site commemorating the birth of Kamehameha. Thoughtful visitors show respect in visiting these and other religious sites, where offerings of flower leis and rocks wrapped in leaves are modern-day evidence of worship. *Hawi, HI 96719. At the northern tip of the island.*

◆ **Puukohola Heiau National Historic Site.** Dedicated in 1791, this massive stone temple built by Kamehameha in honor of his war god is the last major religious structure of the pre-Christian era. It was the mighty Kamehameha's effort to gain spiritual power for his conquests. The result was unification of the islands into one kingdom, of which he was the first ruler. *Kawaihae, HI 96743; tel. 808-882-7218. Open daily 7:30-4. Just north of Mauna Kea Resort, beside Spencer Beach Park.*

NATURE

◆ **Hawaii Forest and Trail.** Naturalist Rob Pacheco provides the expertise and gear and leads small groups into the upland forest or over to watch the volcano by night. Unforgettable nature hikes. Will pickup and deliver Kohala Coast visitors. Call for reservations. *Box 2975, Kailua-Kona, HI 96745; tel. 808-322-8881, 800-464-1993; fax 808-322-8883. Admission.*

◆ **Hawaiian Walkways.** Guide Hugh Montgomery knows the ancient coastal trails well and will escort hikers on day and overnight trips there or into the high country. Call for reservations. *Box 2193, Kamuela, HI 96743; tel. 808-885-7759, 800-457-7759. Admission.*

◆ **Mauna Kea Observatories Support Services.** The best place on earth to peer into deep space is atop Mauna Kea, where seven nations operate astronomical labs in the alpine chill at nearly 14,000 feet. The visitors center at 9,000 feet conducts public astronomy programs. Call for details. *177 Makaala, Hilo, HI 96720; tel. 808-961-2180.*

SAFETY TIPS

Swim only when seas are calm, and check with lifeguards or others before entering the water. Watch out for sharp-edged lava or coral when swimming, snorkeling, or walking along beaches and tidepools. Wear reef walkers.

TOURIST INFORMATION

◆ **Hawaii Visitors Bureau, Big Island Chapter.** *75-5719 W. Alii Dr., Kailua-Kona, HI 96740; tel. 808-329-7787. Open Mon.-Fri. 8-4:30.*

◆ **Kohala Coast Resort Association.** *69-275 Waikoloa Beach Dr., Kamuela, HI 96743; tel. 808-885-4915. Open Mon.-Fri. 9-5.*

CHAPTER 19

Kahalu'u

Hot, dry, and sunny, the 40-mile Kona Coast of the Big Island is any sun-worshiper's perfect tropical destination. Call it Arizona-by-the-Sea with coconut trees. There's cactus, too. The Hawaiian word *kona*, incidentally, means leeward, which explains why this is the sun-baked, dry side of the island.

Kailua-Kona is a small seaside community of 10,000 permanent residents that you'll recognize as a tourist haven the moment you see Ali'i Drive. This beach-front drag skirts the southwest coast, embracing

Beauty	A
Swimming	B
Sand	B+
Hotels/Inns/B&Bs	A
House rentals	B
Restaurants	B
Nightlife	C
Attractions	B
Shopping	C
Sports	A
Nature	A

hotels, shops, and restaurants. It leads directly to the best beaches.

In and around Kailua-Kona, there are big empty beaches, small crowded beaches, and handy roadside beaches. There's even a beach at a royal Hawaiian palace in the heart of town. Beaches come in three shades: black sand, salt-and-pepper sand, and, in one instance, white sand, which is a rarity on this black lava coast (it's even called White Sands Beach).

Best beach on the Kona Coast is Kahalu'u (*Kaw-HA-LOO-oo*), a wide expanse of salt-and-pepper sand on a palm-fringed tropical lagoon. The water is usually full of swimmers, snorkelers, and every afternoon at high tide, endangered Hawaiian sea turtles, which glide in to feed on the green algae that flourishes on the lava rocks.

Offshore, from December through April, humpback whales cruise the deep coastal waters that teem with manta rays, spinner dolphins, and other sea creatures. Some of these, such as ahi, mahimahi, and opakapaka, end their days as the daily special, for this is one of the world's best sport-fishing grounds. Only a mile offshore of Honokohau Harbor, trophy Pacific blue marlin and other pelagic fish follow thermal bands in the deep sea. The record, a 1,649-pound marlin hooked on May 16, 1984, is the largest landed so far.

Some local products owe their existence to the 13,679-foot Mauna Loa volcano, which looms over the neighborhood. Rich volcanic soil imparts the distinctive taste to Kona coffee, the only coffee grown in the United States, and also to the cacao beans that go into world-class Kona chocolate.

The Kona Coast is full of history. Ancients established a "place of refuge" on the serene black-sand beach at Honaunau Bay, now the site of a national historical park.

A few miles west, on mile-wide Kealakekua Bay, a white obelisk marks the place where Captain James Cook met his end. Having "discovered" what he named the Sandwich Islands (after the Earl of Sandwich) on January 18, 1778, the British navigator returned a year later. He was killed on the black sands by Hawaiians who decided he was not their god, Lono.

HOW TO GET THERE

◆ The Big Island of Hawaii is a 35-minute jet flight from Honolulu International Airport. From Keahole Airport in Kailua-Kona (15 minutes from the center of town), turn right on Queen Kaahumanu Hwy. (Hwy. 19) and drive south 7 mi. Turn right at Palani Rd. and drive toward the waterfront. To reach the center of Kailua-Kona, turn left on Ali'i Dr., the coastal road. Rental cars are available through the hotels and at the airport, but be aware that there are few gas stations in West Hawaii.

KAHALU'U BEACH PARK

A gorgeous tropical beach with reef-protected lagoons, Kahalu'u is the most popular beach on the Kona Coast, as it was in
olden days. Early Hawaiians built grass
houses and stone heiau on this shore and
called it *Kahalu'u*, which means "The
Diving Place."

Beauty	A
Swimming	B
Sand	A
Amenities	A

Today, it attracts 1,000 people a day almost year-round. They
troop beneath the coconut trees lining the salt-and-pepper
shore and splash in turquoise pools fringed by a black lava rock
breakwater. At 4.3 acres, Kahalu'u is not the biggest beach on
the Big Island, but it's one of the best-equipped, with off-road
parking, beach-gear rentals, a food concession, and visiting
Hawaiian artisans.

It also has Larry Silva, a knowledgeable lifeguard who grew
up on Oahu's North Shore and knows the sea. The view from
his lifeguard stand takes in a New England-style blue-and-white
church on a black lava point, the panoramic Kona Coast, and
1,000 happy, smiling people at the beach. *Drive 5 mi. south on
Ali'i Dr. until you see Kahalu'u Beach Park. Turn right and park in
lot on the south side of beach.*

Swimming: Excellent on left side of protected bay.

Sand: Grainy black-and-white volcanic sand.

Amenities: Rest rooms, showers, picnic tables, pavilion, beach-
gear rentals, snack bar. Lifeguard on duty.

Sports: Snorkeling, scuba diving.

Parking: Ample free parking in lot.

KAMAKAHONU BEACH

Everyone in Hawaii calls it King Kam
Beach because King Kamehameha the
Great lived here from 1812 until his death
in 1819. But it's real name is Kamakahonu
(*Kaw-maw-KA-ho-nu*), or "Eye of the
Turtle," after a rock that looked like a tor-
toise, that is now buried under Kailua Pier.

Beauty	A
Swimming	B
Sand	A
Amenities	B

No matter what you call this beach, everybody sooner or

later hits this sandy equivalent of the town square. The location is ideal, just north of the Kailua Pier, the departure point for charter fishing boats, commercial dive boats, and snorkel cruises down the Kona Coast. Always busy and crowded, this small cove features King Kamehameha's reconstructed royal compound, now a national historical monument. *Off Ali'i Dr. in the center of Kailua-Kona.*
Swimming: Calm, shallow waters, not always clean because of heavy charter fishing and dive boat traffic.
Sand: Imported golden sand.
Amenities: Rest rooms on the pier. No lifeguard.
Sports: Swimming.
Parking: A few free spaces on the street. Pay parking behind King Kamehameha Kona Beach Hotel.

OLD KONA AIRPORT RECREATION AREA

Open, raw coastline, this long stretch of beach adjoins the abandoned Kona Airport, which was closed in 1970 (runways too short for big tourist planes and too noisy for small-town folks). Little known by tourists, this beach-front park is

Beauty	B
Swimming	B
Sand	B
Amenities	C

Kailua-Kona's prime recreation center for picnicking, surfing, and fishing. *From Hwy. 11, turn onto Makala Blvd. and drive tward the waterfront. Turn right on Kuakini Hwy. and drive 1 mi.*
Swimming: Excellent in tide pool lagoons.
Sand: Salt-and-pepper sand.
Amenities: Rest rooms, outdoor showers, picnic tables, barbecue grills. No lifeguard.
Sports: Surfing, snorkeling, fishing from shore and with a spear.
Parking: Ample free parking.

WHITE SANDS BEACH PARK

Blink and you'll miss it as you cruise along Ali'i Drive. Or it may not be there at high tide. It's sometimes called Disappearing Beach because it does just that. Recovered from Hurricane Iniki, White Sands Beach has been restored with imported sand.

Beauty	A
Swimming	A
Sand	B
Amenities	B

From town, drive 4 mi. south on Ali'i Dr. until you see White Sands Beach.

Swimming: Good swimming since the sandbar blocks waves and slows the undertow.

Sand: White.

Amenities: Rest rooms, showers. Lifeguard on duty.

Sports: Surfing in winter, when big waves roll ashore.

Parking: Limited roadside parking.

KEALAKEKUA BAY

Mile-wide Kealakekua (*Kay-ah-la-KAY-koo-ah*) Bay is a diver's dream, an under-water park full of tropical fish, turtles, dolphins, manta rays, and eels. In 1969, the entire bay was declared off-limits to fishing, creating a marine preserve that

Beauty	A
Swimming	A
Sand	B
Amenities	NA

today is the most popular dive spot on the Kona Coast. It is visited daily by dozens of snorkel and glass-bottom boats that set out from the Kona Pier and Keahou Bay. The bay is the last anchorage of Captain James Cook, who was killed here on February 14, 1779, in what British historians call "the fatal catastrophe." *Book a cruise to Kealekukua Bay on a snorkel boat, a glass-bottom boat, or a sailboat. Excursions start and end at Kailua Pier in Kailua-Kona.*

Swimming: Excellent swimming and diving in calm, protected water.

Sand: Black lava rock and pebbly sand.

Amenities: There are rest rooms, food, and dive gear on boats. No lifeguard, but crews are trained in emergency procedures.

Sports: Snorkeling, scuba diving.

HULIHE'E PALACE

This small, handy beach is good for a quick in-town dip, especially on hot Kona afternoons. Hulihe'e (*Hoo-lee-HAY-ay*) is also an excellent place to snorkel because of abundant tropical fish. *Entering town from the north, drive about 1 block south on Ali'i Dr. until you come to Hulihe'e Palace on the right. The beach is*

Beauty	B
Swimming	B
Sand	B
Amenities	B

at the south end of the seawall.

Swimming: Once favored by kings and queens, this is still a royal place to swim. No strong currents or tide; small surf except in winter storms.

Sand: Coarse sand, black lava rocks.

Amenities: Urban beach. Food, drink, and facilities available in nearby stores and restaurants. No lifeguard.

Sports: Excellent snorkeling.

Parking: Free parking one block inland in public lot.

HOTELS/INNS/B&Bs

Kona Coast as a destination is more moderately priced and more diverse than its expensive Kohala neighbors to the north. There are a few luxury resorts, but they're the exception. The fishing village of Kailua-Kona is home to many condominiums and a few hotels, plus there are lots of charming B&Bs hidden throughout the area.

◆ **Kona Village Resort** (very expensive). Staying here is like living a dream of Polynesian life. Built on an ancient village site, the 125 bungalows reflect Pacific island architecture. But old-time grass huts were never like these, clustered among the flowers by the sea, private, romantic, secluded. Right outside the door is a petroglyph field with rare ancient drawings of sails and fishing. *Box 1299, Kailua-Kona, HI 96745; tel. 808-342-84340, 800-367-2111; fax 808-329-4602. 15 mi. north of Kailua-Kona.*

◆ **King Kamehameha's Kona Beach Hotel** (expensive). Large (455 rooms), older beach-front hotel with all bases covered—pool, beach, tennis, restaurants, and lounges. Also, historic sites with free tours every day. Overlooking Kailua Pier, where ships dock and marlin are weighed every afternoon. *75-5660 Palani Rd., Kailua-Kona, HI 96740; tel. 808-329-2911, 800-367-2373; fax 808-923-2566. On the right as you enter the village of Kailua-Kona.*

◆ **Holualoa Inn Bed & Breakfast** (moderate). Four rooms in elegant country estate with spectacular coast views from a high perch over Kailua-Kona area. Estate-grown Kona coffee with breakfast. Pool. Walking distance to art galleries. *Box 222, Holualoa, HI 96725; tel. 808-324-1121, 800-392-1812. A 15-minute drive from Kailua-Kona on Hwy. 11, then up Hualalai Rd.*

◆ **McCandless Ranch Bed & Breakfast** (moderate). Two units beautifully furnished in Monarchy-period style with liberal use of precious koa wood. One room is in the family ranch house overlooking the sea. The other is a separate one-bedroom cottage with indoor/outdoor living room and kitchen. There's a pool in front. It's your once-in-a-lifetime chance to see vanishing Hawaiian crows, which live on this ranch at an altitude of 6,000 feet. *Hookena, HI 96726; tel. 808-328-9313. South of Kona about 20 mi. in Hookena.*

◆ **Merryman's Bed & Breakfast** (moderate). Four rooms are available in a cedar home at the 1,500-foot level above Kealakekua. *Box 474, Kealakekua, HI 96750; tel. 808-323-2276, 800-545-4390.*

◆ **Manago Hotel** (inexpensive). Family-operated hotel for Hawaii travelers since 1917. Famed for its one Japanese-style room with *furo* and tatami mats. *Box 145, Captain Cook, HI 96704; tel. 808-323-2642; fax 808-323-3451. High on the slope of Mauna Loa on Hwy. 11 in Captain Cook.*

◆ **Patey's Place** (inexpensive). Hostel with single or shared rooms. Also, tours around the island. *75-195 Ala Onaona, Kailua-Kona, HI 96740; tel. 808-326-7018, 800-972-7408; fax 808-326-7640. Call from the airport courtesy phone.*

◆ **Rainbow Plantation** (inexpensive). Here's a place where you can sleep among coffee trees. Seven acres devoted to coffee, macadamia nuts, and tropical fruits and flowers surround this B&B. Fresh-roasted Kona coffee for sale, as well as fruit, nuts, and plants. Beaches are about a 20-minute drive downhill. *Box 122, Captain Cook, HI 96704; tel. 808-323-2393, 800-494-2829; fax 808-323-9445. High above the coast near Captain Cook.*

HOUSE RENTALS

◆ **Kanaloa at Kona Condominiums** (expensive). These ocean-front vacation condos are spacious and lavishly furnished, with palatial bathrooms and all housekeeping facilities. The well-managed complex has tennis courts and a pool. *78-261 Manukai St., Kailua-Kona, HI 96740; tel. 808-322-9625; fax 808-322-3818. Waterfront in Keauhou Resort, just south of Kailua-Kona.*

RESTAURANTS

◆ **Chart House** (expensive). Reliable Chart House fare: steaks, prime rib, grilled chicken, fresh fish and seafood, terrific salad bar. Mud Pie tops the dessert menu. *75-5770 Ali'i Dr., Kailua-Kona, HI 96740; tel. 808-329-2451. Open daily for dinner. In Kailua-Kona, a splash away from Kailua Bay.*

◆ **Huggo's** (moderate). Fresh fish, steaks, salad bar, desserts, and bar on a comfortable perch just above the wave tops. The kind of place every seaside town should have. Photos on the walls illustrate amazing fish tales. One of several spots along the Kona Coast where you can watch giant manta rays feed on tiny fish drawn to the night lights. Live music most evenings. *75-5828 Kahakai Rd., Kailua-Kona, HI 96720; tel. 808-329-1493. Open Mon.-Fri. for lunch and daily for dinner and entertainment. On the Kailua-Kona waterfront.*

◆ **Palm Cafe** (moderate). Pacific Rim cuisine in an open-air restaurant overlooking an ocean cove, with such signature dishes as Mahimahi Malia (served on noodle crisps with lobster sauce and coconut cream). Also, Kona pizza with Portuguese sausage and kimchi, and daily pasta specials. Ocean view spectacular at sunset. *75-5819 Ali'i Dr., Kailua-Kona, HI 96740; tel. 808-329-7765. Open daily for dinner. At Coconut Grove Marketplace.*

◆ **Sam Choy's Restaurant** (moderate). Choy is one of the creative chefs of the Hawaii regional cuisine school. He prepares fresh island fare in dishes with local, Asia/Pacific, and Western flair. Reservations for dinner advised. *735576 Kauhola 1, Kailua-Kona, HI 96740; tel. 808-326-1545. Open Mon.-Sat. for breakfast and Wed.-Sat. for dinner. North of Kailua-Kona village in the Koloko Light Industrial Center complex by the Costco store.*

NIGHTLIFE

◆ **Don Drysdale's Club 53.** Sports bar with TV for watching events. Light-fare menu and cocktails. *Kona Inn Shopping Village, Kailua-Kona, HI 96740; tel. 808-329-6651. Open daily. Waterfront in Kailua village. Drysdale's Two is at the Keauhou Shopping Village.*

◆ **Kona Village Luau.** Many consider this the best commercial luau in the state, mostly because of its genuine hospitality and ample, authentic feast, including all the opihi (limpets) you can eat, as well as kalua pig baked in an underground oven out front. The Polynesian show is not too slick—more like a backyard family party. *Box 1299, Kailua-Kona, HI 96745; tel. 808-325-5555, 800-367-5290. Friday nights at 5. Admission. 8 mi. north of Keahole Airport.*

ATTRACTIONS

◆ **Classic Aviation Bi-planes.** Flight-seeing in replica of 1935 Waco biplane with open cockpit big enough for two passengers. Also, aerobatic flights. Call for reservations. *Box 1899, Kailua-Kona, HI 96745; tel. 808-329-8687, 800-695-8100; fax 808-329-0781. Admission. At Keahole Airport.*

◆ **Ellison S. Onizuka Space Center.** Small museum of space travel dedicated to the memory of Kealakekua's own astronaut, killed in the *Challenger* accident. Moon rock on display, plus a maneuvering unit where you can strap in and rendezvous with a space object. Video theater. *Box 833, Kailua-Kona, HI 96745; tel. 808-329-3441. Open daily 8:30-4:30. Admission. At Keahole Airport.*

◆ **Royal Kona Coffee Mill & Museum.** Self-guided tour, video of coffee farming in Kona, gift shop, and free coffee. *Box 829, Captain Cook, HI 96704; tel. 808-328-2511. Open daily 9-5. On Hwy. 11 in Honaunau.*

SHOPPING

◆ **Alapaki's.** Local artisans' works, including bowls, carvings, and sculptures made of local woods. Hawaiian quilt pillow kits, feather art, kukui (candlenut) items, and hula instruments, such as feathered *uliuli* rattles and coconut *pahu* drums. *Keauhou Shopping Center, Keauhou-Kona, HI 967050; tel. 808-322-2007. Open daily. From Kailua-Kona, drive south 5 mi. on Ali'i Dr. to intersection with Kamehameha III Rd. Look for shopping center on left.*

◆ **Holualoa Gallery.** Local potter/painter displays own works and works of other local artists. *Box 773, Holualoa, HI 96725; tel.*

808-322-8484. Open Tue.-Sat. 10-5. In Holualoa artists village on Hwy. 180, about 15 minutes' drive above Kailua-Kona.

◆ **Island Orchid Co.** Hawaiian tropical flowers, direct from local growers. *75-6082 Ali'i Dr., Kailua-Kona, HI 96740; tel. 808-326-2266, 800-622-0230. Open Mon.-Sat. In Casa de Emdeko.*

◆ **Kealakekua's Grass Shack.** A wide variety of items: Hawaiian carved koa wood bowls, Niihau shell leis, woven lauhala (pandanus tree leaves) hats, black coral. Old-fashioned Hawaiian music tapes and records. Tapa cloth and other Pacific crafts. *Box 1, Kealakekua, HI 96750; tel. 808-323-2877. Open daily. 15 minutes' drive south of Kailua-Kona on Hwy. 11.*

◆ **Kimura Lauhala Shop.** One of the few remaining shops of its kind, it specializes in handcrafted items of lauhala. *Box 32, Holualoa, HI 96725; tel. 808-324-0053. Open Mon.-Sat. 9-5. In Holualoa, a 15-minute drive above Kailua-Kona.*

◆ **Summerhouse.** Country collectibles, Hawaii-style. *Kaiwi Square, Kailua-Kona, HI 96740; tel. 808-329-7223. Open Mon.-Sat.*

BEST FOOD SHOPS

SANDWICHES: ◆ **Don Drysdale's Club 53.** Sandwiches, soups, snacks, salads, buffalo burgers. *Kona Inn Shopping Village, Kailua-Kona, HI 96740; tel. 808-329-6651. Open daily.*

SEAFOOD: ◆ **Kona Seafood Inc.** This seafood market has the freshest fish and the best prices in the Kona district. *Box 407, Honaunau, HI 96726; tel. 808-328-9777. Open daily. In the new seafood market at the 106-mi. marker on Hwy. 11 at Honaunau.*

FRESH PRODUCE: ◆ **KTA Super Stores.** *Kona Coast Shopping Center, Kailua-Kona, HI 96740; tel. 808-329-1677. Open daily.*

BAKERY: ◆ **French Bakery.** French breads, pastries, cookies, sandwiches. *Kaahumanu Plaza, Kailua-Kona, HI 96740; tel. 808-326-2688. Open Mon.-Sat.*

ICE CREAM: ◆ **Baskin Robbins.** *Lanihau Center, Kailua-Kona, HI 96740; tel. 808-329-5144. Open daily.*

BEVERAGES: ◆ **Kona Healthway.** *Kona Coast Shopping Center, Kailua-Kona, HI 96740; tel. 808-329-2296. Open daily.*

WINE: ◆ **Kona Wine Market.** *75-5626 Kuakini Hwy., Kailua-Kona, HI 6740; tel. 808-329-9400. Open daily.*

SPORTS

FISHING

Home of world-record Pacific blue marlin, Kona is a sport-fishing capital with a calendar full of big-money tournaments. Boats don't have to go far to catch deep-water fish, because the ocean depth gauge starts dropping to 14,000 feet right outside Honokohau Harbor. If you want to splurge and charter a fishing boat, this is the place to do it.

◆ **Kona Activities Center.** Sets up individual charters or group fishing tournaments. By reservation. *75-252 Nani Kailua Dr., Kailua-Kona, HI 96740; tel. 808-329-3171.*

◆ **Kona Charter Skippers Association.** Full range of prices and options on boats from 26 to 62 feet in length. By reservation. *75-5663 Palani Rd., Kailua-Kona, HI 96740; tel. 808-329-3600, 800-762-7546.*

BOATING

◆ **Capt. Dan McSweeney's Year-Round Whale Watch.** McSweeney knows his whales and guarantees passengers will see at least one or come again free. Besides the seasonal humpbacks that winter in Hawaii, six other species are out there, plus dolphin. A video-camera mounted under the boat films the mammals as they swim below. Proceeds benefit the Wild Whale Research Foundation. Three- to four-hour tours by reservation. *Box 139, Holualoa, HI 96725; tel. 808-322-0028; fax 808-322-2732. Open Tue., Thu., and Sat. Jul.-Dec.; daily Dec.-Apr. Cruises from Honokohau Harbor.*

◆ **Capt. Zodiac Raft Expeditions.** Zippy ride down the South Coast to Kealakekua for snorkeling. Historical narration and sea cave exploration on the way. Snacks and drinks are included. Whale watching in season. By reservation. *Box 5612, Kailua-Kona, HI 96745; tel. 808-329-3199, 800-422-7824; fax 808-329-7590.*

◆ **Captain Bob's Glassbottom Boat.** One-hour tour of the Kona Coast, showing what's above and below the water. Boat glides over thousands of tropical fish, various kinds of coral, lava tubes and arches, and a steep drop-off, not to mention turtles, flying fish, and whales in winter season. *78-7047 Mamalahoa Hwy., Holualoa, HI 96725; 808-322-3102. Operates daily.*

DIVING

◆ **Fair Wind Snorkel & Dive.** Morning cruises from Keauhou Bay to Kealakekua underwater park, with a barbecue lunch and snorkeling. Introductory or advanced dives are available. Afternoon cruises for snorkelers and divers. Custom charters available for sunset cocktail and dinner cruises aboard a 50-foot catamaran. *78-7130 Kaleiopapa St., Kailua-Kona, HI 96740; tel. 808-322-2788, 800-677-9461; fax 808-324-1772. Sails daily.*

◆ ***Kona Aggressor II.*** Four-day to weekly charters on luxury live-aboard 80-foot catamaran for up to ten diver passengers. Jacuzzi, chef, video equipment. By reservation. *74-5588 Pawai Pl., Bldg. F, Kailua-Kona, HI 96740; tel. 808-329-8182, 800-344-5662; fax 808-329-2628.*

◆ **Kona Coast Divers.** Day and night dives, high-tech training, custom boats. By reservation. *75-5614 Palani Rd., Kailua-Kona, HI 96740; tel. 808-329-8802.*

BICYCLING

◆ **Chris' Adventures Bike or Hike.** Statewide tour operations. Includes Coffee Trek, a day-long bike/snorkel tour on Wednesdays and Sundays. *Box 869, Kula, HI 96790; tel. 808-326-4600, 800-224-5344.*

◆ **DJ's Rentals.** This shop rents motorized bikes ranging from mopeds to Harley Davidsons. *75-5663 Palani Rd., Kailua-Kona, HI 96740; tel. 808-329-1700. Open daily. Across from King Kamehameha hotel.*

GOLF

◆ **Kona Country Club/Ali'i Country Club.** Two 18-hole courses: the par-72 Kona (ocean) course and the par-72 Ali'i (hillside) course, both designed by William Bell. Pro shop, rentals, restaurant, clubhouse, lessons, driving range. *78-7000 Ali'i Dr., Kailua-Kona, HI 96740; tel. 808-322-3431, 808-322-2595; fax 808-322-3361. Open daily. Admission. Keauhou Resort area, just south of Kailua-Kona.*

TENNIS

◆ **Mauna Loa Village Resort (Holua Sports).** Complex of 14 courts with lighting on 7. Private and group lessons, daily clinics, tennis aerobics, rentals, ball machines. *78-7190 Kaleipapa Rd., Kailua-Kona, HI 96740; tel. 808-322-0091, 800-829-9661. Open daily. Admission. In the Keauhou Resort area, just south of Kailua-Kona.*

HORSEBACK RIDING

◆ **Fallbrook Trail Rides.** Guided one- and two-hour rides, just up from Kailua-Kona on grassy bridle paths through a fern forest. Ocean views and wildlife, including pheasant and turkey. *Box 1243, Kailua-Kona, HI 96740; tel. 808-322-1818.*

HISTORY

◆ **Ahuena Heiau, Inc.** Ancient Ahuena Heiau is considered Hawaii's most significant historic site. It was first restored by King Kamehameha after he settled his family and court at Kailua-Kona in 1812, having united the islands. The 15th-century stone platform, surrounded by 14-foot-tall wooden images, was the site of Kamehameha's funeral rites in 1819 and the place where his wife and son brought down the Hawaiian religion by simply eating together, violating a strict kapu (taboo). *75-5660 Palani Rd., Kailua-Kona, HI 96740. Outdoor monument that may be seen anytime. Waterfront by King Kamehameha hotel.*

◆ **Hulihe'e Palace.** Victorian summer palace of the Hawaiian royalty a century or so ago. Built in 1838. Now a museum with rare artifacts. *75-5718 Ali'i Dr., Kailua-Kona, HI 96740; tel. 808-329-1877. Open daily 9-4. Admission. Central Kailua-Kona waterfront.*

◆ **Place of Refuge National Historic Park.** Peaceful six-acre ancient refuge meant protection of the Hawaiian gods and absolution by their priests for fugitives, guilty or innocent. Reconstructed temple site, artifacts. Good interpretive programs demonstrate weaving and other ancient skills. Annual summer cultural festival in late June. *Box 129, Honaunau, HI 96726; tel. 808-328-2288. Open daily 6 a.m.-midnight. Admission. Beach front at Honaunau, 4 mi. south of Kealakekua Bay.*

NATURE

◆ **Hawaii Forest & Trail.** Experienced naturalist leads small groups on hikes into native forests and up into the volcanic high country, including a trek on Hualalai, the volcano behind the Kona Coast. Walks tailored to participants' abilities. Lunch and drinks provided. By reservation. Airport or hotel pick up. *Box 2975, Kailua-Kona, HI 96745; tel. 808-322-8881, 800-464-1993. Admission.*

◆ **The Exploration Company.** Eco-tours for the whole family. Kayak to the Captain Cook monument and old Hawaiian village ruins during a four-hour paddle passing several historic sites. Other adventures: a walk in the cloud forest, a nighttime manta ray watch, and whale watching in winter. Call for reservations. *75-5669 Ali'i Dr., Kailua-Kona, HI 96740; tel. 808-327-9409. Admission.*

TOURIST INFORMATION

◆ **Hawaii Visitors Bureau, Big Island Chapter.** *75-5719 W. Ali'i Dr., Kailua-Kona, HI 96740; tel. 808-329-7787. Open Mon.-Fri. 8-4:30.*

CHAPTER 20

Waipio

On the Big Island's north coast of Hamakua, seven valleys open to the Pacific in 12 miles. The best known is Waipio (*Why-PEE-o*), because it is the most accessible. It also happens to have a spectacular black-sand beach.

Beauty	A
Swimming	B
Sand	B
Hotels/Inns/B&Bs	C
House rentals	NA
Restaurants	B
Nightlife	NA
Attractions	C
Shopping	D
Sports	A
Nature	A

The mile-long strand stretches in a coal-black line between the deep blue sea and the green floor of the lush, U-shaped valley once inhabited by Hawaii's kings. From the bay at its mouth, Waipio Valley sweeps back six miles between vertical walls with 2,000-foot-high waterfalls. Here, 40,000 Hawaiians once lived in a Garden of Eden amid ever-green taro, red bananas, and wild guavas.

In 1823, William Ellis marveled at "the beauty of the romantic valley with its numerous inhabitants, cottages, plantations, fishponds, and meandering streams, on the surface of which the light canoe was moving to and fro."

It's still an idyllic spot today, and possibly quieter. Only about 50 people live in the valley, tending taro, fishing, and soaking up the ambience of this special place.

The beach is unforgettable, fronted by big dunes and creased with a stream. The water is bold and full of rip currents. Winter brings monster waves that create dangerous conditions for all but experienced surfers.

In the 1960s, the Peace Corps used Waipio Valley to train candidates for tropical assignments in Southeast Asia, Latin America, and Africa, and public access was limited. Today, it should be a required stop for all who come to the Big Island on vacation. Although the valley is located on the windward coast, rainfall is much less than the saturation levels of nearby Hilo.

Most visitors drive to the lookout to stand in awe and take photographs. It's a perfect picnic spot, too. But steadfast beach-goers will book three nights to explore the beach, the valley, and the waterfalls. There are a few places to stay in the valley, or you can check into one of the inns or B&Bs around Honokaa (*see* Hotels/Inns/B&Bs).

Some hardy folks hike the mile-long trail into the valley, and even hardier ones hike back out. Others take the Waipio Valley Shuttle, a four-wheel-drive van that readily negotiates a slope every bit as steep as San Francisco's Nob Hill. It heads down a paved, one-lane road that hugs the cliff as it descends 2,300 to the valley floor.

The 90-minute excursion loops out to the beach and up into the valley. You can be dropped off for exploring or horseback riding, then catch a later shuttle back up to the lookout.

HOW TO GET THERE

◆ The Big Island of Hawaii is a 35-minute jet flight from Honolulu International Airport. From Keahole Airport in Kailua-Kona (1 1/2 hours from Waipio Valley Lookout), turn left on Queen Kaahumanu Hwy. (Hwy. 19) and drive 34 mi. to Kawaihae Rd. Turn right and head for the town of Waimea, where you turn left onto Mamalahoa Rd. (still Hwy. 19). Take this into the town of Honokaa and turn left onto Kukuihaele Rd. (Hwy. 240), which leads to Waipio Valley Lookout in about 9 mi. Rental cars are available at the airport. Be aware that there are few gas stations after Kailua-Kona, although you will find them in Waikoloa Village and Waimea.

WAIPIO BEACH

Swimming: Often dangerous because of riptides and strong currents in the open ocean.
Sand: Coarse black lava, hot underfoot.
Amenities: No public facilities. No lifeguard.
Sports: Surfing, surf casting. Bring your own gear. There are no shops or rentals in the area.
Parking: Ample free parking at Waipio Valley Lookout.

HOTELS/INNS/B&Bs

Accommodations in and around Waipio Valley are the opposite of those in Hawaiian resort areas with hundreds of tourists. Only a few people each day can descend the barely passable four-wheel-drive track down the 1,000-foot cliff to enter the valley. A handful of lodgings accommodates guests for short stays. In Honokaa, the nearest town to the valley, there are homey country stores, cafés, and B&Bs.

◆ **Waipio Valley Treehouse** (expensive). A 200-square-foot tree house 30 feet up in a monkeypod tree and two cottages constitute Linda Beech's unusual bed-and-breakfast. She taps the 1,000-foot Papala Falls for power and solar-heats spring water for hot tubs. Solar power operates refrigerators as well. All units have kitchens, housekeeping necessities, books, and games. Swimming in waterfall pool. Beach is an easy two-mile hike. *Box 5086, Honokaa, HI 96727; tel. 808-775-7160. Transportation provided from Waipio Lookout.*

◆ **Waipio Wayside B&B Inn** (moderate). Five-room inn in a renovated sugar plantation home, about a ten-minute drive from Waipio Lookout. Ask for the Library Room, which overlooks the ocean and has a double bed, full bath, and 400 books. *Box 840, Honokaa, HI 96727; tel. 808-775-0275, 800-833-8849; fax 808-775-0275. 2 mi. up from Honokaa, toward Waipio Valley on Hwy. 240. Look for sign and a long white picket fence.*

◆ **Hale Kukui** (inexpensive). Perched 600 feet above the water on an ocean cliff overlooking Waipio Valley and the sea, it has a fabulous view for 20 miles along the Big Island's north coast. Guest cottage can be used as either a studio, two-bedroom, or three-bedroom unit. Natural pool for swimming. *Box 5044, Kukuihaele, HI 96727; tel. 808-775-7130, 800-444-7130. From Honokaa, take Hwy. 240 all the way to the end. Turn right, then, 100 feet later, turn right again on a twisty paved road. Go 1/8 mi.*

◆ **Luana Ola Guest Cottages** (inexpensive). Two cottages on two acres near shops, restaurants, and theater. Both sleep up to four, with kitchenette and laundry. Great views of Hamakua Coast, sunsets, and the island of Maui across the channel. *Box 430, Honokaa, HI 96727; tel. 808-775-7727, 800-357-7727. From Honokaa's main street, go toward the sea on Maile St. Take the second left, Kawila St., and look for the sign on the left.*

◆ **Waipio Hotel** (inexpensive). Five rooms with no electricity, no refrigeration, and no hot showers at this rustic forest lodge in the Waipio Valley. Yet there's always a problem getting reservations. *25 Malama Pl., Hilo, HI 96720; tel. 808-775-0368. From Waipio Valley Lookout, go down steep road to the valley floor. Pass taro fields, cross over a stream, and look for the hotel on the right.*

RESTAURANTS

◆ **Hotel Honokaa Club** (moderate). Casual dining in a newly restored restaurant at this old sugar planter's hotel. Ocean view. Hearty American fare, including roast beef and ribs, but everyone seems to go for the Japanese dinner with miso soup, pickled vegetables, ahi sashimi, and grilled butterfish with miso or teriyaki sauce. *Box 247, Honokaa, HI 96727; tel. 808-775-0678. Open daily for breakfast, lunch, and dinner.*

◆ **Jolene's Kau Kau Korner** (inexpensive). Tasty Hawaiian-style plate lunches feature Korean *kalbi* ribs, Spam, rice, potato salad, and macaroni. *45-3625 Mamane St., Honokaa, HI 96727; tel. 808-775-9498. Open Mon.-Fri. for lunch and dinner, Sat. for lunch. At the corner of Mamane and Lehua, as you come into town.*

ATTRACTIONS

◆ **Waipio Valley Shuttle.** Off-road tour of Waipio Valley—90 minutes with narration of local history and lore, transportation to and from Waipio Lookout. Reservations required. *Box 5128,*

Honokaa, HI 96727; tel. 808-775-7121; fax 808-775-9911. Open Mon.-Sat. Tours leave hourly 8-4. Admission. Meet at Waipio Lookout.

◆ **Waipio Valley Wagon Tours.** Mule-drawn wagon ride through the lush tropical valley, along a stream and through a green jungle thick with mountain apple and fragrant ginger. Reservations required. *Box 1340, Honokaa, HI 96727; tel. 808-775-9518; fax 808-775-9538. Operates four rides Mon.-Sat. starting at 9:30. Admission. Transportation provided from Waipio Lookout.*

SHOPPING

◆ **Hawaiian Macadamia Plantation.** Stop in to purchase the tasty nuts grown in Honokaa, which calls itself the macadamia nut capital of the world. *Honokaa, HI 96727; tel. 808-775-7743. Open daily. Heading toward Waipio Lookout on Hwy. 240, it's at the bottom of the hill, 1 mi. past the post office.*

SPORTS
HORSEBACK RIDING

◆ **Waipio Naalapa Trail Ride.** Two-hour guided trail ride through Waipio Valley with guide who knows area history and legend. Reservations required. *Box 992, Honokaa, HI 96727; tel. 808-775-0419; fax 808-775-9318. Rides Mon.-Sat. at 9:30 and 1. Transportation to and from Waipio Look.*

◆ **Waipio On Horseback.** Guided horseback trail rides and off-road van tours of Waipio Valley twice daily. *Box 183, Honokaa, HI 96727; tel. 808-775-7291; fax 808-775-9888. Rides and tours Mon.-Sat. at 9:30 and 1:30. Meet at Waipio Lookout for transportation into valley.*

HISTORY

◆ **Katsu Goto Memorial.** Katsu Goto, one of the first indentured Japanese immigrants, arrived in Honokaa in the late 1800s to work on a sugar plantation. He learned English, quit the plantation, opened a shop, and aided his fellow immigrants in labor disputes with American sugar planters. He was murdered, and his body was hung from a lamp post in Honokaa on October 23, 1889, a victim of local-style justice. *Honokaa, HI 96727. Next to the library at the Hilo end of town.*

NATURE

◆ **Kalopa State Park Nature Trail.** Seven-mile self-guided hike through 615-acre upland reserve of native Hawaiian rain forest, which has many species of rare plants. *Tel. 808-775-7114. Off Hwy. 19, about 4 mi. in the direction of Hilo from Honokaa.*

TOURIST INFORMATION

◆ **Hawaii Visitors Bureau, Big Island Chapter.** *250 Keawe St., Hilo, HI 96720; tel. 808-961-5797. Open Mon.-Fri. 8-12, 1-4:30.*

CHAPTER 21

Leleiwi

Everyone will tell you that Hilo is a great place if you're a fern. It's usually moist and damp, with an average annual rainfall of 128 inches, highest in Hawaii for a coastal area. While that's ideal growing conditions for such exotic tropical flowers as orchids and anthuriums, it's less than perfect for beachgoers in search of rays.

Umbrellas outsell bikinis in Hilo (*HEE-lo*), and there's not much call for sunscreen. It's sort of a tropical version of Seattle. But this quaint town on the Big Island's northeast coast has genuine appeal, a multitude of flowers, and striking black-sand beaches. When the sun shines in Hilo, people bloom and flowers wilt.

Beauty	A
Swimming	B-
Sand	B
Hotels/Inns/B&Bs	A
House rentals	C
Restaurants	B
Nightlife	C
Attractions	A
Shopping	A
Sports	A
Nature	A

It's an exciting terrain by any standard. Some of Hawaii's most beautiful waterfalls are a short drive from town, and red-hot Kilauea, the world's most active volcano, rumbles occasionally at a safe distance. The big, blue Pacific is at the doorstep.

Hilo has a fine collection of beaches, if you know where to look. Swimmers take the plunge at Leleiwi Beach Park, one of Hawaii's most beautiful coastal playgrounds. Bayfront Beach Park, an underappreciated black-sand beach, stretches for nearly a mile at the head of Hilo Bay, right in the center of town. Picnickers prefer Coconut Island, and surfers head for either Honoli'i Beach Park or James Kealoha Park, known locally as Four Miles.

An old seaport and planter's town that almost died when the Hawaii sugar industry collapsed, Hilo (population 45,000) is enjoying a comeback as a historic district, with old stores revived as galleries, restaurants, and shops. Even murky Hilo Bay is making a recovery since the sugar mills shut down.

Several inexpensive bay-front hotels and new bed-and-breakfasts make Hilo one of the best vacation bargains in Hawaii, but be forewarned: It can rain three days out of seven. That's why Hilo never attracted the hordes of tourists found in Kailua-Kona, on the other side of the island. A neighborhood volcano may also make tourists wary. In the spring of 1984, Mauna Loa erupted and sent a river of lava to within four miles of town. It made for an exciting day at the beach.

LELEIWI BEACH PARK

Unlike any other beach in the islands, scenic Leleiwi (*Lay-lay-EE-vee*) is a tropical study in green, blue, and black. The black pebble beach curves in and out around palm-fringed, green-water ponds dotted by black rock islets that stand out

Beauty	A
Swimming	B
Sand	B
Amenities	B

against the cobalt-blue Pacific. It's a photographer's delight.

Open-air baths fit for a king or queen, these shallow pools are

HOW TO GET THERE

◆ The Big Island of Hawaii is a 35-minute jet flight from Honolulu International Airport. From Hilo Airport (10 minutes from downtown Hilo), turn right on Kanoelehua Ave. (Hwy. 11) and drive about 1 mi. to where it intersects with Bayfront Hwy. and Banyan Dr. Go straight on Banyan Dr. for waterfront hotels. Turn left on Bayfront Hwy. to reach Bayfront Park. At the same spot, you turn right on Kalaniana'ole Ave. to reach Leleiwi Beach. Rental cars and small four-wheel-drive vehicles are available through the hotels and at Hilo Airport.

generally free of currents and are ideal for families with children, especially in the protected inlets at the center of the beach park.

Lelewei is one of the most popular snorkel spots in Hawaii, with an abundance of tropical fish and endangered sea turtles seeking safe haven in this natural refuge. Next door, the Richardson Ocean Center is a marine life education facility with interpretive displays. *From downtown Hilo, drive east on Bayfront Hwy. and, where it intersects with Kanoelehua Ave. (Hwy. 11), bear left on Kalaniana'ole Ave. and drive 4 mi. to the beach.*
Swimming: Shallow, calm water, ideal for beginners.
Sand: Not exactly sandy, the coast is lined mostly with smooth black pebbles of eroded lava chunks.
Amenities: Rest rooms, showers, marine education center. Lifeguards on duty.
Sports: Body boarding on gentle miniwaves. Snorkeling.
Parking: Ample off-road parking.

JAMES KEALOHA BEACH PARK

A beautiful bay with islands, lagoons, and fishponds, Kealoha Beach Park is named in honor of James Kealoha (*Kay-ah-LO-hah*), a Hilo grocer's son who was elected Hawaii's first lieutenant governor after Hawaii became the 50th state in 1959. He

Beauty	A
Swimming	B
Sand	B
Amenities	B

died in 1983 at the age of 75. Locals call it Four Miles, because it's exactly four miles from the downtown post office, once the center of all measured miles in Hilo. *From downtown Hilo, drive east on Bayfront Hwy. and, where it intersects with Kanoelehua Ave. (Hwy. 11), bear left on Kalaniana'ole Ave. and drive 3 mi. to the beach.*
Swimming: Excellent in the lagoon for children.
Sand: Mostly black-lava sand with occasional patches of crushed white coral.
Amenities: Rest rooms, showers, picnic tables, pavilion. Lifeguard on duty.
Sports: Body boarding, surfing.
Parking: Ample off-road parking.

HILO BAYFRONT BEACH PARK

It was once the jewel in the crown of this coast. In the days of steamships, visitors arrived on this famous strand in rowboats to discover a tropical scene like no other: a broad, flat beach meeting the curve of the bay, black sand as fine as pepper, a

Beauty	A
Swimming	B
Sand	B
Amenities	C

small beach town under coconut palms at the foot of a snow-capped, nearly three-mile-high volcano.

The scene remains, but the beach has changed dramatically. After several tidal waves scoured Hilo, the town was relocated inland and uphill. Hilo Bay, the principal seaport for the Big Island, was dredged to accommodate deep-draft vessels. Sugar-mill wastes spoiled the beach and the bay, virtually ending fishing, crabbing, and the old Hawaiian way of life.

Since the sugar mills went bankrupt, the water quality has improved, but the tepid bay water needs stirring. A Save the Bay coalition suggested breaching the Hilo Bay breakwater to replenish the water, but no action was taken. *Coming from the airport on Hwy. 11, just before town take the Bayfront Hwy. exit to the beach.*

Swimming: The bay water is still murky.

Sand: Fine black sand is hot underfoot when the sun shines.

Amenities: Portable toilets. No lifeguard.

Sports: Sailing, kayaking. The Kamehameha Canoe Club and the Puna Canoe Club launch outrigger canoes here.

Parking: Ample off-road parking.

HONOLI'I BEACH PARK

This small black-sand beach rates a mention only because it's the most popular surf break on this coast. Honoli'i (*Ho-no-LEE-ee*) is also a scenic, shady spot thanks to a waterfall-fed steam that runs through the park to the ocean. *Drive 5 mi. out of*

Beauty	A
Swimming	D
Sand	B
Amenities	C

town on the Belt Rd. (Hwy. 19). Turn left at Pauka'a and follow the old road to the beach.

Swimming: A small pool at the north end of the beach is safe for swimming. Ocean swimming is not advised for beginners. The boulder-strewn bottom drops to deep water fast, and rip currents swipe the shore.

Sand: Grainy black sand mixed with dirt from runoff and bits of beach glass.

Amenities: Rest rooms, showers, paved path from road to beach. No lifeguard.

Sports: High surf makes it ideal for surfers.

Parking: Roadside.

HOTELS/INNS/B&Bs

This charming, historic gateway to the volcanoes is a delightful old city where the yards are filled with beautiful orchids and the hotels, although far from fancy, are reasonable and uncrowded.

◆ **Hawaii Naniloa Hotel** (moderate). Not luxurious by today's standards, perhaps, but replete with amenities: pools, restaurant, bar, shops, spa. Free car included in room rate. *93 Banyan Dr., Hilo, HI 96720; tel. 808-969-3333, 800-367-5360; fax 808-969-6622. Ocean front on Banyan Dr.*

◆ **Hilo Hawaiian Hotel** (moderate). This 285-room bay-front hotel is near the Queen Liliuokalani Japanese Garden, with Coconut Island a short way offshore. Pool, restaurant, bar, evening music, ocean views. Rate includes free rental car or free sixth night stay. Local travelers often stay here. *71 Banyan Dr., Hilo, HI 96720; tel. 808-935-9361, 800-367-5004; fax 808-961-9642. On Banyan Dr., fronting Hilo Bay.*

◆ **Arnott's Lodge and Hiking Adventures** (inexpensive). Rock-bottom rates, starting with bunks, for budget travelers. Besides a place to sleep, the lodge offers to take guests hiking to see the volcano, stargazing atop Mauna Kea, and discovering other parts of the Big Island outdoor wonderland. *98 Apapane Rd., Hilo, HI 96720; tel. 808-969-7097, 800-368-8752; fax 808-961-9638. Free pickup from Hilo Airport.*

◆ **Haili House** (inexpensive). Hawaiian-style bed-and-breakfast with five bedrooms in a 1922 home decorated in vintage decor. Front-porch lanai for watching the town and complimentary use of umbrellas for strolling. *239 Haili St., Hilo, HI 96720; tel. 808-969-7378. Across from Lyman House Museum in midtown Hilo.*

◆ **Pi'ihonua Bed & Breakfast** (inexpensive). Separate studio above a garage sleeps up to four (children welcome), with kitchenette and Hawaiiana decor. Located beside lush forest preserve, in the direction of Rainbow Falls. *875 Ainako Ave., Hilo, HI 96720; tel. 808-935-6041; fax 808-961-2589. 1 mi. off Kaumana Dr. on Rte. 200 above Hilo.*

HOUSE RENTALS

◆ **Hawaii's Best Bed & Breakfasts.** Islandwide bed-and-breakfast and vacation-rental accommodations, including some in Hilo. *Box 563, Kamuela, HI 96743; tel. 808-885-4550, 800-262-9912; fax 808-885-0559. Open daily.*

RESTAURANTS

◆ **Cafe Pesto** (moderate). Wood-fired pizzas, calzones, pastas, seafood, soup, and salads, all done with flair in a kind of Italian/Southwest/Pacific approach. You'll get the idea after a taste of Asian duck tacos, seafood paella, and ceviche pasta salad. *308 Kamehameha Ave., Hilo, HI 96720; tel. 808-969-6640. Open daily for lunch and dinner. In the restored historic South Hata Building, facing Hilo Bay in downtown Hilo.*

◆ **Harrington's** (moderate). Pleasant, casual indoor/outdoor restaurant overlooking a quiet bay. Specialties include fresh fish, seafood, prime rib, and "Slavic steak" with a tasty sauce. Live music, usually contemporary Hawaiian, Wednesday through Sunday. *135 Kalanianaole Ave., Hilo, HI 96720; tel. 808-961-4966. Open daily for dinner. Near the end of Banyan Dr.*

◆ **Lehua's Bay City Bar & Grill** (moderate). American food with Hawaiian touches, such as grilled chicken with lime marinade and papaya salsa. Entertainment until 2 a.m. on weekends. *11 Waianuenue Ave., Hilo, HI 96720; tel. 808-935-8055. Open daily for lunch and dinner. Bay front in downtown Hilo.*

◆ **Roussel's** (moderate). New Orleans-influenced dishes with local ingredients. A Creole touch right in Hilo, the restaurant stages a Mardi Gras parade every year. *6060 Keawe St., Hilo, HI 96720; tel. 808-935-5111; fax 808-935-1285. Open daily for dinner, Mon.-Fri for lunch. In downtown Hilo.*

NIGHTLIFE

◆ **Waioli Lounge.** Hawaiian contemporary groups perform nightly. Free *pupu* ("appetizers") served from 4 to 6 p.m. *Hilo Hawaiian Hotel, 71 Banyan Dr., Hilo, HI 96720; tel. 808-935-9361. Open daily.*

ATTRACTIONS

Hilo's abundant rainfall (averaging 128 inches per year) and rich volcanic soil make for fabulous gardens, and much of Hawaii's commercial flower and fruit crop is grown here. Tour the gardens, nurseries, and public areas to see this riot of orchids, anthuriums, ginger, and other showy blooms.

◆ **Hawaii Tropical Botanical Gardens.** A rain forest expedition through 20 Eden-like acres of tropical flowers and trees grown into giants in the sea mists of Onomea Bay. Torch gingers taller than a man, rare orchids, bamboo groves, and spiky bromeliads, all in a natural outdoor setting. Sea turtles float in the picturesque bay. *RR 143-A, Papaikou HI 96781; tel. 808-964-5233. Open Mon.-Sat. 8:30-4:30, Sun. 9-4:30. Admission. 4 mi. north of Hilo on the Hawaii Belt Rd. (Rte. 19) at Onomea.*

◆ **Mauna Loa Macadamia Nut Orchards.** Visitors center at world's largest (5,000 acres) mac nut plantation features video, self-guided orchard and factory tour, free samples of the delectable treat. *Hilo, HI 96720; tel. 808-966-8618. Open daily 8:30-5. Off Hwy. 11 on Macadamia Rd. 8 mi. up from Hilo.*

◆ **Nani Mau Gardens and Botanical Museum.** Twenty acres of landscaped gardens to tour on foot or on a narrated tram ride. Botanical museum, restaurant, gift shop. *421 Malalika St., Hilo, HI 96720; tel. 808-959-3541. Open daily 8-5. Admission. Driving up Rte. 11 from Hilo Airport, take a left on Makalika between mile markers 3 and 4.*

◆ **Suisan Fish Auction.** The catch of the day by the Hilo fishing fleet is unloaded, weighed, and then sold at auction in a rapid-fire mixture of English and Hawaiian. Onlookers watch the buyers walk from pallet to pallet selecting yellowfin tuna (ahi), other tropical fish, and squid. *85 Lihiwai, Hilo, HI 96720; tel. 808-935-8051; fax 808-935-2115. Opens Mon.-Sat. at about 7:30 a.m. A short walk from Banyan Dr. hotels along the shore.*

SHOPPING

◆ **Dreams of Paradise.** Nature art of the Big Island plus koa furniture, antiques, textiles, gourmet foods. Mail orders too. *308 Kamehameha Ave., Suite 106, Hilo, HI 96720; tel. 808-935-5670. Open daily. Downtown Hilo bay front.*

◆ **Mauna Kea Galleries.** Gallery of antique and vintage Hawaiian and Polynesian art, including rare books, photos, paintings, heirloom quilts, artifacts. *276 Keawe St., Hilo, HI 96720; tel. 808-969-1184. Open Mon.-Wed., Fri., Sat. In downtown Hilo.*

◆ **Sig Zane Designs.** Contemporary Hawaiian garb by a local designer. Women's clothing and aloha shirts for men. *122 Kamehameha Ave., Hilo, HI 96720; tel. 808-935-7077; fax 808-934-7028. Open Mon.-Sat. In downtown Hilo.*

BEST FOOD SHOPS

SANDWICHES: ◆ **Bear's Coffee.** Sandwich fare plus 30 kinds of fresh-roasted coffee. *106 Keawe St., Hilo, HI 96720; tel. 808-935-0708. Open Mon.-Sat. for breakfast and lunch. In downtown Hilo.*

SEAFOOD: ◆ **Suisan Co. Ltd.** *85 Lihiwai, Hilo, HI 96720; tel. 808-935-9349. Open Mon.-Sat.*

FRESH PRODUCE: ◆ **Hilo Farmers Market.** Outdoor market for produce and flowers. *Kamehameha Ave., Hilo, HI 96720. Open Wed., Sat. In downtown Hilo, on Kamehameha at Mamo.*

BAKERY: ◆ **Lanky's Pastries & Deli.** Pastries and breads baked fresh. *Hilo Shopping Center, Hilo, HI 96720; tel. 808-935-6381. Open daily.*

ICE CREAM: ◆ **Hilo Homemade Ice Cream.** *1477 Kalanianaole Ave., Hilo, HI 96720; tel. 808-969-9559. Open daily.*

BEVERAGES: ◆ **Safeway Stores.** *111 E. Puainako St., Hilo, HI 96720; tel. 808-959-3502. Open daily.*

WINE: ◆ **Safeway Stores.** Large selection of wines and beers. *111 E. Puainako St., Hilo, HI 96720; tel. 808-959-3502. Open daily.*

SPORTS
FISHING

Visitors will see lots of fishermen dropping lines in Hilo Bay from the city shores, but no charter fishing boats operate from Hilo Harbor.

BOATING

Despite its busy harbor and beautiful bay, Hilo lacks commercial cruises and boat trips.

SURFING

◆ **Local Style.** Surfboard rentals, sales. *111 E. Puainako Ave., Hilo, HI 96720; tel. 808-959-6121. Open daily. In Prince Kuhio Plaza.*

◆ **Orchid Land Surfshop.** Custom surfboards, body boards, sportswear. *832 Kilauea Ave., Hilo, HI 96720; tel. 808-935-1533. Open daily. Near Kaikoo Mall.*

DIVING

◆ **Nautilus Dive Center.** Sales, rentals, air, five-day certification. *382 Kamehameha Ave., Hilo, HI 96720; tel. 808-935-6939. Open daily.*

BICYCLING

◆ **Mid-Pacific Wheels.** Bike sales, repairs, parts, rentals. *1133C Manono, Hilo, HI 96720; tel. 808-935-6211. Open Mon.-Sat.*

GOLF

◆ **Hilo Municipal Golf Course.** Public 18-hole par-71 course, with token fees, club rentals, pro shop, restaurant, driving range. *340 Haihai St., Hilo, HI 96720; tel. 808-959-7711; pro shop tel. 808-*

959-9601. Open daily. Admission.
◆ **Naniloa Country Club.** Naniloa Hotel's own nine-hole par- 35 course, with covered driving range, rentals, restaurant, and lounge. Open to nonguests. Low fees. *120 Banyan Dr., Hilo, HI 96720; tel. 808-935-3000; fax 808-969-6622. Open daily. Admission.*

HISTORY

Hilo is dedicated to revitalizing its quaint downtown in the wake of repeated devastating tidal waves (the most recent in 1960) and the demise of sugar plantations and other economic mainstays. To help find the history, get a Hilo Historic Walking Tour map at the Lyman Museum.

◆ **Hilo Sampan Co.** Hilo Sampans, a colorful Filipino version of a van, have been revived, creating a fun way to get around town. Drivers point out downtown historic sites and suggest the best places to get such local treats as *mochi* ice cream and *lilikoi* cream cheese. Call for route and other details. *101 Aupuni St., Suite 1001, Hilo, HI 96720; tel. 808-935-6955. Open Mon.-Sat. 8-4. Tickets available from drivers and at several outlets around town.*

◆ **Lyman Museum and Mission House.** Built in 1839 by Rev. David Lyman, this missionary home displays slice-of-life relics of the era. An adjoining building houses displays recounting the history of Hawaii's many ethnic groups, brought to the islands to work on sugar plantations. Mineral and shell collections too. *276 Haili St., Hilo, HI 96720; tel. 808-935-5021. Open Mon.-Sat. 9-5, Sun. 1-4. Admission. In downtown Hilo.*

NATURE

Hilo's abundance of waterfall valleys, which punctuate the landscape north of the city, includes two famous sites that are good for picnics. Rainbow Falls and nearby Boiling Pots are above Hilo, off Kaumana Drive. Akaka Falls is reached on Route 220 from Honomu, approximately eight miles north on Highway 19. At Akaka Falls State Park, the easy 3/4-mile loop trail leading to Kapuna Falls and 420-foot Akaka Falls is lined with ginger, heliconia, bamboo, orchids, and other plants.

TOURIST INFORMATION

◆ **Destination Hilo Association.** *Box 1391, Hilo, HI 96720; tel. 808-935-5294, 800-445-6329. Open Mon.-Fri. 8-noon.*

◆ **Hawaii Visitors Bureau, Big Island Chapter.** *250 Keawe St., Hilo, HI 96720; tel. 808-961-5797. Open Mon.-Fri. 8-4:30.*

CHAPTER 22

Volcano Coast

Of all Hawaii's beaches, these are the most unusual: too hot to walk on, too new to be named. They are the red-hot lava beaches under construction on the Big Island's volcano coast. They are the newest beaches on earth.

Here, since 12:31 a.m. on January 3, 1983, when Kilauea (*Kee-lo-WAY-ah*) volcano began its current continuous eruptive phase, the southeast coast of Hawaii has been growing daily. In the longest eruption in recorded Hawaiian history, the volcano pumps out 650,000 cubic yards

Beauty	A
Swimming	NA
Sand	A
Hotels/Inns/B&Bs	A
House rentals	C
Restaurants	B
Nightlife	C
Attractions	A
Shopping	C
Sports	NA
Nature	A

of lava every day, enough to build a four-foot-wide, four-inch-deep sidewalk from Honolulu to New York City in two days. No one knows when it will stop.

On its seven-mile flow from the summit to the sea, the lava has crossed Chain of Craters Road several times and smothered the National Park Visitors Center. It destroyed the famous black-sand beach at Kalapana and the Waha'ula heiau, built in 1275 by Pa'ao, the Polynesian navigator and devotee of human sacrifice. More than 100 homes have gone up in smoke at a cost of more than $20 million.

Hawaiians believe it's all the work of Madame Pele, the legendary goddess of fire who both creates and destroys. Anyone with a yen to see her work in progress should drop in at Hawaii Volcanoes National Park, probably the most exciting in

America. Founded in 1916, it is the twelfth national park and the only one with active volcanoes, a tropical rain forest, a black lava desert, and a preserve for endangered native Hawaiian birds.

It also has some amazing beaches. The 377-square-mile park takes in 30 miles of mostly new shoreline, from Waha'ula to Kalu'e, including beaches that appear and disappear. The black-sand beach at Kamoamoa, for example, was created in 1987 and vanished five years later under new lava flows. Even while they're around, these beaches are too dangerous for swimming. Don't even think about it.

Hawaii is famous for black-sand beaches, which may be seen more safely in such places as Hilo, but adventure-seekers can't pass up this chance to watch nature creating beaches before their eyes. When red-hot lava meets the cold water, it crackles and hisses and burns underwater, sending up great plumes of steam until the ocean finally puts out the fire and turns the lava into black sand.

At night, it's one of the greatest spectacles on earth, a fabulous light show with explosions of fire and running rivers of lava—red rivulets flowing right beneath your feet and finally boiling red-orange into the sea.

Caution: Stand in awe, but do not remove any lava rock souvenirs. Myth has it that Pele's revenge for such a deed will bring a string of bad luck. Lots of rocks are returned every day by mail from miserable miscreants begging rangers to put them back.

HOW TO GET THERE

◆ **The Big Island of Hawaii is a 35-minute jet flight from Honolulu International Airport. From Hilo Airport (45 minutes from Hawaii Volcanoes National Park and the village of Volcano), turn left on Hawaii Belt Rd. (Hwy. 11) and drive 29 mi. to the park entrance. On the Big Island, rental cars and small four-wheel-drive vehicles are available through the hotels and at Hilo Airport.**

CHAIN OF CRATERS BEACHES

Since the beaches of Hawaii Volcanoes National Park come and go according to the whim of Madame Pele, it is best to refer to them collectively as Chain of Craters beaches.

Beauty	A
Swimming	NA
Sand	A
Amenities	C

The coast off Chain of Craters Road is where the action is, so much so that the flowing lava has closed the road. Visitors may hike in a mile from the road barricade to witness new beaches being formed. They cool quickly in the waves that lap ashore. With luck—and extreme caution—you may actually be able to walk on a new black-sand beach in Hawaii.

Bear in mind, however, that the site changes daily and risks can vary greatly. Besides volcanoes, the coast is subject to fissures and full-scale earthquakes. Avoid sea cliffs. They often collapse into the sea. Be prepared, too, for extreme heat and sulfuric smoke, a considerable hindrance, even though one early visitor, Mark Twain, observed more than 100 years ago that it "is not unpleasant to a sinner."

To ensure survival, check with park rangers at the Visitors Center before setting out to see the lava and again when you arrive near the site. Rangers are on the Chain of Craters Road from 9 to 7 every day. When they are not present, visitors proceed at their own risk. The park is open 24 hours a day, year-round, including holidays. For a volcano-eruption update, call 808-967-7977. *From the park entrance, drive 23 mi. down Chain of Craters Rd. to the barricade that establishes the safety zone before the lava flow. The road will be covered with pahoehoe (hardened lava), which looks like chocolate frosting.*
Swimming: Very dangerous. Not advised, even for experienced swimmers.
Sand: Newly created black volcanic sand.
Amenities: Rest rooms, sun shelter. No lifeguard.
Sports: None. Just bring your camera.
Parking: Ample parking on Chain of Craters Road.

HOTELS/INNS/B&Bs

Many pilgrims to Kilauea and Hawaii Volcanoes National Park stay in Hilo, 29 miles away and about a 45-minute drive up good roads. But a savvy few who like the high-country air stay in the village of Volcano near the park. It's mostly residential, a favorite second-home and retirement spot for beach-dwelling Hawaii people. Accommodations tend toward the rustic.

◆ **Kilauea Lodge and Restaurant** (moderate). Built in 1938 for the YMCA and later converted to a 10-acre private estate, the lodge includes a large main dining room, 12 B&B rooms, and a refurbished historic bungalow. *Box 116, Volcano, HI 96785; tel. 808-967-7366. In the village of Volcano.*

◆ **Volcano House** (moderate). A rustic 42-room lodge with the longest history of tourist accommodations in the Islands. The volcano's fiery performances drew the first awestruck tourists in the 1860s, and a grass shelter was built at the rim of Halemaumau Crater. It was the progenitor of Volcano House, which has perhaps the world's only restaurant and bar with front-row seats for any eruptions that occur in the huge black pit steaming with fumaroles and eerie glows. *Box 53, Hawaii Volcanoes National Park, HI 96718; tel. 808-967-7321; fax 808-967-8429. Inside the national park near the entrance. Follow signs.*

◆ **Carson's Volcano Cottage** (inexpensive). A B&B cottage with a fireplace to ward off the high-country evening chill. Also three rooms in main house. Jacuzzi among the tree ferns. Can reserve other cottages and rooms in the area. Five minutes from Hawaii Volcanoes National Park. *Box 503, Volcano, HI 96785; tel. 808-967-7683, 800-845-LAVA. From Hilo, take the first right after the 25-mi. marker onto Jade St. Drive about 1/2 mi. and turn right on 6th. Watch for sign on right.*

◆ **Chalet Kilauea** (inexpensive). Three themed rooms and a "treehouse" split-level suite. Fireplace, hot tub. Surrounded by a forest of lehua trees and tree ferns. Also cottage and home rentals. *Box 998, Volcano, HI 96785; tel. 808-967-7786, 800-937-7786. Off Wright Rd. at Laukapu Rd. in Volcano village.*

◆ **Hale Ohia** (inexpensive). This former summer estate of a prominent Hawaii family is now a bed-and-breakfast with rooms and cottages. *Box 758, Volcano, HI 96720; tel. 808-967-7986, 800-455-3803. Across Hwy. 11 from Volcano village, 1 mi. south of the national park.*

◆ **My Island Bed and Breakfast** (inexpensive). Rooms and breakfast in a century-old missionary-style home at the 4,000-foot elevation, near the national park. Also reservations for 29 other B&B homes on the Big Island. *Box 100, Volcano, HI 96785; tel. 808-967-7216; fax 808-967-7719. On Old Volcano Hwy. just below the village.*

HOUSE RENTALS

◆ **Hawaii's Best Bed & Breakfasts.** Reservations for cottages and rooms in the Volcano area. *Box 563, Kamuela, HI 96743; tel. 808-885-4550, 800-262-9912; fax 808-885-0559.*

◆ **Hawaiian Islands Bed & Breakfasts.** Reservations for cottages and rooms in the Volcano area. *572 Kailua Rd., Kailua, HI 96734; tel. 808-261-7895, 800-258-7895; fax 808-262-2181.*

◆ **Volcano Reservations.** Handles rentals for homes, cottages, inns. *Box 998, Volcano, HI 96785; tel. 808-967-7244, 800-736-7140; fax 808-967-8660.*

RESTAURANTS

◆ **Kilauea Lodge & Restaurant** (moderate). Best dinner in town presented in a warm, inviting atmosphere alongside a souvenir-encrusted stone hearth with a crackling fire. Surprisingly diverse menu for a restaurant atop a volcano. If they're serving ohelo-berry pie for dessert, get some—the berries grow nowhere else. Reservations recommended. *Box 116, Volcano, HI 96785; tel. 808-967-7366. Open daily for dinner. In Volcano village.*

◆ **Volcano Golf & Country Club Restaurant** (moderate). Club restaurant open to the public. Specials include fresh mahimahi, garlic-pepper chicken, and Loco Moco, an island favorite made with steamed rice, fried eggs, and a hamburger patty topped with brown gravy. *Box 46, Hawaii Volcanoes National Park, HI 96718; tel. 808-967-8228. Open daily for breakfast and lunch; Fri., Sat. for dinner. Off Hwy. 11 near entrance to the national park. At the 30-mi. marker, turn right onto Golf Course Rd.*

◆ **Kilauea General Store and Deli** (inexpensive). Sandwiches, salads, soups, chili, and stew. Breakfast plate. Full line of baked goods. *Box 959, Volcano, HI 96785; tel. 808-967-7555. Open daily for breakfast and lunch. In Volcano village.*

NIGHTLIFE

Volcanoes are the only hot spots in this part of Hawaii. Hawaii Volcanoes National Park and the Hawaii Natural History Association cosponsor "After Dark in the Park," a series of programs to help people understand more of the magic of Kilauea and its environs. The free programs are presented Tuesdays at 7 in the auditorium of Kilauea Visitors Center at the park. For details, call the Division of Interpretation (808-967-7184).

ATTRACTIONS

Here you can witness Creation in action: molten earth steaming forth from a fiery womb or glowing red under your feet as you walk on recently cooled lava. Hawaii Volcanoes National Park, established in 1916, lets you watch Kilauea volcano at work with relative safety. Down by the sea, new real estate gets added daily to the Big Island. But the 377-square-mile park has many other marvelous features, such as a dormant caldera (the volcano's fire pit) that you can drive across, miles of hiking trails, fern forests, and a lava tube to walk through.

◆ **Akatsuka Orchid Gardens.** Cut flowers and plants to ship, plus a free orchid for stopping by. *Volcano, HI 96785; tel. 808-967-8234. Open daily 8:30-5. On Hwy. 11, at the 22-mi. marker.*

◆ **Thomas A. Jaggar Museum.** Top-notch small museum answers many questions about volcanic activity. It approaches the subject from the scientific viewpoint, with seismographs and exhibits, and explores the Hawaiian version through the legends of Pele, the temperamental fire goddess who vents her emotions through eruptive handiwork. *Box 74, Hawaii Volcanoes National Park, HI 96718; tel. 808-967-7643. Open daily 8:30-5. In the national park.*

◆ **Volcano Art Center.** This nonprofit group, which promotes Hawaiian arts and cultural heritage, operates a fine gallery of local works, including paintings, clothing, jewelry, and wood carvings. The center also sponsors many special cultural events and performances and operates Elderhostel programs for senior citizens from around the country. *Box 104, Hawaii Volcanoes*

National Park, HI 96718; tel. 808-967-8222; fax 808-967-8512. Open daily 9-5. In an old building next to the Kilauea Visitors Center in the park.

◆ **Volcano Heli-tours.** Air tours over active eruption sites to witness a boiling crater spilling hot lava over the side for its long crawl to the sea. A never-to-be-forgotten sight, although new FAA rules keep the choppers to a minimum height of 1,500 feet. *Box 626, Volcano, HI 96785; tel. 808-967-7578, 800-967-7578. Flights daily, weather permitting. Office open Mon.-Fri. 9-3. Admission. Departs from lawn across from Volcano Golf & Country Club.*

◆ **Volcano Winery.** Tasting room for new winery that creates Symphony wine from white grapes grown on the slopes of Mauna Loa. Also white wines with tropical-fruit flavors, such as guava chablis. Sample the new Volcano blush wine, made from grapes and jaboticaba, an exotic fruit from Brazil that grows wild in backyards of Volcano. *Box 843, Volcano, HI 96785; tel. 808-967-7772. Open daily 10-5. From 30-mi. marker on Hwy. 11, turn right on Golf Course Rd. Drive past the golf club about 1/4 mi. to the winery gate. Proceed down gravel lane to parking area.*

SHOPPING

◆ **Kilauea General Store.** Campers' supplies. Garden room filled with cut flowers and plants, including cymbidium orchid sprays in spring and fall. Don't go home without a jar of Lilikoi Gold, a passion-fruit butter spread made by owner Kathy Tripp's mother. It's worth climbing a volcano for. *Box 959, Volcano, HI 96785; tel. 808-967-7555. Open daily. In Volcano village.*

◆ **Volcano Store.** In spring and fall, the selection of locally grown cymbidium orchids, on stems heavy with a dozen or so flowers, will dazzle flower lovers. Prices are half as much as in major markets. *Box 307, Volcano, HI 96785; tel. 808-967-7210. Open daily. By the post office.*

BEST FOOD SHOPS

SANDWICHES: ◆ **Kilauea General Store.** Deli sandwiches, drinks, fresh-baked tropical-fruit breads, and cookies. *Box 959, Volcano,*

HI 96785; tel. 808-967-7555. Open daily. In Volcano village.

FRESH PRODUCE: ◆ **Volcano Store.** Groceries and other essentials. *Box 307, Volcano, HI 96785; tel. 808-967-7210. Open daily. By the post office.*

BAKERY: ◆ **Alii Bakery & Drive Inn.** Stop in for Taro bread, Japanese *an pan*, and other specialties baked on premises. *Volcano, HI 96785; tel. 808-967-7103. Open daily. Next to Volcano Store.*

BEVERAGES: ◆ **Volcano General Store.** *Box 307, Volcano, HI 96785; tel. 808-967-7210. Open daily. By the post office.*

WINE: ◆ **Kilauea General Store.** Selections include local Volcano fruit wines. *Box 959, Volcano, HI 96785; tel. 808-967-7555. Open daily. In Volcano village.*

SPORTS
GOLF

◆ **Volcano Golf & Country Club.** Par-72 18-hole semiprivate golf course with pro shop, restaurant and bar, driving range, reasonable fees. *Box 46, Hawaii Volcanoes National Park, HI 96718; tel. 808-967-7331; fax 808-985-8891. Open daily. Just outside the entrance to the national park.*

NATURE

Anyone may hike from Chain of Craters Road to the lava-flow site, but guided hikers may gain closer, safer access. Self-guided hikes at Hawaii Volcanoes National Park include a ten-minute walk to Halemaumau Crater overlook; a 30-minute walk on Devastation Trail (the cinder outfall of the 1959 Kilauea Iki eruption); a 20-minute walk through a fern tree forest, and a two-hour trek into Kilauea Iki, across lava flows still steaming from the 1959 eruption.

◆ **Hawaii Forest and Trail.** Big Island naturalist Rob Pacheco offers guided expeditions after dark to "see the red"—red-hot lava boiling down to the sea from Kilauea caldera. *Box 2975, Kailua-Kona, HI 96745; tel. 808-329-1993, 800-464-1993. Admission.*

SAFETY TIPS

Kilauea is the world's most active volcano. If you want to get up close, wear sturdy hiking shoes and follow rangers' orders. Bring water; wear sunscreen. If you go at night to see the active flows, bring a good flashlight and realize that your safety is up to you. Active flows top 2,000 degrees and can emit nasty sulfuric gases or explode into steam when cold seawater meets hot lava.

TOURIST INFORMATION

◆ **Hawaii Visitors Bureau, Big Island Chapter.** *250 Keawe St., Hilo, HI 96720; tel. 808-961-5797; fax 808-961-7563. Open Mon.-Fri. 8-12, 1-4:30.*

◆ **Hawaii Volcanoes National Park.** Brochures about the park, information, videos, books, and other materials about volcanoes. Daily updates about volcanic activity and where to view it. *Box 52, Hawaii Volcanoes National Park, HI 96718; tel. 808-967-7311. Park open 24 hours a day. Visitors center open daily 7:30-5.*

CHAPTER 23

Hulopoe

F ew travelers have seen Lanai (*Lah-NIGH-ee*), except as a sunset backdrop from Maui. Few have snorkeled its crystal waters teeming with tropical sea life, even though it is ranked among the world's top diving spots. Surprisingly, few beach lovers have enjoyed the beauties of Hulopoe Beach, one of Hawaii's finest.

Beauty	A
Swimming	B
Sand	B
Hotels/Inns/B&Bs	A
House rentals	D
Restaurants	A
Nightlife	C
Attractions	C
Shopping	D
Sports	A
Nature	A

Now that word of Lanai's virtues is spreading, however, the island's focus has shifted from agriculture to tourism. For decades, growing pineapples was the sole interest here, and the handful of hardy visitors staying at the island's one lodge were awakened before dawn by the blast of the whistle calling workers to the fields.

Despite its wild beauty, Lanai doesn't resemble anybody's idea of a tropical paradise. Deprived of rain by Maui's mountains, the 141-square-mile island looks like a wrinkled kidney bean dropped in the sea. Red earth is slashed with deep gorges that stretch to the sea from the misty summit of 3,366-foot Mount Lanaihale.

Even with the recent addition of two luxury resorts complete with championship golf courses, the island has a frontier quality that beckons the adventurer. Besides its intriguing beaches and sea caves, there is plenty of backcountry to explore. Small Axis deer far outnumber the human population (2,800), and there are just 40 miles of blacktop road on the island.

Snorkelers and scuba divers on local craft or excursion boats from Maui see Lanai at its captivating best, a vista of sheer volcanic cliffs, white beaches, and abandoned settlements. A shipwreck is lodged on one of its coral reefs, and pocket coves and pinnacle islets dot the landscape.

Until recently, Lanai was called the Pineapple Island, reflecting the glory years when James Dole's empire led the world in production. The sun-drenched fields are still there, but commercial harvesting has ended. Lanai's staple now is tourism, and the workers have gone inside to wait tables and make beds.

Dole's modern-day counterpart is David Murdock, a Los Angeles tycoon who acquired most of the island a decade ago and built Lanai's first luxury hotels, the Lodge at Koele and the Manele Bay Hotel. These excellent resorts provide an exalted base camp for adventure. Guests can rent four-wheel-drive vehicles, walk the beaches, or hike mountain trails, then give their red-dirt-stained clothes to a butler. Activities are concierge-dependent: Dial 9 for horseback riding.

HULOPOE BEACH

Hulopoe (*Hoo-lo-PO-ee*) is a picture-post-card crescent of golden sand bordered by lava reefs. The water is clear, and there's a tide pool carved in the lava big enough for swimming. Palms and other trees on the upper beach offer shade from the sun.

Beauty	A
Swimming	B
Sand	B+
Amenities	B

This is Lanai's beach park, protected on either side by head-

HOW TO GET THERE

◆ Lanai is a 35-minute flight by small plane from Honolulu International Airport. Resort shuttles pick up guests at Lanai Airport. Three airlines serve the island: Hawaiian Air, Box 30008, Honolulu, HI 96820; tel. 808-838-1555, 800-367-5320; IslandAir, 99 Kapalulu Pl., Honolulu, HI 96819; tel. 808-833-7108, 800-323-3345; or Mahalo Airlines, 90 Nakolo Pl., Suite 215, Honolulu, HI 96819; tel. 808-833-5555, 800-4-MAHALO.

lands. At the far end, the Manele Bay Hotel looks down from the heights. The near headland separates the beach from Manele Bay, the neighboring boat anchorage. Take the old trail that leads along it to Sweetheart Rock. It's a 15-minute walk, and the view down the coast is spectacular. Spinner dolphins often play in Hulopoe Bay, and whales go by in winter. *From Lanai City, take Manele Rd. all the way to the end (about 8 mi.).*

Swimming: Hulopoe's warm waters, always in the mid-70s or higher, are usually safe for swimming and snorkeling, but wave and water conditions vary with the winds. Swimming conditions are posted. Plantation workers dynamited the lava years ago to create the tidal pool, so there's always a safe place for children to splash and swim.

Sand: Soft, golden-tan. The bottom of the near-shore swimming area is flat sandstone with lava rocks in some places.

Amenities: Clean rest rooms, outdoor showers, barbecue grills, and picnic tables. Lifeguard on duty.

Sports: The beach cabana at the Manele Bay Hotel rents Boogie boards, snorkeling equipment, and other beach gear.

Parking: The landscaped parking area is free and ample.

SHIPWRECK BEACH

Shipwreck Beach is every beachcombers' dream of wild, windswept strand. Known to islanders as Kaiolohia, it's commonly referred to as Shipwreck Beach because of a rusty Liberty ship that has been stuck on a reef offshore since around the time of World War II.

Beauty	A
Swimming	D
Sand	C+
Amenities	NA

From the parking lot at the end of Keomuku Road, a hiking trail along the beach leads to Polihua Beach, ten miles north. A side trail leads inland to some petroglyphs (ancient rock carvings). *From Lanai City, take Keomuku Rd. all the way to the end (about 8 mi.). The road is paved most of the way but steep; four-wheel-drive is recommended.*

Swimming: Given the strong currents in the channel between Lanai and Maui, this is not a safe place to swim.

Sand: White, grainy, and covered with driftwood and choice debris, including the occasional blue-green glass fishing float.

Amenities: None. No lifeguard.
Parking: Small, unpaved lot at the end of the road.

HOTELS/INNS/B&Bs

The island's three hotels, all operated by the same company, give visitors a choice of modern luxury or rustic simplicity. In addition, some homeowners rent accommodations in the small town of Lanai City, about eight miles away from the nearest swimming beach.

♦ **The Lodge at Koele** (very expensive). Unlike any other luxury hotel in Hawaii, this one is miles from the beach, set 2,000 feet above sea level in the misty highlands outside Lanai City. Local people are fascinated by it because, with formal gardens, a conservatory, a gazebo, and a reflecting pool, it breaks the mold for Hawaiian resorts. Done in the grand manner, the 100-room lodge has a great hall with giant stone fireplaces and enough stuffed furniture to pass for an *Architectural Digest* outlet store. In the lavishly decorated guest rooms, even the floors are appointed with hand-painted vines and flowers. If you like it very quiet, ask for a room in the wing that's closest to Lanai City. *Box 774, Lanai City, HI 96763; tel. 808-565-7300.*

♦ **Manele Bay Hotel** (very expensive). Like many Hawaiian seaside palaces, this 250-room hotel is perched on a cliff overlooking a sparkling bay, but it offers many extras beyond this basic requirement. One is a great view of Hulopoe Beach below. Others are the waterfalls and gardens flanking the property, lush with hibiscus, plumeria, and bougainvillea. The hotel's architecture is Mediterranean and the decor eclectic. For the best rooms, reserve one of the ground-level, ocean-front suites to the right of the central pool area and toward the wild hill. They offer a special sense of seclusion and have the best view of the beach. *Box 310, Lanai City, HI 96763; tel. 808-565-7700.*

♦ **Hotel Lanai** (moderate). Built in the 1920s for plantation guests, this ten-room hotel lives on as a country lodge overlooking Lanai City. The one-story wooden building is bordered by a lawn and flower beds under a stalwart stand of pines. Rooms, recently redecorated, are small and clean. Rooms 1, 2, 9, and 10 are the best, though not the most spacious; they open to a covered lanai, allowing guests to step outside and enjoy the pine-scented tropical air. *Box 520, Lanai City, HI 96763; tel. 808-565-4700.*

◆ **Dreams Come True** (inexpensive). Three B&B rooms, each with private bath, are available in what was once a plantation manager's house. The rooms feature canopy beds with large pillows and are decorated with antiques from Southeast Asia. Avocados, passion fruit, papaya, limes, and other fruit grow outside and may be on your plate for breakfast. *Box 525, 547 12th St., Lanai City, HI 96763; tel. 808-565-6961.*

◆ **Phyllis McOmber's** (inexpensive). This new wood-frame hunting lodge contains three bedrooms (all with single beds) and sleeps up to eight guests. It's conveniently located, less than two blocks from the town square in the center of Lanai City. *Box 2160, Lanai City, HI 96763; tel. 808-565-6071.*

HOUSE RENTALS

◆ **Dreams Come True.** *Box 525, 547 12th St., Lanai City, HI 96763; tel. 808-565-6961.*

RESTAURANTS

For a small island, Lanai offers a wide variety of menus, ranging from local to luxurious. Restaurants at the Manele Bay Hotel and the Lodge at Koele are among the best in the state, with imaginative offerings based on Hawaiian regional cuisine. They make good use of fresh fish, local venison, and Lanai-grown vegetables, fruits, and herbs. Each hotel has a formal dining area and an informal one, and the golf clubhouses serve lunch.

◆ **Ihilani Restaurant** (very expensive). Pacific Rim cuisine is the specialty at this antique-filled room overlooking the sea. *Manele Bay Hotel, Box 310, Lanai City, HI 96763; tel. 808-565-7700. Open daily.*

◆ **The Dining Room** (very expensive). The atmosphere is hushed in this formal dining room bursting with artworks. Try the island venison prepared by chef Phillipe Padovani. *The Lodge at Koele, Box 774, Lanai City, HI 96763; tel. 808-565-7300. Open daily.*

◆ **Hotel Lanai** (moderate). The enclosed veranda and wood-paneled dining room of this venerable lodge attract diners from around the world. It's also popular with local residents, who come in for dinner, usually for fresh ahi tuna with two scoops of rice. *Box 520, Lanai City, HI 96763; tel. 808-565-4700. Open daily.*

♦ **Pool Grille** (moderate). Cheeseburgers, salads, and iced tea served by the pool overlooking the Pacific. *Manele Bay Hotel, Box 310, Lanai City, HI 96763; tel. 808-565-7700. Open daily.*

♦ **Terrace Restaurant** (moderate). In the back of the Great Hall, you can find soup, sandwiches, and other light fare alongside a window that overlooks the reflecting pond and its gazebo. *The Lodge at Koele, Box 774, Lanai City, HI 96763; tel. 808-565-7300. Open daily.*

♦ **Blue Ginger Cafe** (inexpensive). Joe Abilay, a Filipino chef formerly with Maui's Kaanapali Beach Hotel, specializes in *bento* boxes (Japanese box lunches) and stir-fried chicken and vegetables. Simple local dishes and pizza are also on the menu. Indoor and outdoor seating. *409 Seventh St., Box 290, Lanai City, HI 96763; tel. 808-565-6363. Open daily for breakfast, lunch, and dinner.*

NIGHTLIFE

Lanai buttons up early. Residents looking for a good time go to the Hotel Lanai for drinks. The two luxury hotels offer evening entertainment that ranges from lectures to hula performances.

SHOPPING

Boutiques in the hotels sell sportswear and Hawaiian gifts, but the old-fashioned general stores around Dole Park Square in Lanai City offer a different kind of shopping experience, one vanishing rapidly from contemporary Hawaii. They sell foods of every description, from champagne to dried cuttlefish, as well as clothes, hardware, and other goods. Investigate any of these places for a cool drink or a Lanai T-shirt. If you can't wait for a day of full-blown shopping, jump on the next boat to Maui (*see* Boating).

♦ **Akamai Trading Co.** Jewelry, clothing, and souvenirs compete for attention with furniture and appliances. *Box 9, 408 Eighth St., Lanai City, HI 96763; tel. 808-565-6587.*

SPORTS

Its rugged coast and spectacular marine life have established Lanai as a must for snorkelers and scuba divers. There's plenty of horseback riding and hiking, too, and golfers will appreciate the two championship courses.

FISHING
Charter fishing trips leave from the Manele Bay Small Boat Harbor in quest of Pacific blue marlin, tuna, and mahimahi. Reservations can be made through either luxury resort.

BOATING
Sunset cruises and dive and snorkeling expeditions departing from the Manele Bay Small Boat Harbor can be booked through the concierge at either of the luxury resorts. An all-day boat trip is possible to Lahaina, Maui.

DIVING
Local snorkeling and scuba diving guides will take you to sites teeming with fish. Boats leave from the Manele Bay Small Boat Harbor. Make reservations through the concierge at either luxury resort.

BICYCLING
The two luxury resorts provide mountain bikes for guests.

GOLF
♦ **Challenge at Manele.** Designed by all-time golf great Jack Nicklaus, this course is well named, especially in light of the water hazard on the 12th hole: a wave-lashed coast of jagged lava. *Manele Bay Hotel, Box 310, Lanai City, HI 96793; tel. 808-565-7700.*

♦ **The Experience at Koele.** Set on the gentle slopes of Mount Lanaihale by designers Greg Norman and Ted Robinson, this spectacular course is the only one in Hawaii with bent-grass greens. *The Lodge at Koele, Box 774, Lanai City, HI 96763; tel. 808-565-7300.*

TENNIS

Both luxury resorts have courts. At the Manele Bay Hotel, there's a pro shop and an instructor.

HORSEBACK RIDING

♦ **The Lodge at Koele.** From these elegant stables, you can trot around the fields or take off for cooler altitudes. *Box 774, Lanai City, HI 96763; tel. 808-565-7300.*

HISTORY

Exploring Lanai is best done by four-wheel-drive vehicle or on foot. Bring your hiking boots. Hotel concierges will arrange for vehicles or guided tours.

♦ **Keomoku Village.** A picturesque wooden church and a cemetery are all that's left of a bustling 1890s sugar town that later served as a ranching community, until it was abandoned in the 1950s. About three miles beyond it is Lopa Beach, a good spot to swim and snorkel. Accessible only by four-wheel-drive. *From Lanai City, take Keomuku Rd. to the end (about 8 mi.). At the beach, turn right onto an unpaved road. The village is 6 mi. down the beach.*

♦ **Kaunolu.** Site of King Kamehameha's summer fishing retreat 200 years ago. Ruins of house platforms, grave sites, shelters, a heiau temple platform, and petroglyphs dot the area. Accessible only by four-wheel-drive vehicle. *From Lanai City, take Kaumalapau Hwy. Turn left on Kaupili Rd. for 2.2 mi. to the rugged Kaunolu Trail. The site is 3 mi. down the trail.*

♦ **Petroglyphs.** Fascinating figures are carved into 34 huge boulders on a hillside above Palawai Basin. One is a detailed drawing of a voyaging canoe. The carvings are visible from Manele Road about two miles outside of Lanai City on the way to Hulopoe Beach. *Accessible from dirt roads off Manele Rd. Motivated explorers will find the way and scramble up the hill for a look.*

NATURE

♦ **Garden of the Gods.** An unusual stand of red and gold basalt rocks, eroded by wind, rain, and the hoof beats of thousands of

Axis deer. This badlands is especially worth visiting at sunrise or sunset, when the light plays tricks on the land. Accessible only by four-wheel-drive vehicle. *6 mi. northwest of Lanai City at the end of Polihua Rd. From there, the directions get complicated, so ask your concierge for a map.*

♦ **Munro Trail.** The most demanding of Lanai's many fine walking paths, it weaves through the heights for 18 miles, offering great views of four other islands.

TOURIST INFORMATION

♦ **Hawaii Visitors Bureau.** Brochures, maps, and guides available free. *2270 Kalakaua Ave., Suite 801, Honolulu, HI 96815; tel. 808-923-1811. Open Mon.-Fri. 8-4:30.*

♦ **Destination Lanai.** *Box 700, Lanai City, HI 96763; tel. 808-565-7600.*

CHAPTER 24

Papohaku

Molokai has 106 miles of shoreline but only a few great beaches. Ancient Hawaiian fishponds run for miles along the south shore, and the world's steepest sea cliffs deny access to remote pocket beaches on the north. On the east and west shores of this long, narrow island (it looks like a snail without a shell) there are miles of beaches, but they are either remote, inaccessible, or swept by strong currents. The 26-mile Kaiwi Channel, between Molokai and Oahu, is considered one of the world's most dangerous.

Beauty	A
Swimming	C
Sand	A
Hotels/Inns/B&Bs	C
House rentals	B
Restaurants	C
Nightlife	D
Attractions	B
Shopping	C
Sports	B
Nature	A

Yet the 35-mile-long island has two outstanding beaches: Papohaku, which stretches wide as a football field for two miles, and Halawa, spectacular with its black sand and rugged setting.

Actually, the so-called Friendly Island of Molokai (*MO-lo-kigh-ee*) doesn't claim to be a major beach destination. It's more comfortable playing the role of a quiet country island only 30 minutes by plane from Oahu but several decades back in time. Farming, fishing, and ranching are the primary activities. With wide-open landscapes at one end and lush jungled cliffs at the other, Molokai keeps close to nature and to a thriving sense of Hawaiian culture. People of Hawaiian blood make up a majority of the nearly 7,000 inhabitants living on an island of 260 square miles. Most reside in the little port town of Kaunakakai, a handful of stores built with the kind of false fronts that show up in Hollywood westerns.

The island's only resort sits on a bluff overlooking Kepuhi Beach, on the island's blunt west end, from which you can see the lights of Oahu twinkling in the evening. Counting hotel rooms and condominiums, Kaluakoi Resort has a total of 500 units, but they come with few frills. There are no phones or TV sets in the rooms. Its golden-sand beach includes dunes and beach rock, but swimming is risky at almost any time of year.

Just to the south, on the other side of 110-foot-high Puu O Kaiaka, is the broad, beautiful—and often empty—expanse of Papohaku Beach. Unfortunately, a shore break and strong undertow make swimming risky here too. This beach is best used for walking, contemplating nature, fishing, collecting shells, and sunbathing.

Safe pocket beaches dot the eastern shore of Molokai, otherwise dominated by the stone weirs and silty waters of ancient fishponds, some of which are being restored and used again as fish nurseries. At the extreme east end, Halawa Valley, once a thriving taro farm community until tidal waves swept it away, makes a fern-filled spot for wilderness hiking and camping.

Molokai's north coast is a formidable rampart of 3,250-foot-

HOW TO GET THERE

◆ Molokai is a short flight by small plane (IslandAir, Hawaiian Airlines, Mahalo Airlines, Air Molokai) from Honolulu International Airport's commuter terminal. From Molokai's Ho'olehua Airport (30 minutes from Papohaku Beach Park), take Maunaloa Hwy. (Hwy. 460) west 8 mi. to Kaluakoi Rd. Turn right and drive about 4 1/2 mi. down to the West Shore. Turn left at Kaluakoi Resort and drive 1 mi. to the entrance to Papohaku Beach Park on right.

◆ Rental vehicles are available at Ho'olehua Airport, but they're in short supply. Make a reservation in advance.

high cliffs, described in *The Guinness Book of World Records* as "the highest sea cliffs yet pinpointed anywhere in the world." With waterfalls, lush valleys, and remote beaches known only to kayakers and sailors, this is a world apart. If you hit the beach at Pelekunu Bay, you're either shipwrecked or a real adventurer.

PAPOHAKU BEACH PARK

People who are refreshed and calmed by spending time on a beach will want to save early mornings or late afternoons for walking Papohaku (*PAH-po-ha-koo*), one of the longest broad stretches of golden sand in Hawaii. It's best to stay back from

Beauty	A
Swimming	C
Sand	A
Amenities	B

the water line unless conditions are calm, however. With no outer reef to break the waves, they are powerful and unrestrained, and their backwash can knock children and even adults off their feet and pull them into the sea.

In May, Molokai throws a festival under the trees at Papohaku Beach Park, celebrating its claim of being the birthplace of the hula. It's a wonderful day of Hawaiian dance, chanting, music, crafts, and local foods. *Drive west on Maunaloa Hwy. (Hwy. 460). Turn right on Kaluakoi Rd. and drive. 4 1/2 mi. down to the West Shore. Turn left at Kaluakoi Resort and drive 1 mi. to the entrance to Papohaku Beach Park on right.*

Swimming: Unsafe for swimming unless calm; rip currents.
Sand: Golden and so soft and plentiful that it was mined for many years.
Amenities: Rest rooms, showers. No lifeguard.
Sports: Body boarding.
Parking: Paved lot in park.

KEPUHI BEACH

Kepuhi (*KAY-poo-hee*), a picturesque golden strand with black lava rocks, fronts the Kaluakoi Golf Course, which in turn fronts the hotel and villas. Like neighboring Papohaku, it's a beach to be enjoyed mostly on shore. A rock cliff, Puu o

Beauty	A
Swimming	C
Sand	A
Amenities	B

Kaiaka, separates the two beaches and has a path to the top. *Drive west on Maunaloa Hwy. (Hwy. 460). Turn right on Kaluakoi Rd., and drive 4 1/2 mi. downhill to the resort. The public right-of-way is on the resort side of the cliff, and a public parking lot is at the end of the road.*
Swimming: Rarely safe unless calm.
Sand: Golden and soft.
Amenities: Rest rooms and food at the resort. No lifeguard.
Sports: Bodysurfing.
Parking: Ample free parking on paved lot.

SANDY BEACH

On the way to Halawa Valley, a small, reef-protected pocket beach of golden sand by the side of Kamehameha V Highway is Molokai's most popular swimming beach. The rocky bottom often leads to stubbed toes, however. Great

Beauty	A
Swimming	B
Sand	A
Amenities	C

view of West Maui Mountains across the 8 3/4-mile Pailolo Channel. *Drive east on Mauanaloa Hwy. to the town of Kaunakakai and continue east on Kamehameha V Hwy. for 7 mi. past Wave Crest. Look for beach on right at mile marker 21.*
Swimming: Safe for small children.
Sand: Golden and soft.
Amenities: Rest rooms. No lifeguard.
Sports: Bodysurfing.
Parking: Roadside.

HALAWA BEACH PARK

In the lee of 300-foot-high Cape Halawa, the easternmost point of Molokai, Halawa Valley is scenically spectacular with 250-foot Moaula Falls, a black-sand beach, and a wave-lashed island offshore. Swimming is safe close to shore. Launch a kayak in

Beauty	A
Swimming	C
Sand	B
Amenities	D

summer from Halawa (*HAH-la-vah*) Beach when the Pacific is flat and paddle down Molokai's awesome north shore to the remote, rocky beaches of Wailau, Pelekunu, and Hauupu.

Paddle some more and you'll land at Kalaupapa National Historical Park. It's the former home of exiled lepers and Father Damien de Veuster, a heroic Belgian priest who died tending the afflicted. *Drive east on Maunaloa Hwy. (Hwy. 460) to the town of Kaunakakai. Go through the town on Kamehameha V Hwy. (Hwy. 450) and stay on the coastal road for 24 1/2 mi. The road veers inland across Cape Halawa and winds uphill 3 mi. It narrows as it reaches the rim of Halawa Valley, then descends on a steep, twisty road to the valley floor and the beach.*

Swimming: Safe in summer.

Sand: Black and coarse.

Amenities: Rest rooms. No lifeguard.

Sports: Bodysurfing, surfing.

Parking: Ample free parking under shade trees in dirt lot.

HOTELS/INNS/B&Bs

Molokai has one resort, Kaluakoi, which is comprised of a hotel, condominiums, a restaurant, shops, and facilities for golf, tennis, and other sports. Other tourist facilities on the island include a handful of condominium complexes, an old hotel near Kaunakakai, and some bed-and-breakfast rooms in homes.

◆ **Colony's Kaluakoi Hotel & Golf Club** (moderate). Built in 1977, this resort is typical of some older resorts in Hawaii: a blend of beautifully landscaped and manicured grounds, Hawaiian architecture, so-so food, and often cheerless rooms that need renovating. But the price is right, and the choices are few on Molokai. The setting makes for a peaceful retreat with easy golf access. Honolulu residents slip over here for weekends. *Box 1977, Kepuhi Beach, HI 96770; tel. 808-552-2555, 800-277-1700. On Kaluakoi Rd. at the west end of the island.*

◆ **Kamalo Plantation Bed & Breakfast** (inexpensive). Glenn and Akiko Foster's home on five acres has lush tropical gardens and trees and its own ancient Hawaiian village ruins. Two rooms and a separate cottage are available. *HCO 1, Box 300, Kaunakakai, HI 96748; tel/fax 808-558-8236. At the east end of the island.*

HOUSE RENTALS

◆ **Kaluakoi Villas** (moderate). The best way to enjoy beachfront living at Kaluakoi Resort is to pay a bit more and get one of the "cottages" that front the golf course and the sea. They have kitchenettes, gardens, lanais, and soaring interiors with Polynesian roofs. Ask for 3B: It's near the pool and restaurant, with a short walk to the beach that doesn't cross the busy golf course. *1131 Kaluakoi Rd., Maunaloa, HI 96770; tel. 808-552-2721, 800-367-5004; fax 808-552-2201. At Kaluakoi Resort.*

◆ **Wavecrest Resort Rentals** (moderate). Small complex of one- and two-bedroom resort condos near east end swimming beaches. *HCO 1, Box 541, Kaunakakai, HI 96748; tel. 808-558-8103, 800-367-2980. From Molokai Airport, drive east on Mauanaloa Hwy. to the town of Kaunakakai. Continue east on King Kamehameha V Hwy. to mile marker 13.*

RESTAURANTS

◆ **JoJo's Cafe** (moderate). House specialties: fresh fish, shrimp and lamb and chicken curries. *Maunaloa, HI 96770; tel. 808-552-2803. Open Mon., Tue, and Thu.-Sat. for lunch and dinner.*

◆ **Kualapuu Cookhouse** (moderate). Home-style cooking, with freshly made pies and cakes. *Box 174, Kualapuu, HI 96757; tel. 808-567-6185. Open Mon.-Sat for breakfast and lunch and Mon.-Fri. for dinner. Near Molokai airport.*

◆ **Banyan Tree Terrace Restaurant** (inexpensive). A favorite local hangout specializing in fresh fish and prime rib. Weekend dancing to live bands. *Box 856, Kaunakakai, HI 96748; tel. 808-553-5342. Open daily for breakfast, lunch, and dinner. In Pau Hana Inn, on the waterfront near Kaunakakai.*

◆ **Molokai Drive Inn** (inexpensive). Breakfast, box picnic lunches to go, and that Hawaiian standard, the plate lunch. Also shakes and malts. *Kaunakakai, HI 96748; tel. 808-553-5655. Open daily for breakfast, lunch, and dinner. In the village.*

◆ **Ohia Lodge** (inexpensive). Basic buffets and menus in an informal setting. *Kaluakoi Hotel, Kepuhi Beach, HI 96770; tel. 808-552-2555. Open daily for breakfast, lunch, and dinner.*

NIGHTLIFE

◆ **Ohia Lounge.** Cocktail lounge with live Hawaiian music. *Kaluakoi Hotel, Kepuhi Beach, HI 96770; tel. 808-552-2555. Open daily.*

◆ **Pau Hana Inn.** Molokai's liveliest spot on weekend nights is the inn's indoor/outdoor bar and oceanfront lanai. *Box 856, Kaunakakai, HI 96748; tel. 808-553-5342. Open daily. On the waterfront near Kaunakakai.*

SHOPPING

◆ **Big Wind Kite Factory.** Brilliantly colored fanciful kites made on the premises, plus imported goods. One kite sock is made to resemble a hula dancer with lei and fluttering grass skirt. *Box A, Maunaloa, HI 96770; tel. 808-552-2364. Open daily. In the village.*

◆ **Laughing Gecko.** Gifts, art, antiques, Hawaiiana, and handicrafts from Molokai. *Kepuhi Beach, HI 96770; tel. 808-552-2320. Open daily. In the Kaluakoi Hotel.*

◆ **Mapulehu Glass House.** Tropical flowers for shipment to the mainland or fruit and flowers for your condo. Free guided tours of the gardens. *HCO 1, Box 500, Kaunakakai, HI 96748; tel. 808-558-8160. Open daily. At the east end of the island.*

◆ **Molokai Island Creations.** Women's and children's clothes and gifts. Tank tops with original prints, swimwear, and books on the Hawaiian Islands. *Box 576, Kaunakakai, HI 96748; tel. 808-553-5926. Open daily. In the village.*

◆ **Plantation Gallery.** Wood carvings, quilt patterns, Hawaiiana, books, and Pacific Rim arts and crafts. *Box A, Maunaloa, HI 96770; tel. 808-552-2364. Open daily. In Maunaloa village.*

BEST FOOD SHOPS

SANDWICHES: ◆ **Molokai Pizza Cafe.** Pizza, sandwiches, pasta, fish, frozen yogurt. *Box 1232, Kaunakakai, HI 96748; tel. 808-553-3288. Open daily. In the village.*

SEAFOOD: ◆ **Misaki's Inc.** *Kaunakakai, HI 96748; tel. 808-533-5505, 808-553-5515. Open daily. In the village.*

FRESH PRODUCE: ◆ **Outpost Natural Foods.** *Box 1009,*

Kaunakakai, HI 96748; tel. 808-553-3377. Open daily except Sat. In the village.

BAKERY: ◆ Kanemitsu Bakery & Restaurant. Tasty fresh-baked Molokai bread from here is a popular gift in Hawaii. *79 Ala-Malama St., Kaunakakai, HI 96748; tel. 808-553-5855. Open daily. In the village.*

ICE CREAM: ◆ Molokai Drive Inn. *Kaunakakai, HI 96748; tel. 808-553-5655. Open daily. In the village.*

BEVERAGES: ◆ Wavecrest General Store. *HCO1 Box 510, Kaunakakai, HI 96748; tel. 808-558-8335. Open daily. On King Kamehameha V Hwy. at mile marker 13.*

WINE: ◆ Molokai Wines & Spirits Unlimited. *Box 240, Kualapuu, HI 96748; tel. 808-553-5009. Open daily. In the village of Kaunakakai.*

SPORTS
FISHING

◆ **Alyce C.** Full- or half-day fishing charters off Molokai and Lanai. *Box 825, Kaunakakai, HI 96748; tel. 808-558-8377. Open daily. Departs from Kaunakakai Harbor.*

◆ **Shon-a-lei II.** Full- and half-day or overnight fishing charters. Whale-watching in winter. *Box 1018, Kaunakakai, HI 96748; tel. 808-553-5242, 800-998-3474. Open daily. Departs from Kaunakakai Harbor.*

BOATING

◆ **Fun Hogs Hawaii.** Kayaks for rent, for use with or without a guide. *Box 424, Hoolehua, HI 96729; tel. 808-552-2555. Open daily. At a shop in the Kaluakoi Hotel.*

◆ **Molokai Charters.** Sailing charters and a cruise to Lanai for snorkeling and a picnic. Whale-watching in season. *Box 1207, Kaunakakai, HI 96748; tel. 808-553-5852. Daily departures.*

SURFING

◆ **Molokai Fish and Dive.** Surfboard rentals and other gear for rent or sale. *Box 576, Kaunakakai, HI 96748; tel. 808-553-5926. Open daily. In the village.*

DIVING

◆ **Bill Kapuni's Snorkel & Dive Adventure.** Snorkel and diving trips at what Bill calls the last unspoiled reef in Hawaii. Air, equipment rentals, instruction. *Box 1962, Kaunakakai, HI 96748; tel. 808-553-9867. Open daily. Boat departs from Kaunakakai Harbor.*

BICYCLING

◆ **Fun Hogs Hawaii.** Mountain bike rentals. *Box 424, Hoolehua, HI 96729; tel. 808-552-2555. Open daily. At a shop in the Kaluakoi Hotel.*

GOLF

◆ **Kaluakoi Golf Course.** Par-72, 18-hole course designed by Ted Robinson. Pro shop, rentals, driving range, and putting green by the sea. *Kepuhi Beach, HI 96770; tel. 808-552-2739; fax 808-552-0144. Open daily. Admission. Ocean front at Kaluakoi Resort.*

TENNIS

Colony's Kaluakoi Hotel has four courts with lighting, which are free to guests, fee for nonguests. Rents equipment, too. Wavecrest has two courts for guests.

HORSEBACK RIDING

◆ **Great Molokai Ranch Trail.** Molokai Ranch has opened trails on its 53,000-acre spread to guided tours. Horseback riders will enjoy the mountain trails and the beach ride, which ends with a picnic on a private cove. The beach is strewn with seashells and offers a cooling swim when wave conditions allow. Kayaking or canoeing also available. *Box 259, Maunaloa, HI 96770; tel. 808-552-2681, 800-254-8871. Open daily. Outfitters' headquarters in a barn in Maunaloa.*

HISTORY

◆ **Smith/Bronte Landing Site.** A historical marker near the spot where Ernie Smith and Emory B. Bronte crash-landed their single-engine Travelair *City of Oakland* in 1927. They emerged unhurt to become the first civilians to fly to Hawaii from the

U.S. mainland. They had taken off from Oakland, California, and completed the 2,397-mile trip in 25 hours and two minutes. *Kaunakakai, HI 96748. On King Kamehameha V Hwy. near Wavecrest.*

NATURE

◆ **Kamakou Nature Conservancy Preserve.** Wilderness hiking by permit only in a native forest that spans a slice of Molokai, from dry lowlands to boggy mountaintop rain forest. Four-wheel-drive vehicle road access, depending on weather. Overnight camping available nearby. *For permits, contact Maui District Forester, Box 1015, Wailuku, HI 96793. For information, contact the preserve manager at Box 220, Kualapuu, HI 96757; tel. 808-553-5236.*

◆ **Ma'a Hawaii: Molokai Action Adventures.** Hunting with rifle or bow for deer, boar, goat. Cultural tour of Molokai's fishponds and heiau temple site. Also hiking, snorkeling, diving, kayaking, and fishing. Call for reservations. *Box 1269, Kaunakakai, HI 96748; tel. 808-558-8184.*

TOURIST INFORMATION

◆ **Hawaii Visitors Bureau.** Brochures, maps, and guides available free. *2270 Kalakaua Ave., Suite 801, Honolulu, HI 96815; tel. 808-923-1811; fax 808-922-8991. Open Mon.-Fri. 8-4:30.*

◆ **Molokai Visitors Association.** *Box 960, Kaunakakai, HI 96748; tel. 808-553-3876, 800-800-6367; fax 808-553-5288. Open Mon.-Fri. 9-5.*

CHAPTER 25

Keamano

I t's your once-in-a-lifetime experience: an escape to the "forbidden" island of Niihau (*NEE-ee-how*), a 6-by-18-mile island northwest of Kauai and once off-limits to outsiders. A New Zealand woman bought it from King Kamehameha in 1863 for $10,000 in gold, and to this day, it is inhabited only by her descendants and a tribe of 230 native Hawaiians, who live there voluntarily in isolation from the rest of the world, to maintain their traditional way of life.

Beauty	A
Swimming	C
Sand	A
Hotels/Inns/B&Bs	NA
House rentals	NA
Restaurants	NA
Nightlife	NA
Attractions	C
Shopping	C
Sports	C
Nature	A

Visitors have been welcome since 1987, when helicopter service was introduced to provide emergency medical care for the islanders. Running tourist excursions helps pay for the upkeep on the helicopter.

Although the trip is only a 20-minute hop from Kauai, it takes you back more than two centuries in time. The island probably looks much as it did in 1778, when Captain James Cook dropped anchor here, laying claim to what he called the Sandwich Islands. Depending on rainfall, the island is either a brown, lifeless desert or a green velvet landfall, scattered with bright patches of yellow-orange Ilima flowers. As the helicopter circles the island, you can spot the sunken Lehua Crater off the north shore, soar over 1,281-foot Mount Paniau, see wild pigs racing across dry lake beds, or hover above *paniolos* (cowboys) on horseback.

You may also catch a glimpse of the little seacoast village of

Puuwai, which remains off-limits to all who call on Niihau, the last truly Hawaiian place. Here, *kanaka maoli* (native people) still speak the Hawaiian language, scratch out a living as cattle and sheep ranchers, and pay scant heed to the world beyond. Almost entirely self-sufficient, the local people take water from the clouds, fish from the sea, and vegetables from the garden.

For the adventurous, the Niihau outing provides a true wilderness experience on a remote Hawaiian island. The helicopter lands at two beaches where you can alight and go exploring. Each stop provides a different experience, and both are wonderful.

But come prepared. There are no hotels, fast-food outlets, or boutiques on the island. Pack a lunch and a water bottle. If you plan to snorkel, bring your own snorkel and mask.

KEAMANO BEACH

That long-sought beach with no foot-prints, Keamano (*Kay-ah-MAH-no*) is one of the most isolated places you are ever likely to visit. Nearly a mile long, this crescent of golden sand rises to graceful dunes tufted with sea grass and Ilima

Beauty	A
Swimming	B
Sand	A
Amenities	C

flowers. Visitors are free to comb the long, 100-foot-wide beach, which grows flatter as it curves west toward the sunken crater of Lehua Island, a seabird rookery three-quarters of a mile offshore. You can watch for whales, search for opihis (a conical shellfish) in black lava tide pools, or visit with villagers,

HOW TO GET THERE

◆ Niihau is reached by helicopter, with flights leaving from Burns Field on the island of Kauai. The airport is on Lele Rd. off Hwy. 50 in West Kauai, between the towns of Hanapepe and Waimea. The 3-hour excursion costs $200 per person. Call ahead for reservations. Niihau Helicopters, Box 370, Makaweli, HI 96769; tel. 808-335-3500.

who may have exquisite hand-strung shell necklaces for sale.

In or out of the water, you'll be well rewarded at Keamano. The swimming is delightful, and snorkeling in the crystalline pools of the bay, alone with big, tame fish, is at first eerie, then thrilling.

Keamano is also the perfect vantage point from which to observe migrating humpback whales on their seasonal commute between Alaska and Hawaii. Because Niihau is the westernmost of the inhabited Hawaiian Islands, it provides a front-row seat for whale watchers. Scarcely 100 yards offshore, the humpbacks cavort for hours, slapping their tails and leaping straight out of the water in a spectacular display.

Swimming: Free of sharks, the clear, 70-degree water makes for excellent swimming and snorkeling. The bottom is sandy and steep and can be dangerous in winter. The best place to swim and snorkel is in the large, shallow pool on the western side of the bay, which is protected by a finger of black lava rock.

Sand: Golden coral sand is strewn with Niihau's precious little red, white, and yellow shells.

Amenities: A tin-roof pavilion is the only shelter from the sun.

KEANAHAKI BEACH

Second stop on the tour is Keanahaki (*Kay-ahna-HOCK-ee*) Beach. On the way, the helicopter dips to within 100 feet of the tiger sharks in Shark's Cove. Over the years, the white-tipped sharks have learned that this is a good spot to prey on

Beauty	A
Swimming	D
Sand	A
Amenities	NA

monk seals or cattle that have escaped while being loaded onto ships for market.

Keanahaki is on the bay where Captain Cook is said to have landed, and in fact, it resembles engravings done by Cook's shipboard artists, John Webber and William Hodges. The beach, which faces the open ocean on the windward side of Niihau, is a small pocket of golden sand often strewn with driftwood, seashells, bottles, glass floats from fishing nets, and other flotsam prized by beachcombers. When the tide is low, you may find tiny shells, no bigger than grains of rice, that islanders string into necklaces.

The chopper visit here is too brief to permit swimming, which should be considered dangerous anyway.

Swimming: Strong currents and deep water rule out swimming here.

Sand: A nice stretch of golden coral sand, but tides often bring in mounds of plastic garbage.

Amenities: None.

SHOPPING

Sometimes the women of Puuwai come to meet the helicopter and spread out their prized shell leis (necklaces) to be admired and purchased. Niihau's artisans create some of Hawaii's finest handiwork. They collect the tiny shells on the beach, pierce them, and string them into delicate necklaces. Longer versions of the leis made on Niihau are worth thousands of dollars and are usually found only in museums or in families where they are prized heirlooms. Expect to pay at least $100 for a Niihau shell necklace, about half of what it would cost elsewhere in Hawaii.

SPORTS

HUNTING

♦ **Niihau Safaris.** Hunting was opened to outsiders in 1993 in an effort to curb damage done to the island's fragile vegetation by wild pigs and goats. Hunters arrive by helicopter and spend the day stalking their prey with shotgun, rifle, or bow and arrow. Excess meat is donated to guides and residents. *Box 370, Makaweli, HI 96769; tel. 808-335-3500.*

SAFETY TIPS

Come prepared for a no-frills wilderness experience, and don't forget your hat, sunglasses, and sunscreen.

TOURIST INFORMATION

♦ **Hawaii Visitors Bureau.** *2270 Kalakaua Ave., Suite 801, Honolulu, HI 96815; tel. 808-923-1811. Open Mon.-Fri. 8-4:30.*

Now Save Money on All Your Travels by Joining

Frommer's
TRAVEL BOOK CLUB

The Advantages of Membership:

1. Your choice of any **TWO FREE BOOKS.**

2. Your own subscription to the **TRIPS & TRAVEL** quarterly newsletter, where you'll discover the best buys in travel, the hottest vacation spots, the latest travel trends, world-class events and festivals, and much more.

3. A **30% DISCOUNT** on any additional books you order through the club.

4. **DOMESTIC TRIP-ROUTING KITS** (available for a small additional fee). We'll send you a detailed map highlighting the most direct or scenic route to your destination, anywhere in North America.

Here's all you have to do to join:

Send in your annual membership fee of $25.00 ($35.00 Canada/Foreign) with your name, address, and selections on the form below. Or call 815/734-1104 to use your credit card.

Send all orders to:

The following Frommer's guides are available from your favorite bookstore, or you can use the order form on the preceding page to request them as part of your membership in Frommer's Travel Book Club.

FROMMER'S COMPLETE TRAVEL GUIDES

(Comprehensive guides to sightseeing, dining and accommodations, with selections in all price ranges—from deluxe to budget)

Acapulco/Ixtapa/Taxco, 2nd Ed.	C157	Jamaica/Barbados, 2nd Ed.	C149
Alaska '94-'95	C131	Japan '94-'95	C144
Arizona '95	C166	Maui, 1st Ed.	C153
Australia '94-'95	C147	Nepal, 3rd Ed. (avail. 11/95)	C184
Austria, 6th Ed.	C162	New England '95	C165
Bahamas '96 (avail. 8/95)	C172	New Mexico, 3rd Ed.	C167
Belgium/Holland/Luxembourg,		New York State, 4th Ed.	C133
4th Ed.	C170	Northwest, 5th Ed.	C140
Bermuda '96 (avail. 8/95)	C174	Portugal '94-'95	C141
California '95	C164	Puerto Rico '95-'96	C151
Canada '94-'95	C145	Puerto Vallarta/Manzanillo/	
Caribbean '96 (avail. 9/95)	C173	Guadalajara, 2nd Ed.	C135
Carolinas/Georgia, 2nd Ed.	C128	Scandinavia, 16th Ed.	C169
Colorado '96 (avail. 11/95)	C179	Scotland '94-'95	C146
Costa Rica, 1st Ed.	C161	South Pacific '94-'95	C138
Cruises '95-'96	C150	Spain, 16th Ed.	C163
Delaware/Maryland '94-'95	C136	Switzerland, 7th Ed.	
England '96 (avail. 10/95)	C180	(avail. 9/95)	C177
Florida '96 (avail. 9/95)	C181	Thailand, 2nd Ed.	C154
France '96 (avail. 11/95)	C182	U.S.A., 4th Ed.	C156
Germany '96 (avail. 9/95)	C176	Virgin Islands, 3rd Ed.	
Honolulu/Waikiki/Oahu, 4th Ed.		(avail. 8/95)	C175
(avail. 10/95)	C178	Virginia '94-'95	C142
Ireland, 1st Ed.	C168	Yucatán '95-'96	C155
Italy '96 (avail. 11/95)	C183		

FROMMER'S $-A-DAY GUIDES

(Dream Vacations at Down-to-Earth Prices)

Australia on $45 '95-'96	D122	Ireland on $45 '94-'95	D118
Berlin from $50, 3rd Ed.		Israel on $45, 15th Ed.	D130
(avail. 10/95)	D137	London from $55 '96	
Caribbean from $60, 1st Ed.		(avail. 11/95)	D136
(avail. 9/95)	D133	Madrid on $50 '94-'95	D119
Costa Rica/Guatemala/Belize		Mexico from $35 '96	
on $35, 3rd Ed.	D126	(avail. 10/95)	D135
Eastern Europe on $30, 5th Ed.	D129	New York on $70 '94-'95	D121
England from $50 '96		New Zealand from $45, 6th Ed.	D132
(avail. 11/95)	D138	Paris on $45 '94-'95	D117
Europe from $50 '96		South America on $40, 16th Ed.	D123
(avail. 10/95)	D139	Washington, D.C. on $50	
Greece from $45, 6th Ed.	D131	'94-'95	D120
Hawaii from $60 '96 (avail. 9/95)	D134		

FROMMER'S COMPLETE CITY GUIDES

(Comprehensive guides to sightseeing, dining, and accommodations in all price ranges)

Amsterdam, 8th Ed.	S176	Minneapolis/St. Paul, 4th Ed.	S159
Athens, 10th Ed.	S174	Montréal/Québec City '95	S166
Atlanta & the Summer Olympic		Nashville/Memphis, 1st Ed.	S141
Games '96 (avail. 11/95)	S181	New Orleans '96 (avail. 10/95)	S182
Atlantic City/Cape May, 5th Ed.	S130	New York City '96 (avail. 11/95)	S183
Bangkok, 2nd Ed.	S147	Paris '96 (avail. 9/95)	S180
Barcelona '93-'94	S115	Philadelphia, 8th Ed.	S167
Berlin, 3rd Ed.	S162	Prague, 1st Ed.	S143
Boston '95	S160	Rome, 10th Ed.	S168
Budapest, 1st Ed.	S139	St. Louis/Kansas City, 2nd Ed.	S127
Chicago '95	S169	San Antonio/Austin, 1st Ed.	S177
Denver/Boulder/Colorado Springs,		San Diego '95	S158
3rd Ed.	S154	San Francisco '96 (avail. 10/95)	S184
Disney World/Orlando '96 (avail. 9/95)	S178	Santa Fe/Taos/Albuquerque '95	S172
Dublin, 2nd Ed.	S157	Seattle/Portland '94-'95	S137
Hong Kong '94-'95	S140	Sydney, 4th Ed.	S171
Las Vegas '95	S163	Tampa/St. Petersburg, 3rd Ed.	S146
London '96 (avail. 9/95)	S179	Tokyo '94-'95	S144
Los Angeles '95	S164	Toronto, 3rd Ed.	S173
Madrid/Costa del Sol, 2nd Ed.	S165	Vancouver/Victoria '94-'95	S142
Mexico City, 1st Ed.	S175	Washington, D.C. '95	S153
Miami '95-'96	S149		

FROMMER'S FAMILY GUIDES

(Guides to family-friendly hotels, restaurants, activities, and attractions)

California with Kids	F105	San Francisco with Kids	F104
Los Angeles with Kids	F103	Washington, D.C. with Kids	F102
New York City with Kids	F101		

FROMMER'S WALKING TOURS

(Memorable strolls through colorful and historic neighborhoods, accompanied by detailed directions and maps)

Berlin	W100	Paris, 2nd Ed.	W112
Chicago	W107	San Francisco, 2nd Ed.	W115
England's Favorite Cities	W108	Spain's Favorite Cities (avail. 9/95)	W116
London, 2nd Ed.	W111	Tokyo	W109
Montréal/Québec City	W106	Venice	W110
New York, 2nd Ed.	W113	Washington, D.C., 2nd Ed.	W114

FROMMER'S AMERICA ON WHEELS

(Guides for travelers who are exploring the U.S.A. by car, featuring a brand-new rating system for accommodations and full-color road maps)

Arizona/New Mexico	A100	Florida	A102
California/Nevada	A101	Mid-Atlantic	A103

FROMMER'S SPECIAL-INTEREST TITLES

Arthur Frommer's Branson!	P107	Frommer's Where to Stay U.S.A.,	
Arthur Frommer's New World		11th Ed.	P102
of Travel (avail. 11/95)	P112	National Park Guide, 29th Ed.	P106
Frommer's Caribbean Hideaways		USA Today Golf Tournament Guide	P113
(avail. 9/95)	P110	USA Today Minor League	
Frommer's America's 100 Best-Loved		Baseball Book	P111
State Parks	P109		

FROMMER'S BEST BEACH VACATIONS

(The top places to sun, stroll, shop, stay, play, party, and swim—with each beach rated for beauty, swimming, sand, and amenities)

California (avail. 10/95)	G100	Hawaii (avail. 10/95)	G102
Florida (avail. 10/95)	G101		

FROMMER'S BED & BREAKFAST GUIDES

(Selective guides with four-color photos and full descriptions of the best inns in each region)

California	B100	Hawaii	B105
Caribbean	B101	Pacific Northwest	B106
East Coast	B102	Rockies	B107
Eastern United States	B103	Southwest	B108
Great American Cities	B104		

FROMMER'S IRREVERENT GUIDES

(Wickedly honest guides for sophisticated travelers and those who want to be)

Chicago (avail. 11/95)	I100	New Orleans (avail. 11/95)	I103
London (avail. 11/95)	I101	San Francisco (avail. 11/95)	I104
Manhattan (avail. 11/95)	I102	Virgin Islands (avail. 11/95)	I105

FROMMER'S DRIVING TOURS

(Four-color photos and detailed maps outlining spectacular scenic driving routes)

Australia	Y100	Italy	Y108
Austria	Y101	Mexico	Y109
Britain	Y102	Scandinavia	Y110
Canada	Y103	Scotland	Y111
Florida	Y104	Spain	Y112
France	Y105	Switzerland	Y113
Germany	Y106	U.S.A.	Y114
Ireland	Y107		

FROMMER'S BORN TO SHOP

(The ultimate travel guides for discriminating shoppers—from cut-rate to couture)

Hong Kong (avail. 11/95)	Z100	London (avail. 11/95)	Z101